REDEMPTION IN '64

REDEMPTION IN '64

THE CHAMPION CLEVELAND BROWNS

John M. Harris

BLACK SQUIRREL BOOKS®
Kent, Ohio

BLACK SQUIRREL BOOKS® 🐿®
Frisky, industrious black squirrels are a familiar sight on the Kent State University campus and the inspiration for Black Squirrel Books®, a trade imprint of The Kent State University Press. www.KentStateUniversityPress.com

© 2018 by The Kent State University Press, Kent, Ohio
All rights reserved
Library of Congress Catalog Number 2018008745
ISBN 978-1-60635-343-1
Manufactured in the United States of America

No part of this book may be used or reproduced, in any manner whatsoever, without written permission from the Publisher, except in the case of short quotations in critical reviews or articles.

Portions of *Redemption in '64* were originally published in "The Last Champions," *Timeline* Jan.–Mar. 2015, Vol. 32, Issue 1, pp. 2–15 and are reprinted with the permission of The Ohio History Connection.

Library of Congress Cataloging-in-Publication Data
Names: Harris, John M. (John McCormick), 1954- author.
Title: Redemption in '64 : the champion Cleveland Browns / John M. Harris.
Other titles: Redemption in 1964 | Cleveland Browns
Description: Kent, Ohio : The Kent State University Press, [2018] | "Portions of "Redemption in '64" were originally published in "The Last Champions," Timeline, Jan-Mar 2015, Vol. 32, Issue 1, pp. 2-15 and are reprinted with the permission of The Ohio History Connection"--T.p. verso. | Includes bibliographical references and index.
Identifiers: LCCN 2018008745 | ISBN 9781606353431 (paperback : alk. paper)
Subjects: LCSH: Cleveland Browns (Football team : 1946-1995)--History. | National Football League--History--20th century. | Football--United States--History--20th century--Anecdotes.
Classification: LCC GV956.C6 H37 2018 | DDC 796.332/640977132--dc23
LC record available at https://lccn.loc.gov/2018008745

For Sheryl

CONTENTS

Acknowledgments	ix
Prologue	1
One	12
Two	20
Three	35
Four	42
Five	50
Six	59
Seven	67
Eight	74
Nine	82
Ten	98
Eleven	110
Twelve	121
Thirteen	132
Fourteen	138
Fifteen	147
Sixteen	160
Seventeen	166
Eighteen	175
Nineteen	184
Epilogue	199
Notes	211
Index	229

ACKNOWLEDGMENTS

This book grew out of an article I wrote on the fiftieth anniversary of the Cleveland Browns' 1964 NFL championship season. The story in *Timeline*, a publication of the Ohio History Connection, caught the attention of Kent State University Press, which asked me to write a book about the '64 Browns. As a lifelong (and long-suffering) Cleveland fan, I was delighted at the opportunity to delve deeply into the season, the title game, and its participants.

This book and the *Timeline* article couldn't have been produced without the help of a number of individuals, beginning with Tony Dick, formerly the Browns' manager of alumni relations. Tony put me in contact with former players and with fans of the championship team, and he also made the club's scrapbooks available to me.

I had the privilege of speaking with a dozen former Cleveland Browns and Baltimore Colts, and a handful of them were especially patient and generous with their time. Frank Ryan and his wife, Joan, opened their Grafton, Vermont, home to me and answered innumerable queries about their personal and professional lives. Dick Schafrath, John Wooten, and Jim Ninowski helped place issues of the era into their proper context—among them football strategy, race relations, and the complicated genius Paul Brown. Howard Schnellenberger provided insights into Blanton Collier's time as coach of the University of Kentucky Wildcats. Kay Collier McLaughlin, Blanton's daughter, steadfastly preserves her father's legacy, and she made sure I had whatever information I needed about him and her mother, Forman. Kay's biography of her father, the aptly named *Football's Gentle Giant*, is a treasure trove of information about him and the men he coached and with whom he worked.

Others I had the opportunity to interview included former Browns Walter Beach, Dale Lindsey, Paul Warfield, and Paul Wiggin and former Colts Gary Cuozzo, Tom Matte, and Don Shula (a former Browns player as well as coach of the Colts).

Lady Gilmore explained the Browns' place in Cleveland's African American community, and Doris McFarland supplied information about Paris, Kentucky, the hometown of Blanton and Forman Collier. Jon Kendle, archivist at the Pro Football Hall of Fame in Canton, made the Cleveland Browns archives available to me. Jonathan Knight and Roger Gordon read the first draft of the manuscript and provided valuable suggestions and edits. Tony Tomsic, a Cleveland native and renowned sports photographer, including for the *Cleveland Press* and *Sports Illustrated,* provided photos for this book and an account of what it was like to watch the '64 title game from the sideline.

A posthumous note of gratitude goes to my parents and maternal grandparents, all of whom instilled in me a love for football, especially the Cleveland Browns.

PROLOGUE

Cleveland Browns owner Art Modell stood on the sideline of Cleveland Municipal Stadium looking as though he'd just swallowed a slug. Dressed in a camel-hair overcoat to shield himself against the wind whipping off Lake Erie, he appeared older than his thirty-nine years, lines creasing his forehead, his dark eyes hollow. Beside him stood Baltimore Colts owner Carroll Rosenbloom, smiling under a corduroy cap that covered his gray-blonde toupee. Rosenbloom appeared oblivious to the cold and unruffled by the fact that his club was about to play for the 1964 National Football League championship.

"I just hope you guys don't embarrass us," Modell said.

"Don't worry," Rosenbloom responded. "This thing will be just fine."[1]

Modell had as much reason to worry as Rosenbloom had to be confident. The Browns were a one- or two-touchdown underdog, depending on who was laying the bets. Baltimore was quarterbacked by Johnny Unitas, the league's Most Valuable Player, and the Colts led the NFL in scoring in 1964, totaling the third-most points in league history to that date. The Browns played a "rubber band defense": they bent but didn't break, conceding short completions but nothing long. As a result, they gave up more yards than any team in the league. The prevailing thought was Unitas and the Colts would put up so many points Cleveland would be unable to keep pace.

Modell had much more than bragging rights riding on the game's outcome. His reputation and judgment were also at stake. Three years earlier, he'd left New York for Cleveland after buying a majority share of the club, and after two seasons as owner he shocked the NFL by firing the team's founder and only head coach, Paul Brown, a man whom many considered the greatest coach in pro football history. It was a bold and risky move. Arthur Daley of the *New York Times* said, "The dismissal defies comprehension," and Whitey Kelley of the *Charlotte Observer* said it would have been more believable to hear Jimmy Hoffa give a nomination speech for Bobby Kennedy. To some, Brown's firing was the beginning of the end for professional football in Cleveland. From its birth in 1946, the franchise had boasted local ownership, a local coach, and a team stocked with local players. Now it was just another business venture, owned by some guy from Brooklyn. "Baseball has ceased to exist as a money-making major league sport in Cleveland," wrote Bud Furillo, a columnist for the *Los Angeles Herald-Examiner*. "Now that Brown has passed from the scene, you can summon the gravediggers for football, too."[2] A loss to the Colts would prove Modell's naysayers right: Cleveland couldn't win a championship without Paul Brown.

Modell had made millions as a pioneer in television production and later in advertising. He gave it up to become involved in professional football. Cleveland especially excited him because the Browns were the most successful franchise in the league and because this made him a partner with Paul Brown. Modell readily admitted he was starstruck. A tug-of-war for control of the franchise began immediately. The first time the two met, Modell tried breaking the ice by telling a joke. Brown stared at him without a word. Modell wanted to learn about the team, and he liked to be near the players, so he visited the team's practices every day. Brown never acknowledged him, and Modell showed up less and less. Eventually he quit going.

Modell was swept up in the game's passion, and no city was more passionate about its team than Cleveland. Municipal Stadium regularly was filled to capacity, with eighty thousand or more spectators for home games, and the Browns were the city's main topic of conversation. "I've never seen anything quite as emotional as football," Modell said. "Even when I was putting out twelve hours a week of live TV programming the pressures were not comparable."[3] He watched the Browns games from a box above the field, packs of Marlboros and antacids arrayed before him. He banged the counter in front of him, cigarette butts flying from an ashtray and antacid tablets bouncing to the floor. "Watching Art Modell watch the Cleveland Browns is often more interesting than watching the game," one observer noted. Modell groaned, cried, pleaded, clawed at his hair, and lit cigarette after cigarette, "the match cupped inside his hand like Humphrey Bogart."[4]

Paul Brown, though, was stoic and strict (he was described as having all the warmth of a glacier). He had developed a set of rules, and he—and everyone associated with the Browns—lived by them. To Brown's way of thinking, the rift between him and the upstart ad man didn't stem from a difference in personalities, as many assumed. "It was a basic conflict," he said, "between two different styles and two different philosophies of operating—one from knowledge and experience; the other from a complete lack of either."[5]

In the Browns' first thirteen years of existence, the team won four All-America Football Conference titles and three more NFL championships. They missed the playoffs only once during that run. Brown stated from the outset he wanted to create the football equivalent of Ben Hogan, Joe Louis, and the New York Yankees. He succeeded. But the game was beginning to pass him by when Modell arrived in 1961. His rigidity, so successful with the post–World War II players on whose backs he'd built his juggernaut, failed to impress the new breed of player. Few of them had played on Cleveland's championship teams, and they weren't so accepting of Brown's iron fist. They chafed privately and publicly, and the hated New York Giants crowed that Brown was so predictable in his play-calling they knew what was coming before the Cleveland offense lined up. The Browns finished 7–6–1 in 1962, and Modell fired Brown. Tex Maule mused in *The Game*, a history of the NFL published prior to the 1964 season: "The wisdom of Modell's decision will be up for regular audit as the years roll by."[6]

The title game was played two days after Christmas, and kickoff was set for 1:30 P.M. The stadium lights were already on as the teams took the field for warm-ups, breaths steaming out from under their helmets. The temperature at Hopkins Airport was thirty-two degrees, but it was estimated to be twenty on the field—"a real teeth-clicker of a day," according to one reporter. Winds swirled through the stadium, kicking up dust from the baseball infield. The flags rimming the roof flapped in gusts reaching thirty miles per hour. Groundskeeper Harold Bossard had lined the field with a dozen heaters in hopes of thawing it out, and at game time the grassy part was spongy with divots, not bad conditions considering the time of year. But the baseball infield in the stadium's closed end was hard as pavement. Bossard tried to drive a metal stake into it, and it bent. *New York Herald Tribune* columnist Red Smith claimed there was no windbreak between Hudson Bay and Euclid Avenue. It was the kind of day that prompted calls for the championship game to be played in a warm-weather, neutral site. But, Smith wrote, "whenever anything is written about settling the title playoff permanently in some city like Miami, a blizzard of indignant mail blows in from fans who insist they enjoy suffering."[7]

In the two weeks between the end of the season and the title game, much was made of the potential for a frigid and windy day. The May Company advertised twenty pounds' worth of gear for dealing with the cold, including a thermos, five layers of clothing, scarf, stocking cap, pennant, stadium seat, even a facemask with eyeholes and mouth holes. J. Glen Smith, city health commissioner, recommended wearing thermal underwear, woolen socks, and lined gloves. Blankets would be especially beneficial for women because they could be wrapped around the knees and lower legs. "In fact," Dr. Smith said, "this might be one time when women would be better off wearing slacks in public." He also warned against overindulging in alcohol. Even one shot of whiskey per quarter to stay warm could lead to pneumonia. "And you know how it is with so-called medicinal doses of whiskey," he said. "Pretty soon you're doubling the dosage, and by the end of the game you've had it."[8]

Despite the cold and the odds laid by bookies, Cleveland fans remained faithful, if not necessarily confident. The game sold out soon after the Browns defeated the New York Giants in their season finale, and scalpers weren't getting much action. "Everybody that really wants to go already has tickets," said a knowledgeable guy at Hotel Manger's Purple Tree Lounge.[9] Prices were set by the league—$10, $8 and $6—and the Cleveland management estimated it could sell 130,000 tickets if it had the seats.

Bob Migliorino, a twenty-one-year-old Cleveland native, was among those fortunate enough to secure a ticket. His father, in charge of street sales for the *Plain Dealer*, obtained two. Migliorino worked part-time at a Sears store at 107th and Lorain, and a few days before the game he was folding underwear when his supervisor walked by. He asked her for the day off to go to the game. The supervisor—they called her "Sourpuss"—told him he had a choice: he could go to the game or he could keep his job. "That's no problem," Migliorino replied. "I don't work here anymore." He walked upstairs to the paymaster, collected what he was owed, and never looked back. "I couldn't believe that anyone in Cleveland, Ohio, wouldn't let you go to the game," he said.[10]

About 10,000 Baltimore fans were expected to trek to Cleveland, including the 150-piece Colt band and its majorettes. Also planning to make the trip were the Bugle Boys, a half-dozen horn-tooting fanatics, who made so much racket during the regular season that other Colts fans complained. Baltimore general manager Don Kellet investigated and allowed the boys to continue their bugling. "We want the Cleveland people to know we are there," said R. J. Gilliland, a Baltimore travel agent organizing the trip for members of the Colt Corral fan club. "We intend to be enthusiastic but we will not be hostile."[11] Modell hired the largest police force in NFL history, 200 officers, including men and women in plainclothes.

The contest pitted two men in their second seasons as head coaches in the NFL: Cleveland's Blanton Collier and Baltimore's Don Shula. It also was a match of mentor and student. At fifty-eight, Collier was one of the oldest coaches in the league, while Shula was the second youngest, at thirty-four. Collier joined the Browns when the team was formed, and he spent eight years as Paul Brown's top assistant. He left the team in 1954 to become head coach of the University of Kentucky, returning to Cleveland in 1962 after Kentucky bought out his contract. He became Cleveland's head coach—the second in the team's history—after Modell fired Brown.

Shula was a native of Painesville, attended John Carroll University, and played defensive back for the Browns. His position coach was Collier, and he later served as Collier's assistant at Kentucky. Shula said Collier influenced his decision to go into coaching, and he continually applied what he'd learned from him. "He was just an extraordinary teacher," Shula said, "covered everything bit by bit, detail by detail."[12] Shula was named NFL coach of the year in 1964 after leading the Colts to eleven straight wins and a 12-2 record. Cleveland fans expressed disappointment Collier was overlooked for the honor.

Five days before the title game, Modell announced Collier had signed a new three-year contract, replacing the three-year deal he had signed when the Browns hired him before the 1963 season. In the previous two years, Collier had achieved the best record of any coach in the league, 20-7-1. The salary wasn't revealed, though it unquestionably included a pay raise. Unlike most coaches, who ranted and ruled by intimidation, Collier, a soft-spoken Kentuckian, was first and foremost a teacher. Where most coaches would yell at a running back who'd fumbled—"Hang onto the goddamn ball!"—Collier would patiently explain how best to secure the ball. Some questioned whether he was too easygoing, but his players bought into his methods, and it showed in their play. In 1963, the Browns improved from seven to ten wins and finished second behind the Giants in the East. And now they were the conference champions. "I know of no man who has played for Blanton who does not respect him," star fullback Jim Brown said. "In a grim and sometimes brutal business, he has one quality that makes him stick out—sincerity. Blanton never jives anyone. If he wanted to he wouldn't know how."[13]

The Browns' success marked a dramatic reversal of fortune for Collier. He had replaced Bear Bryant at Kentucky in 1954, and though he was named Southeastern Conference coach of the year his first season, he'd been unable to maintain the same level of success, nor that achieved by the revered Bryant.

His 1961 team finished 5–5, and he and Nikita Khrushchev were hung in effigy from a statue on the lawn of the Fayette County Courthouse. Kentucky fired him, and he returned to Cleveland.

The Eastern Conference title brought him national attention. He was described as modest, quiet, and dignified, and his stock words were often repeated: "You can accomplish anything you want as long as you don't care who gets the credit for it." The portrait painted of him fit what professional football saw as the ideal image of what the sport could and should be—no longer a league of "tramp players" but a place for gentlemen and scholars, even if, as one football writer admitted, that portrait was "corny as Kellogg's." Collier was all those things, but he was much more complicated. He was a football savant; held a master's degree in education; and was a student of psychology, particularly the new discipline of positive thinking. He suffered from degenerative hearing loss, but defensive end Bill Glass considered his impairment a strength. "He felt things more deeply and emotionally than most people do, which made him sensitive of the hurts of others," Glass said. "He could, therefore, get closer to players because he approached them on a more emotional level and not such a coldly, analytical level."[14] He preferred to be addressed as "Blanton" instead of "Coach" or "Mr. Collier," both of which he believed were too formal. Whatever he was called, he was a caring, gentle man who earned respect instead of demanding it.

The Collier family arrived en masse at the stadium for the title game—his wife, Forman; the couple's three grown daughters, Kay, Carolyn, and Jane; plus husbands and friends. It was Kay's habit to check the scoreboard above the bleachers in the open end of the horseshoe for the day's other games. But on this day no games were posted. It struck her: No one else was playing. The first Super Bowl was still two years in the future, and despite the existence of the upstart American Football League, in 1964 the NFL title game was the pinnacle of professional football. "This was it. We were it," Kay said. "So much was riding on it."[15]

The Cleveland offense figured to feature Jim Brown. The team ran the ball on 60 percent of its plays, and the majority of those carries went to Brown. In the days leading up to the title game, the Colts studied film of Cleveland games, and Brown never ceased to amaze them. Baltimore's All-Pro defensive end Gino Marchetti told Shula, "He's even better than I thought he was and I thought he was the best."[16]

Brown rushed for nearly 1,500 yards in 1964, leading the NFL for the second straight season, and he scored his 105th touchdown, tying him for the NFL career mark with Hall of Fame receiver Don Hutson. The previous year he'd set the single-season rushing record with 1,863 yards—more than a mile, writers pointed out. His offensive linemen insisted he could have rushed for 2,000 yards, had he not been taken out early during lopsided wins. In his seven years in the league, Brown had run for more yards than any other player in NFL history, and at twenty-seven years old he was considered the greatest running back ever. When he spoke at a Cleveland Touchdown Club luncheon, the emcee introduced him, "Gentlemen, I give you Superman."[17]

Brown always was at the center of any conversation about the Browns, and that certainly was the case in December 1964. His autobiography, *Off My Chest*, written with Myron Cope, was published that fall and excerpted in *Look* magazine and Cleveland-area newspapers. The book marked the "first time a first-rank professional sports star has delivered an utterly candid account of his business while still at the peak of his career," according to the preface. "Jimmy Brown has let the chips fall."[18]

Among those chips was the place of the black athlete in American society, a topic rarely discussed in frank terms at the time. John Carlos and Tommy Smith's black-gloved salute at the Olympics was still four years off. "I have no bones, no muscles that the white man doesn't have," Brown wrote. "I have no resiliency or speed handed down from my jungle heritage. But I do have as much dignity as any white man."[19] His thoughts on race added to momentum building in the civil rights movement. That summer, President Lyndon Johnson signed the Civil Rights Act, prohibiting discrimination in employment and outlawing segregation in public places. Two weeks before the title game, Martin Luther King Jr. accepted the Nobel Peace Prize in Oslo, Norway.

Jim Brown described himself as "Paul Brown's big brute," and not endearingly or with pride. But Paul Brown no longer was in charge of him or the team. "I now find it in myself to speak my full piece in these pages because, very frankly, Paul Brown no longer is my boss," he wrote. "He ceased being my boss after the 1962 football season."[20]

Jim Brown had been highly critical of his then boss during the 1962 season—both publicly and with his teammates—and depending on one's point of view, he could either be credited or blamed for Paul Brown's firing. In any case, Jim Brown was getting plenty off his chest while helping Cleveland to a title.

The Browns needed to establish their running game in order to keep Unitas and the Baltimore offense off the field, but the Colts defense had given up the fewest points in the league in 1964. If the Browns failed to run effectively or if they fell behind, they would need to rely on their passing attack. Quarterback Frank Ryan had thrown an NFL-best twenty-five touchdowns, including five in the title-clinching win over New York two weeks earlier, but despite his success he was considered only so-so, even by many Cleveland fans. Until the previous season, he'd been little more than a second-stringer, both in six years as a pro and during his college career. *Sports Illustrated* wrote the Browns were a "sound, intelligent and even explosive football team," but they stood little chance against the Colts. The biggest difference between the teams, the magazine wrote, was the quarterbacks. Ryan was serviceable, but Unitas "is the best—perhaps the best ever."[21]

Ryan seemed to be coming into his own, but he was no Otto Graham, the team's first quarterback and the only one to guide it to a championship—seven of them, to be exact, during the 1940s and '50s. Ryan was simply the next in a succession of quarterbacks who'd failed to return the Browns to dominance. (He was different from the others in one way; during the offseason he was pursuing his doctorate in mathematics at his alma mater, Rice University.) In addition to having a reputation for becoming rattled, he was criticized for hanging onto the ball too long, for being too deliberate, for throwing too many interceptions, for any number of things. One Sunday afternoon Ryan's wife, Joan, was caught in traffic and arrived late at Municipal Stadium. As she hurried across the parking lot, her two oldest boys in tow, she heard the crowd roar, and roar again. Then the sound of boos cascaded over the rooftop. "We haven't missed the kickoff," one of the boys said. "They just introduced Dad."[22]

The two teams were entitled to five game films from each other, but Collier and Shula agreed to share six, characteristic of their obsession with detail. In studying the films, Cleveland's All-Pro defensive back Bernie Parrish noticed that Baltimore's opponents allowed the Colts receivers to run 10 or 12 yards downfield before engaging them. Laying off them like that played into Baltimore's hands. Its passing game was predicated on precise timing between Unitas and his receivers. The Colts had a staff member use a stopwatch to time their patterns and throws. They figured it took Unitas 1.6 seconds to drop back and set up, after which he had another second or second and a half to throw the ball. More than four seconds and he would be in trouble. But that rarely was a problem: his receivers would come off the line and at the count of three or four make their cut. Unitas would have the ball waiting for them.

But what if the Cleveland cornerbacks pressured the Baltimore receivers closer to the line of scrimmage—Parrish called it "clamping"—and forced them to alter their routes? To Parrish's way of thinking, he and Cleveland's other cornerback, Walter Beach, might be able to disrupt Baltimore's timing. Unitas would be forced to hold onto the ball longer than he wanted, or he'd have to deliver it sooner, or he'd have to take off running.

For the scheme to work, the Cleveland defensive line needed to pressure Unitas. Otherwise, he could sit back and wait for his receivers to break free, regardless of how much clamping Parrish and Beach applied. Collier told defensive tackles Dick Modzelewski and Jim Kanicki that if they stood their ground, if they clogged the middle, ends Paul Wiggin and Bill Glass could rush Unitas from the edges. This was easier said than done, especially for Kanicki, a second-year tackle who would be going against Baltimore's All-Pro and future Hall of Fame guard Jim Parker. Kanicki had begun the year as a backup but became a starter midway through the season when Bob Gain broke his leg. Earlier in the week, the manager of a grocery store approached Kanicki while he was in the meat department. "I just read a story that said the Colts were gonna run at you every time they needed five yards," he said.[23]

Parrish's strategy was inspired but risky. He, Beach, and safety Ross Fichtner would each have to cover a receiver man to man, and all of Baltimore's receivers were outstanding. Raymond Berry was Unitas's favorite target. In 1964, he caught the 506th pass of his career, a new NFL record. Parrish assigned Beach to Berry. He would cover flanker Jimmy Orr, and Fichtner would cover tight end John Mackey. "We all agreed that we didn't have anything to lose by going all out," Parrish said. "Everyone was picking us to lose anyway." Publicly, he exuded confidence. He predicted the Browns would win, and he defended the maligned Cleveland secondary. "I don't go along with any thinking that we won the division title in spite of the defensive backfield," he said.

Privately, he wasn't so sure. "Chances were," he said, "we would all be in trouble that afternoon."[24]

Halfback Lenny Moore took a handoff from Unitas on Baltimore's first play from scrimmage and rambled 15 yards before safety Larry Benz brought him down. Moore had scored twenty touchdowns during the regular season, on the way to being named first team All-Pro. It was an ominous start for the

Browns and their fans. But Cleveland's defensive strategy began working on the next play. Unitas dropped back, the pocket collapsed around him, and he saw his receivers covered. He took off running, gaining 8 yards before Fichtner tackled him. It was a good gain, but that was fine with the Browns. Unitas was much less effective running than passing. The Colts moved to midfield, but Baltimore fullback Jerry Hill fumbled after a hard hit by Wiggin, and Cleveland recovered.

On Baltimore's next possession, Unitas dropped back to pass and saw his receivers covered close to the line of scrimmage. As he waited for someone to break open, the Cleveland pass rush closed in on him, Kanicki nearly grabbing him with a big paw. He was forced to take off running and gained 20 yards before Benz slammed him down at the Cleveland 25-yard line. It was another nice gain by Unitas, but again, Cleveland was forcing him to scramble. He carried three times for 30 yards in the first quarter, outgaining Jim Brown, and didn't complete a pass until about a minute was left in the period.

Early in the second quarter, Baltimore moved to the Cleveland 19-yard line. The drive stalled, and Lou Michaels came on to attempt a field goal. He was kicking into the gusting wind. The snap bounced off holder Bobby Boyd's fingers, and Boyd picked up the ball and began running. For a moment, it looked as though he might break free, but Beach tripped him up for a 9-yard loss. Shula blamed the snap, but Boyd said the wind had pushed the ball away from him and he'd fumbled it. In any case, the Colts had muffed their first scoring opportunity.

Later in the quarter Baltimore had the ball on its 30-yard line and set up a screen pass to Moore. Unitas lofted the ball to him in the left flat, and four blockers set up in front of him. No one stood between Moore and the goal line except linebacker Galen Fiss. The Cleveland captain knifed between two of the blockers. Moore was running more sideways than upfield, and Fiss rolled his body into the halfback's ankles. Moore's feet flew out from under him, and he crashed to the turf. Instead of a likely touchdown, it was a 5-yard loss. The crowd roared. It wasn't the textbook tackle Collier preferred, but it had worked. "He gambled and won," Shula said afterward. "If he had lost, Lenny had blockers ahead and a lane down the sideline."[25]

As the half wore on, Unitas appeared rattled. Parrish and Beach's clamping was knocking his receivers off their routes, and the Cleveland pass rush was hounding him, especially Kanicki, who somehow was getting the better of Parker. With two minutes to go in the half, the Browns snuffed out another

Baltimore drive when Unitas threw behind Mackey, and the ball bounced off the tight end's thigh pad into the air. Linebacker Vince Costello raced over and grabbed it before it hit the ground.

The Cleveland offense wasn't doing much better against the Colts. The best drive was halted when Ryan was intercepted. On third and eighteen from the Baltimore 34-yard line, he threw downfield toward rookie Paul Warfield. The wind held up the ball, Warfield slipped, and Baltimore linebacker Don Shinnick intercepted at the 15-yard line. Ryan was angry with himself because he knew he'd used poor judgment—he'd thrown into the wind, and the Colts were double-teaming Warfield. Ryan sprinted over and knocked Shinnick out of bounds and into the Baltimore sideline. Colts players hovered over Ryan and barked at him as he lifted himself off the turf. "They were just overjoyed with the interception," he said, "and the fact I was there tackling the guy was an opportunity to get up very close and yell at me."[26]

The first half ended in a scoreless tie. *Sports Illustrated* described it as "spectacularly dull." Unitas and Ryan "played with all the flair of a pair of elderly clubwomen in a Sunday afternoon croquet match." Arthur Daley described the first half as "antediluvian football. . . . If it didn't quite have the flying-wedge antiquity, it was strictly grind-it-out stuff and therefore dreadfully dull." Red Smith wrote, "As an example of how the game is played by the greatest teams in the world, it was the best thing that happened to the American Football League in five years. It may also bring back professional wrestling, if not vaudeville." The out-of-town writers were disappointed and bored, but Bob August of the *Cleveland Press* wrote that he "was absolutely astonished at what I was watching. Unitas and the Colts couldn't do a thing with the Browns' defense. Nothing. And I knew Cleveland's offense would eventually break through."[27]

The Colts and their fans were frustrated, but the Cleveland players were inspired. "I remember we went into halftime feeling good about ourselves as a defense," Wiggin said. "We were kind of thrilled." Even the offense, despite its lack of production, was feeling confident. "We were on the verge of breaking loose all through the first half," veteran kicker Lou Groza said. "It was like fishing and getting nibbles. We were very confident at half." Nothing changed in terms of strategy; there was no "rah-rah, go get 'em" in the locker room. "We sat around, got warm," halfback Ernie Green recalled, "and we looked at each other and in unison we said, 'We can beat these guys.'"[28]

CHAPTER ONE

Blanton Collier arose on the morning of January 16, 1963, put on his glasses, and checked the outside temperature. Zero degrees. He smiled at his wife, Forman, and said, "This is a good place to start."[1]

Downstairs in the family home in the Cleveland suburb of Aurora, two of the Colliers' three grown daughters were preparing sausage and eggs, his favorite. The women had plastered the walls with signs heralding their father's new job as head coach of the Cleveland Browns. One featured a line from the Paris, Kentucky, High School fight song, written when Collier was coach there in the years before World War II. "Here's to captain George," it said, "leading his team right on to victory." Collier had a name for boys who made excuses: "George," as in, "I guess we'll just blame it on George." It was typical Blanton Collier; he didn't accept failure, but he didn't ridicule those who made mistakes. Blaming it on George was "somewhere in between," he said, "and there's no disrespect intended."[2] One day he made a mistake, and one of his players said, "Coach, we'll just blame it on George." From then on Collier was known as George. He didn't mind at all.

His daughters Kay and Jane had come up from their home in Lexington, Kentucky, the previous week after he called to say big changes were coming in Cleveland. The Browns they'd known all their lives no longer were going to be those Browns. He was referring to the firing of Paul Brown, the franchise's first and only coach. The Colliers and the Browns were like family, and he wanted the girls to know about it before they read it in the newspapers. Collier had coached with Brown at the Great Lakes Naval Training Station during World War II and spent the next eight seasons coaching with him in Cleveland, helping build the Browns into a powerhouse. Kay and her then husband, Bob Slone, hustled their baby into their car, and Jane, who was attending the University of Kentucky and living with them, rode along.

Paul and Katy Brown had three boys roughly the same age as the Colliers' three girls. The families rented a cottage together on Turkey Foot Lake south of Akron for a week each summer during training camp. Paul and Katy visited the Colliers in Kentucky every off-season, and Paul would play the piano and sing a duet with Kay. The Browns had attended the weddings of Kay and the Colliers' oldest daughter, Carolyn. Kay considered Paul Brown her uncle. "The simple truth of the matter is this: We loved him, because Daddy loved him," she said.[3] Now, on this morning, Blanton Collier was to be introduced to the media as successor to his colleague and best friend.

The night before he had fretted about what he'd be asked at the news conference. First, he knew, would be questions about his relationship with Brown. Beginning in 1946, the year the Cleveland franchise was founded, Collier had served as Brown's number-one assistant, and during the next eight seasons they won title after title, first in the old All-America Football Conference and then in the National Football League. Brown was the master organizer, Collier the football genius. The two had been a perfect match. But few people outside of northeastern Ohio and Kentucky had heard of Collier. Brown had always made time for the press, but he'd never said much about his assistants and he'd never encouraged them to talk to reporters. (In his autobiography, *PB*, Brown devoted more than twenty pages to discussing the Cleveland players he signed and developed in the team's early years. He spent a paragraph mentioning the assistant coaches. He discussed the equipment manager, Morrie Kono, in more depth.) Like everything else in his organization, Brown kept tight control over the message. That had been fine with Collier, who wanted nothing more than to coach and teach football. Now he was becoming the franchise's second head coach, replacing the man synonymous, literally and figuratively, with the Cleveland Browns.[4]

Paul Brown was already a legend in Ohio football before he took the reins of Cleveland's new pro franchise. He had coached the Massillon Washington High School Tigers to multiple state championships and an 80–8–2 record in nine seasons, so dominating Ohio high school football that his fellow coaches urged Ohio State to hire him so they could be rid of him. Two years later he led the Buckeyes to the 1942 national title, the school's first. When the Cleveland management solicited the public for a nickname for the new team, "Browns"—for Paul Brown—was the choice.

Brown's dismissal by owner Art Modell came in the wake of the second worst season of his career in Cleveland—and following a revolt by some of his players, notably superstar fullback Jim Brown. They believed their coach was living in the past, uncompromising, and unwilling to heed input from them or anyone else. Clark Nealon, a *Houston Post* columnist, pointed out that the new breed of player was not so disposed as those in the past to blindly follow the dictums of someone like Paul Brown. "The football player is a little more complex, harder to reach," he wrote, "and more outspoken, notably in the pro ranks where practically every player has his own ideas about coaching and tactics."[5]

The ouster surprised many, but others saw it coming. The owner and coach had a strained relationship, and the players were unhappy they weren't winning championships. Cleveland's last conference title had come in 1957, and its last NFL crown in 1955. That might be acceptable in some cities, but not in Cleveland. From 1946 through the mid-1950s, the Browns had been the most dominant team in professional football, but now they were little more successful than Cleveland's other pro sports team, the lowly Indians.

Brown's firing prompted plenty of discussion, not just in northeastern Ohio but nationally as well. The sentiment of many was that if Paul Brown could be fired, no coach was immune. It proved the axiom that winning—and winning now—matters most. "If Paul Brown, the greatest strategist ever, doesn't have security," said Nay Sanna, football coach at Shaker Heights High School, "then what coach does!"[6]

Modell hadn't technically fired Brown. The fifty-four-year-old coach and general manager had six years remaining on his contract, which paid an estimated $60,000 per year, and Modell said he could remain as vice president—"vice-president of I don't know what," Brown said bitterly. The owner took full responsibility for the move. "I'll stand or fall on the decision," he said. "I think we'll have a spirited club next year, and I hope we'll have a champion. If things fall flat, I'll be a bum." He also expressed surprise at all the commotion. "Things like this happen every day in business," he said. "This is nothing more than an adjustment in the corporate alignment."[7]

In announcing Brown's demotion on January 9, Modell said he would replace him with two men: a head coach and a general manager. He had a handful of prospects in mind. Speculation centered on Ara Parseghian, a former Brown and now head coach of Northwestern; Tom Landry, head coach of the Dallas Cowboys; Otto Graham, head coach of the Coast Guard Academy; and Cleveland assistant Blanton Collier. "Whoever it is," wrote Paul Hornung of the *Columbus Dispatch*, "he'd better be good."[8]

Collier was a logical choice. He would stay true to Paul Brown's organizational tenets—he was in on them from the beginning, after all—but he would be more flexible and, more importantly, more human. The players liked and respected him, and they didn't know who else might be brought in; at least Collier was a known quantity. Modell liked him, too, because, unlike Paul Brown, he was willing to talk football with him. Blanton Collier would talk football with anyone.

He and Forman were sitting down to watch the Pro Bowl on television when they received a call from Harold Sauerbrei, the club's business manager. "Art would like to watch the game with you," he told Blanton. That wasn't unusual. Modell enjoyed stopping by the Collier house to watch football and chat about the players and strategy. The Collier girls knew this day might prove special, though, because of the possibility of their father becoming coach. They stood at the top of the stairs, straining to hear the conversation, but for the first half the men talked only about the players and the game. At halftime Modell offered Collier the job.

Modell's Tower B office in Municipal Stadium was packed for the press conference, despite the freezing cold and a months-long strike that had shuttered Cleveland's two newspapers, the *Plain Dealer* and the *Press*. The daily newspapers in Akron and Canton and a handful of suburban papers still covered the team, however. And some of the Cleveland reporters came even though they didn't have papers to write for; it was that big of a deal. Although the media ostensibly was there to meet Collier, the story was still Brown's dismissal. (Brown claimed Modell axed him during the newspaper strike to avoid publicity, but that made no sense; the Browns' young owner, a former Madison Avenue advertising executive, craved attention.) Collier sat before a bouquet of microphones, flanked by Modell and Sauerbrei, the new general manager. Dressed in a dark suit, a handkerchief tucked into its breast pocket, he began by reading from a piece of paper folded lengthwise, like the pages of a book. "I am honored, flattered, and I think justifiably proud to be offered what is generally considered one of the top positions in all of football—the ultimate in the coaching profession."[9]

He spoke with a slight Kentucky drawl, answering questions methodically and in extensive detail. His demeanor was unlike anything the reporters had seen from a coach before. He sounded as though he were defending a doctoral dissertation. He'd earned a master's in educational administration at the University of Kentucky and, in essence, a doctorate in football in those early years alongside Paul Brown.

Despite his earlier tenure in Cleveland, he was something of a mystery, even to many in the press. None of Paul Brown's assistants were well known unless they'd played for the Browns. Collier hadn't played for Cleveland or any other NFL team. *Plain Dealer* sports editor Hal Lebovitz said he was so low-key he seemed almost invisible. "This was exactly the opposite with Paul Brown," Lebovitz said. "He was *the man*. When he got off a plane, all eyes were on him. Not that he blew any horns. It was just that he was *Paul Brown*, the supreme boss of the team. He naturally commanded attention."[10] Collier didn't have the kind of personality that would sell tickets. He wasn't young or flashy. But Modell didn't need him to promote the club. He had fullback Jim Brown as his "senior partner." What Modell and the team needed was someone who knew football and could connect with the players. Collier was the perfect man for the job.

He had returned to Cleveland in 1962, after eight years as head coach of the Kentucky Wildcats. The situation seemed ideal for both him and Paul Brown. Collier had been fired from Kentucky following the 1961 season for failing to meet boosters' expectations, and Brown needed him to revive the Cleveland offense, which critics, including some Browns players, claimed had become "stereotyped." With Collier in charge of the offense, Cleveland won all its preseason games, and reporters began crediting him for the team's revival. Brown became increasingly defensive, even paranoid, as he struggled to impose his will on his disgruntled players. Now his *assistant* was receiving credit for the team's turnaround. Brown took back control of the offense, calling the plays himself, and rarely asked for his friend's input. "That was just Paul Brown," said quarterback Jim Ninowski. "Everything had to go through him. He wanted all the credit, and none of the blame."[11] By the end of the season, Collier had become a ghostlike figure to the players, hanging around looking for someone to talk to.

And now he was in charge. The reporters wanted to know who would quarterback the Browns and who would call the plays—the coach or the quarterback. Ninowski had started the 1962 season, but Frank Ryan had taken over when Ninowski was injured. Ryan was the front-runner, Collier said. "Basically, the quarterback will call the plays," he added, "but I reserve the right to call them when the opportunity is there."[12]

His response raised eyebrows. It had been a bone of contention that had helped lead to Paul Brown's firing. Brown had always called the plays from the sideline, rotating in his guards with instructions for the quarterback. He was inflexible on the issue, even though Cleveland's opponents claimed he was so predictable they knew what was coming. Other teams allowed their quarterbacks to change plays at the line of scrimmage to match the opponents' defensive alignment, but not Brown. He knew best. It seemed to Ryan as though he lacked confidence in his players.[13]

Those hoping Collier would criticize his old boss's methods were disappointed. Instead, true to his nature, he delivered a long-winded and detailed explanation of how defensive strategy had evolved in recent years, making it essential for offenses to become more adaptive. When the offense comes to the line of scrimmage, he explained, the defense analyzes its formation and adjusts accordingly. The quarterback sees the deck is stacked against him, and he can call a checkoff at the line of scrimmage. In other words, he can substitute a new play and take advantage of the shifted defense. The reporters scribbled furiously to keep up. "We plan to do a considerable amount of this," he concluded. The answer provided insight into Collier's offensive approach, but it said much more: he wasn't wedded to Paul Brown's system. He was his own man. It appeared the Browns were now a modern football team. "Every man left that room knowing much more about football than when he entered it," Lebovitz said.[14]

The questions about play-calling were a warm-up for discussion of Collier's relationship with his ex-boss. He explained that before accepting Modell's offer, he'd gone to talk with Brown. He didn't ask for Brown's advice or permission. It wouldn't have been fair of him to put his friend in that position, he said. "What concerned me was the loyalty I felt toward Paul. I've been loyal to him all my life. I wanted to keep our friendship on a high level."[15]

He made no mention of the previous season's difficulties and Brown's mistreatment of him. He'd never complained, and hadn't even told his wife. Collier was a student of psychology, and he had a relatively good understanding of what his friend was going through. He'd experienced something much like it at Kentucky. He knew Brown needed total control, and that meant everyone did everything by the book, *his* book. It's what had made him successful for so many years. But the new breed of player didn't respond to his will in the same way as the old-timers, many of whom were war veterans used to taking orders. A handful of the current Browns, including captain Mike McCormack, told Modell they'd quit if Brown returned as coach. It was one thing to bend to the coach's every command when the team was winning, but it wasn't so easy to swallow when it was falling short of its potential. "He had an answer for everything," said All-Pro cornerback Bernie Parrish. "It seemed that he never even considered the possibility he might be doing something wrong."[16]

True to his nature, Collier responded with empathy instead of resentment. It's why he remained loyal and why he checked in first with Brown before accepting Modell's offer. "As soon as I told him," Collier related to the reporters, "he said to me, 'Blanton, you have to take the job. You owe it to your family.'"[17]

He said he and Forman stayed up most of the night trying to come to a decision. "I believe I finally took the job because of my family," he said. "They had been dragged through a tough situation at Kentucky. I decided that I owed it to them not to turn down this job."[18]

But Collier wasn't going to accept it without the blessings of his four fellow assistants. They were all Paul Brown men. Fritz Heisler, the offensive line coach, and Howard Brinker, the defensive coordinator, had played for Brown at Massillon Washington High. Heisler had been with the Cleveland franchise from its founding, and Brinker joined the team in 1952. Ed Ulinski, the linebacker coach, was a guard on Cleveland's championship teams in the AAFC and joined the staff in 1954. Chief scout Paul Bixler coached at Canton McKinley High against Brown's Massillon teams, and he joined the Browns in 1954, replacing Collier when he left for Kentucky. The four of them had nearly a century of coaching experience, much of it with the Browns. They already had job offers, but they all agreed to stay on—a sign of their respect for their new boss.

Collier told the press he accepted the job with conflicting emotions he couldn't adequately express. He was replacing the man who had elevated him from coach of a small Kentucky high school to top assistant in professional football, the same man who had brought him back to Cleveland when he was at the low point of his professional career. Nine years earlier, when he'd decided to leave Cleveland for the Kentucky job, he'd written Brown a letter expressing his gratitude.

> The personal depth of our relationship I cannot discuss in a sane manner. As always, I choke up like some kid, so you will have to guess at the extent of my feelings. As to the technical phase of our relationship, I want you and everyone else to know that anything I have ever done in football is a result of the opportunities you have given me. You are the one who took me, an unknown, small-town football coach, and had enough confidence in me to give me my big chance. I will always be deeply grateful to you.[19]

After the press conference Lebovitz said he'd never seen a coach handle himself so well. He'd revealed two aspects of his personality that his players and others close to him already knew: one, he could and would talk the intricacies of football exhaustively; and two, he was genuine, sincere, and open-minded.

Collier held back one thing, though. Paul Brown had dispatched his son, Mike, to ask him to turn down the job, that to take it would be to betray him for Art Modell. After he accepted the job, Collier told his family, "You need to understand that an era has ended in our lives. I know Paul, and I know he will never forgive me."[20]

CHAPTER TWO

The U.S. military promoted athletics as training for combat during World War II and established football teams at its bases. Stocked with professional and college players, the military teams competed against Notre Dame and schools in the best conferences, and the army and navy academies became national powers. Some criticized the idea, but it had the support of the secretary of the navy Frank Knox. "This is a war where you kill or get killed!" he proclaimed. "And I don't know anything that better prepares a man for bodily contact, including war, than the kind of training we get on the football field."[1]

Paul Brown watched as many of his Ohio State players left for the military, and one year after winning the 1942 national championship his Buckeyes finished 3–6, losing to, among others, Iowa Pre-Flight and Great Lakes Naval Training Station. If he wanted to continue competing at the highest level, he needed to be with a military team. He enlisted in the navy and in 1944 began coaching at the Great Lakes base on the southwestern shore of Lake Michigan. The team practiced in the late afternoon, and day after day he noticed a sailor watching and taking notes. "Isn't this chow hour?" he asked. "Oh, I get my food," the man replied. About the same time, the Great Lakes commander told Brown about a yeoman in the physical training department who wasn't much good to him because all he thought about was football. He was a football nut. "What I mean, a complete filbert," the commander said. "Seems to know something, too, as nearly as I can tell. Maybe you can use him." The yeoman, Blanton Collier, was the same sailor who'd been hanging around practice. Collier told Brown he'd done some coaching and was interested in learning more about the game. Brown gave him a test: write up a scouting report on Great Lakes' next opponent. The result surprised and impressed him. "I already had eight or ten men on my staff," he said, "but before the end of the season Blanton was the guy I relied on the most."[2]

Collier had left his hometown of Paris, Kentucky, after the 1943 season and joined the navy. He was thirty-six, too old to be drafted, and had a wife and three daughters at home. He didn't need to enlist, but he was restless. Born in Millersburg, Kentucky, he was raised in Paris, then a town of about 4,000 in Bourbon County. He graduated from Paris High School in 1923 and matriculated to Georgetown College, where he lettered in football and basketball, though he wasn't much of a football player, weighing just 125 pounds. He was more accomplished in academics, majoring in history and English and gaining the nickname "Brainy."

After graduating in 1927 he took a job in the investment business, determined to do something besides teach, the vocation of many in his family. An uncle was head of the Latin Department at Northwestern University. Another uncle taught romance languages at Williams College, and an aunt taught English at Sweet Briar College. He returned to Paris High at age twenty-two to teach algebra, expecting it to be a temporary job until he figured out what he wanted to do. The school had 500 students, including 150 boys in the upper grades. He began coaching football his second year, and eventually he also coached basketball, baseball, and track.

The Paris school superintendent, Lee Kirkpatrick, loved football and insisted Collier go to a coaching clinic at Northwestern. It ran in conjunction with the College All-Star Game, which each summer pitted America's best graduating collegiate players against the NFL champion. "If you're going to be big-time, you'd better see what the big-timers are doing," Kirkpatrick said. Collier attended in 1935. "I went there and was fascinated," he said. "The all-stars lectured to us and we watched them practice. I was bit. I couldn't get enough of it."[3]

In sixteen seasons at Paris, his football teams compiled a record of 73–50–10 and won three conference championships, and his basketball teams won seven conference titles. His last football squad finished 4–0; the team captain was Billy Arnsparger, who later would coach under him at the University of Kentucky and against him with the Baltimore Colts. Paris failed to have another winning season for seventeen years.

He took over the girls' basketball team one winter when the regular coach became ill. One of the reserves, Mary Forman Varden, caught his eye, and he moved her up to the starting five. A romance blossomed. She often told this story and always with the same punch line: "I've been on the first team ever since."[4] Mary Forman—she went by both her first and middle names, as was the custom among women in Bourbon County—was the daughter of the town druggist. Her parents accepted her relationship with Collier, who was nearly five years her senior, but insisted she first go to prep school in Virginia for a year after graduation. She attended Transylvania College in Lexington for two years before coming back to Paris and marrying Collier in 1931. She was twenty, he was twenty-four, and the couple settled into her parents' house. Three daughters followed over the course of the next eleven years: Carolyn, known as "Sis"; Kay; and Jane.

While at Paris, Collier established a reputation as a kind and thoughtful man. A short profile of him published in the school yearbook related his influence on his players' lives, how he had made them "nobler men." Such tributes—from students, players, assistant coaches, sportswriters, just about anyone who came into contact with him—would follow him throughout his life.

The navy assigned him to its training center at Bainbridge, Maryland. Second-class petty officer Collier taught survival swimming and on weekends spent as much time as he could watching football, including Philadelphia Eagles practices. He began having trouble with his hearing while at Bainbridge, and he later traced it back to the hours he spent training sailors underwater at the base's indoor pool. The cause of his hearing loss never was fully pinpointed, but testing determined it likely was an inoperable and progressive nerve disorder. He could hear volume fine, but he had trouble interpreting words. Riding in a car at night, for instance, he could hear his companions talking, but he wasn't sure what they were saying. He received a berth on the USS *Chicago*, a heavy cruiser bound for the South Pacific, but a physical revealed his hearing problem, and he was, in his words, "kicked off." Instead, he was sent to Great Lakes.

Brown and Collier spent the 1945 season developing a T-formation offense featuring a passing game that was quite sophisticated for the time. The Great Lakes team finished with a six-game winning streak and ended the season beating fifth-ranked Notre Dame 39–7, the biggest sports upset of the year in an Associated Press poll of sportswriters. With the football season and the war over, Brown and Collier went their separate ways, Collier to the University of Kentucky as an assistant coach, and Brown to Cleveland as head coach of that city's franchise in the new All-America Football Conference.

Arch Ward, *Chicago Tribune* sports editor, proposed the league and rounded up investors who believed they could compete with the NFL. As with professional baseball, there would be a National and an American league and a championship game at the end of the season between the two leagues—a World Series of football. Ward had a track record for selling sporting events. He created the Major League Baseball All-Star Game and the College All-Star football game, which attracted more than 90,000 fans to Chicago's Soldier Field in 1945.

The timing for a new league seemed ideal because the war had disrupted the NFL's operations. The Cleveland Rams suspended play for a season, and other teams merged; the Pittsburgh Steelers and Philadelphia Eagles became the "Steagles." Professional and college football players returning from the service were looking for a place to play, creating a stable of free agents.

The All-America started with franchises in eight cities: New York, Brooklyn, Buffalo, and Miami in the East Division; Cleveland, San Francisco, Los Angeles, and Chicago in the West. Dan Topping, owner of baseball's Yankees and the NFL franchise in Brooklyn, took charge of the AAFC's New York Yankees; Eleanor Gehrig, widow of the baseball great, was a co-owner. Radio star Don Ameche headed the Los Angeles Dons—along with, among others, film mogul Louis Mayer of Metro-Goldwyn-Mayer, and the movie stars Pat O'Brien and Bing Crosby.

The Cleveland franchise's principle owner was Arthur "Mickey" McBride, a "millionaire taxicab magnate," who also owned real estate in Chicago and Florida. McBride operated the Yellow Cab franchise in Cleveland and recently had taken over Canton's taxi fleet. Early in his career he'd worked as circulation manager of the *Cleveland Press,* and one day a drunk employee charged into his office brandishing a pistol. McBride wasn't there, but the employee took hostages. McBride was phoned and rushed to his office and, as the hostages cowered in fear, ordered the man to hand over the gun. The man surrendered it. "That's the kind of courage Arthur McBride has," the *Cleveland Press* reported. "Tackling the pro football business ought to be a snap for him."[5]

McBride was fifty-five and knew little about football, but his sons attended Notre Dame and were smitten with the game. McBride offered the head coaching job to Irish coach Frank Leahy, and Leahy agreed—the two men shook on it—but Notre Dame's president asked McBride to refrain from hiring him. Not wanting to cause any trouble for his sons, he rescinded the offer.[6] At Ward's recommendation, McBride offered the job to Paul Brown, still serving at Great Lakes. Brown had made $9,000 a year at Ohio State, and Cleveland offered him $25,000 per year for five years, a share of the team's profits, and $1,000 per month as long as he was in the navy—"the best deal ever given a football coach," McBride crowed.[7] Nonetheless, Brown hesitated. He asked McBride whether he truly was wealthy and whether he was willing to spend the money necessary to create a successful franchise. McBride assured him the answer to both questions was yes. Brown kept talking about his loyalty to a "saint," which confused McBride. It was Lynn St. John, Ohio State's athletic director. Brown also noted he held the rank of professor at Ohio State. "I finally asked him if he had ever heard of the Cleveland Trust Bank," McBride said, "and when he said, 'Yes,' I asked him if he could cash in his titles for money. That seemed to be the clincher."[8] Brown wanted complete control over the football operation, and McBride agreed, adding general manager to his title.

Buckeye hardliners accused Brown of betraying them, while others couldn't figure out why he would leave college football for a professional league that hadn't played a game and in a city that didn't appear to care much for football. The Cleveland Rams won the NFL championship in 1945, their final year in the city, but lost more than $50,000. Owner Dan Reeves said he'd hemorrhaged money every year since buying the franchise in 1941. It didn't make sense. With 900,000 people, Cleveland was the nation's sixth-largest city, and it was perfectly situated both geographically and culturally for a pro team to prosper.

Eastern Ohio, along with western Pennsylvania and upstate New York, was the cradle of professional football. The first pro teams dated to the 1890s and were founded in Pittsburgh: Allegheny Athletic Association and the Pittsburgh Athletics. Soon after came the Latrobe Athletic Club, the Indians Athletic Association of Jeannette, and many more. The first pro team in Ohio was the Massillon Tigers (not to be confused with the high school team) in 1903, followed by the Canton Bulldogs in 1904. That same year, teams popped up across the state, in Shelby, Akron, Dover, Salem, and Lorain. To a large extent, the clubs were made up of local boys, many of whom were recent immigrants and who worked in the steel mills and heavy industry thriving in the region. The rules were lax, and the games became violent encounters, bordering on assault and battery. The players could knock heads without fear of arrest while earning a few bucks. The teams provided their growing legions of fans with good, if not clean, entertainment and gave the smaller towns senses of identity. A Massillon victory over Canton, for instance, gave the city bragging rights for a year.

The NFL was organized in 1920 in Canton—"born in poverty, raised in confusion," in the words of the football writer Tex Maule—and in the intervening quarter of a century forty cities had franchises.[9] In Ohio, those included Cleveland, Canton, Dayton, Akron, Massillon, Cincinnati, Columbus, Marion, Toledo, and Portsmouth. The Rams had begun playing in Cleveland in 1937—the nickname was chosen because it fit easily in newspaper headlines—and Reeves bought the club for $100,000. A New York stockbroker, he was a rabid football fan but had no allegiance to Cleveland. The Rams' last appearance in the city was the 1945 championship game, in which 32,178 watched them defeat the Redskins 15–14 on a zero-degree day at Municipal Stadium. Snow was piled on the sidelines, and the Washington band's instruments froze. That more than 30,000 people would show up in such miserable weather was unfathomable to reporters. It demonstrated the city's potential for pro football, but Reeves already was on his way out, leaving for the West Coast more than a decade before the Brooklyn Dodger and New York Giant baseball franchises. On departing he said, "I consider Los Angeles the greatest city for the future of football in the United States." He later admitted he'd offered Cleveland a poor product and had done little to promote it, adding that it had been his plan from the beginning to move to Los Angeles. The Rams debacle was an anomaly; Cleveland was a good sports town, and it was hungry for football.[10]

The new Cleveland franchise ran an ad in the local newspapers asking fans to submit a team nickname, along with an explanation of no more than fifty words. The prize was a $1,000 war bond. A panel of "prominent Clevelanders," including former Cleveland Indians baseball star Tris Speaker, would pick the winner. More than 8,000 people entered, and 2,000 names were proposed. John J. Harnett, a sailor, won, proposing "Panthers," after an earlier Cleveland semipro team. But a man named George Jones pointed out that in the 1920s he had owned the Cleveland Panthers and thus the rights to the name. He threatened to sue. It's likely McBride would have paid him off to obtain the name, but Brown said no. The Panthers had been losers, and he wanted no part of the name. "I won't start out with anything that smacks of failure," he said. McBride recalled the committee, and it chose another popular entry, "Browns," for the coach. A second $1,000 war bond was awarded, this time to William S. Thompson of Euclid. Paul Brown initially refused. He wanted a nickname he could animate, like the Massillon Tiger. He eventually gave in, and he did choose the team colors: seal brown, burnt orange, and white.[11]

The NFL and AAFC began scrambling for players, competing for pros and for college players chosen in their respective drafts. "Now in a player Donnybrook of this type," wrote John Dietrich of the *Plain Dealer*, "it is understood that ethics are out the window and the law of the jungle prevails."[12] In May of 1945, Brown's former assistant and his successor at Ohio State, Carroll Widdoes, complained that Brown was signing players off the Buckeyes' 1942 freshmen squad. The NFL had established a rule that players couldn't be drafted until their class graduated. The '42 freshmen wouldn't graduate until the spring of 1946. "When he was here I heard him in all his speeches advise boys to get their college education first and then sign professional contracts," Widdoes said. "Now that he is in the pro game he is doing an about face."[13] Widdoes pointed specifically to Lou Groza, the tackle and placekicking star of the '42 freshmen team. The Martins Ferry native weighed about 230 pounds and was nicknamed "Big Chief." He was Hungarian, but with his Roman nose and thick black hair he resembled—some thought—the silhouette on the Indian nickel. He joined the service after his freshman year at Ohio State, was stationed in the Philippines with the Army Medical Corps, and played no service ball. Widdoes and Ohio State insisted he come back to school.

Arch Ward said he agreed with the NFL's graduation policy, but the war had changed everything. He noted that college coaches and athletic directors insisted their former players return to school and earn their degrees, but they failed to mention their desire for the players to help fill stadiums on Saturday afternoons. The choice should be left to the players, Ward argued. They left college as boys, but they returned from the war as men.

Brown claimed he knew nothing about players being contacted by the Cleveland franchise, which was highly unlikely, because he had his hand in everything involving the team. "Our league cannot hope to operate until the 1946 season," he said, "and the availability of those 1942 freshmen now in service is contingent upon how long it takes to whip the Japanese."[14] Brown officially became Browns coach on March 2, 1946. Groza already had signed with Cleveland the previous month, while on Okinawa—the only condition was he make it back alive.

Another player the Browns signed early on was Jim Daniell, who played under Brown at Ohio State in 1941 and was an All-American tackle. He entered the service and played at Great Lakes in 1942, then shipped out for the South Pacific, where he served on a destroyer and saw extensive combat on Okinawa, earning a Silver Star for heroism. He was discharged in October 1945 and joined the Chicago Bears midway through the season. Now, at age twenty-six, he chose to reunite with his college coach. He made himself team captain, and Brown uncharacteristically acquiesced.

Brown relied on his contacts throughout college and service football to build his first team. In addition to Groza and Daniell, he signed five other former Buckeyes, among them lineman Lin Houston, who had played for him at Massillon and on the national championship squad, and receiver Dante "Gluefingers" Lavelli from Hudson. The team included fifteen native Ohioans. Brown preferred midwesterners because he thought he could relate best to them. "I knew what we would be getting in terms of life-style and general philosophy," he wrote in his autobiography, *PB*. Conversely, he was "reluctant to dabble with players from the West Coast. Invariably, they played for a year or two, got a taste of some cold weather or missed the life-style of California and began demanding to be traded to teams on the West Coast."[15]

Among the thirty-one original Browns, twenty-one had played in the Big Ten or at colleges in Ohio, Pennsylvania, West Virginia, and western New York. They included linebacker Lou Saban of Indiana, tackle Lou Rymkus of Notre Dame, halfback Edgar "Special Delivery" Jones of Pittsburgh, and quarterback Otto Graham of Northwestern. In addition to withstanding the cold, Brown knew, those players would attract fans from Ohio and throughout the region.

Shortly after his discharge from the navy, Brown held a clinic in Cleveland that attracted about 400 high school and college coaches from a half dozen states. A banquet at the Hotel Hollenden included a speech by James A. "Sleepy Jim" Crowley, one of the famed Notre Dame Four Horsemen and commissioner of the AAFC. With Paul Brown in Cleveland, Crowley said, the league was assured of success in at least one city.

Much of Brown's discussion with the coaches centered on the intricacies of the newly popular T-formation offense, which he and Collier had installed in their final year at Great Lakes. It transformed the position of quarterback, and the coaches were eager to learn how to run it. Most teams were using the single-wing offense, in which the ball was delivered by shotgun snap to halfbacks who ran or threw. In the T formation, the quarterback lined up directly behind the center, with three backs in a parallel line behind him. It was important that he be a good passer as well as runner. Brown was so confident of his superior knowledge and his ability to adapt that he was happy to share what he knew with the other coaches. He handed out notebooks and showed game films from Great Lakes. "We get a lot of good out of this clinic, too," he said. "If we tell all we know each spring, then by fall we've got to keep digging up new stuff, new plays. It keeps us on our toes. If you use the same stuff year after year you get stale."[16]

Brown believed that in Graham he'd found the ideal quarterback to run the T formation. Brown's Ohio State teams faced Graham and Northwestern three times and were beaten twice. The 1941 Buckeyes' only loss was 14–7 to Northwestern, and Graham threw two touchdown passes. A halfback in a single-wing offense at Northwestern, Graham set Big Ten records for pass attempts and completions for a game, season, and career. He also was adept at handling the ball and could command an offense. He was an All-American basketball player at Northwestern and played professionally for Rochester of the National Basketball League in the winter of '46. "Graham, tall and sturdy, with thick black hair and a turned up nose that gives him an eager expression," as a reporter described him, "has been a glamour boy of athletics from his sophomore days at Northwestern."[17] He was an air cadet during the war and spent a season with North Carolina Pre-Flight in 1944, where he was introduced to the T formation. Brown offered him $7,500 per year and $250 a month as long as he remained in the military.

The Browns assembled for their first training camp on July 29, 1946, at the Alpha Xi Delta sorority house on the campus of Bowling Green State University. The seventh member of the coaching staff, Blanton Collier, joined the team that day. Brown had wanted him from the beginning, but Collier's answer didn't come until shortly before training camp. Finally, he telegrammed: "Will be there day after tomorrow." The decision to leave Kentucky for Cleveland, a difficult one for him and Forman, began a push and pull the Colliers would struggle with throughout his career. They were Bourbon County natives, as were their parents before them, and they felt more comfortable there than anywhere else. But Blanton had found the perfect career: he was being paid to teach football, and at the highest level.

Brown made Collier his roommate and assigned him to coach the defensive backs and to design a defensive scheme. Blanton stood in front of the classroom and explained in detail each player's assignment. "Each specific skill, each small point was taught as if it, and you, were the most important part of the team effort," said linebacker Walt Michaels. "I felt that all eleven men believed in the importance of their roles, and their assignments, because of this approach, which really gave us the cohesiveness necessary for success. . . . He had a pet saying, 'To put it another way,' and he could put it a hundred different ways in one session."[18]

Brown soon put Collier in charge of the offensive backs as well, and he knew every player's role on every play. In film sessions, the other coaches would ask him what had happened on the play they were watching: "Whose man was that?" they'd ask. "Who missed that man?"

On offense, he developed the idea of the flanker. He positioned one of the running backs out of the backfield and made him a third receiver, which enhanced the T formation's passing attack. On defense, he introduced hand signals for different formations, changing the alignment on the go to counter the opponent's offensive formation. A fist, for example, meant a five-man line. "Most people don't have any idea that these things originated with him, because he was so quiet," fullback/linebacker Marion Motley said. "He was always behind the scenes, and never took any credit. But we knew, and when we needed to know anything we went to Blanton."[19]

Collier's primary job, though, was to teach Graham how to run the T formation. They talked through, and literally walked through, each play, step by step. Graham never had encountered anyone as thorough as Collier. "Everything had to be perfect. He was a stickler on perfection, but at the same time he had great patience," Graham said. "If I made a mistake, we would keep working—he would try to draw it out of me—give me every possible chance. He believed that if you repeated any skill enough, it would become a habit."[20]

Flush with McBride's money, Paul Brown established a new standard for running a professional football franchise. He stocked the team with born-and-bred Buckeyes, including African Americans. He organized extravagant pregame and halftime entertainment, and he invested heavily in promotion. Following the 1945 NFL season, the Rams' press agent, Nate Wallack, signed on with the Browns and began selling the team in smaller northeastern Ohio cities. The franchise bought promotional space on 110 billboards, half in the city, the rest in Akron, Canton, Massillon, Mansfield, Warren, Youngstown, Lorain, and Elyria. McBride adorned his cabs with advertising and flooded the radio and newspapers with ads promoting the attractive ticket sellers staffing the team's phone banks. By July 1946, the Browns had sold 3,000 season tickets, seven times more than the Rams ever sold. Industrial plants bought large blocks of tickets, and sales were strong outside the city. Ten thousand seats were set aside for schoolchildren, who could attend for twenty-five cents.

Shortly after training camp opened, Brown announced he'd signed Bill Willis, another player with Ohio connections. Willis, a Columbus native and a 1943 All-American lineman at Ohio State, had approached Brown in the spring of 1946 and asked if he could play for the Browns. He had spent 1945 as coach and athletic director at Kentucky State. It was a question not of whether he was good enough but of whether the new league was accepting black players. No African American had played in the NFL since 1933 and to that point only sporadically. Brown told Willis he knew of no rules barring blacks and he'd discuss it at a league meeting. Some owners objected, but Brown ignored them. Willis became the first African American signed by the AAFC, and at the same time he permanently integrated professional football. Jackie Robinson was still a year away from breaking Major League Baseball's color barrier. Paul Brown was the Branch Rickey and Bill Willis the Jackie Robinson of professional football. "Paul set the tone—'the thread follows the needle,' you know," Willis said. "Paul treated every man alike." He didn't make a big deal of it. He didn't boast or take credit. As Jim Brown said later, "He just went out, signed a bunch of great black athletes, and started kicking butt."[21]

Willis immediately impressed at training camp with his speed and strength. He played middle guard and was so quick off the ball that the center, Mo Scarry, yelled for the coaches to see if he was jumping offside. Collier positioned himself behind Willis, and Brown kneeled at the line of scrimmage. The offense ran three more plays, and each time Willis barged past Scarry, never offside, and grabbed Graham before he could hand off to the running back. "He has as much explosive power as anyone I ever saw," Brown said.

Brown's attitude regarding race was enlightened for the time, but he wasn't willing to break custom and room white and black players together in training camp. The team needed another African American. Collier prodded Brown to sign Marion Motley, a 6-foot-1, 235-pound fullback who'd played for them the previous season at Great Lakes. Motley was working in a steel mill in his hometown of Canton, making $65 per week. He was married and the father of three or four children, the number varying in newspaper stories. Collier called him and invited him to camp. "I've always believed that they needed a roommate for Willis," Motley later told football historian Mickey Herskowitz. "I don't think they really felt I'd make the team." But Motley's speed and his ability to block and catch passes quickly made him indispensable. He also was a force on defense as linebacker. Photos from the era show him racing around end, football tucked in his arm, and a fierce expression under his white leather helmet.[22]

Cleveland's African American newspaper, the *Call and Post*, closely followed the progress of Willis and Motley, and their presence made the Browns a favorite of the city's growing black community. In the week leading up to the opener against Miami, the paper reported, "Hotel reservations indicate that Negro football fans from the entire Midwest will converge upon Cleveland for a view of Paul Brown's sensational Negro stars."[23]

Paul Brown had been passionate and obsessive about football since his days as a 135-pound quarterback for the Massillon Washington High Tigers. By the time he was a senior, he insisted that his coach, Dave Stewart, let him call plays and decide on substitutions. "He was a banty rooster, full of authority and self-confidence," Stewart recalled. He enrolled at Ohio State, but soon realized he wasn't big enough to play for the Buckeyes and transferred to Miami University, where he was a capable, if not sensational, runner and passer. In 1932 he returned to Massillon as head football and basketball coach. When he arrived, the school's stadium could hold 5,000 spectators. During his time there, the school built a stadium capable of seating 21,000. In 1940 the school drew 161,000 fans, more than any college in Ohio except Ohio State.[24]

The attraction was more than just a winning team. Brown understood the value of showmanship as well, and while coaching at Massillon he collaborated with the high school's band director, George "Red" Bird, to provide extravagant variety shows at halftime. Marching bands were nothing new, but Bird's shows were replete with melodramas, comedy skits, boogie-woogie, and waltzes. Brown hired Bird in Cleveland and promised the same and more. Bird developed an all-female marching band, the Musical Majorettes, to perform before games and at halftime. He auditioned 200 women and chose 30, ranging in age from sixteen to twenty-four. "Please stress the fact that all these girls are musicians," he told reporters. "This isn't an organization of drum majorettes." A writer for the *Cleveland News* attended a practice prior to the opening game. One of the 30 was married, he reported, and all were in good standing with Local No. 4, American Federation of Musicians. "Some are skinny, some plump, some short and some tall," he wrote. "There are no blubbery seals among them, however. They walk miles each day in their drills. Reducing is an unnecessary evil." The majorettes wore skirts and boots that exposed their knees, and they were compared to the Rockettes because of their precision. They opened their show prior to the team's first game by forming the letters *HI* while a male singer performed "Hi Neighbor." At halftime, the man sang "Old McDonald," while six majorettes wearing animal heads jumped on stools and danced as he sang choruses for the horse, cow, sheep, pig, dog, and duck. Tommy Flynn, the team's 4-foot-7 mascot, dressed in a bowler, Cleveland Browns T-shirt, and checked pants, ran around with a whip, acting as Old McDonald.[25]

From day one, the Browns played their home games in Cleveland's Municipal Stadium. The city's voters had approved a $2.5 million bond in 1928 to help pay for its construction, making it one of the first times the public helped finance a sports stadium. The final cost was $3 million. The Colosseum-like edifice, which opened in 1931, could seat 78,000 people, making it one of the world's largest outdoor venues. The first event was a heavyweight championship bout between Max Schmeling and Young Stribling on July 3, 1931. The Indians played in the stadium for a couple of seasons, but small weekday crowds prompted them to move back to older League Park except for holiday and weekend games. The Tribe moved to the stadium permanently in 1947 and played its World Series games there in 1948 and 1954, attracting crowds of more than 70,000 for each contest.

The Browns opener against the Miami Seahawks drew 60,135 fans, said to be the largest crowd for a regular-season professional football game to that point. The figure was about 12,000 fewer than the Rams' *total* draw in their four home games the previous year. Cleveland beat Miami 44–0. Lou Groza kicked three field goals and attempted a 58-yarder that fell just short. By the day's standards, it was an extraordinary performance. Kickers were position players—Groza was a tackle—who on occasion could knock the ball through the uprights. When Groza entered the game, he brought along a strip of athletic tape tucked in his helmet. The holder, Don Greenwood, took one end of it, and Groza laid the other on the ground, aiming at the center of the crossbar. Sports sections across the country published a series of photos of Groza and Greenwood going through their pre-kick routine.

Lou was the third of four sons of "Big Spot" Groza. Big Spot had worked in a coal mine and received his nickname after a mule kicked him in the eye and gave him a shiner. He left the mines and bought a tavern across the street from a steel mill in Martins Ferry, and the family lived upstairs. Groza's older brother Frank kicked for the high school team, and Lou went along and shagged. He kicked the ball back and soon had graduated to kicking over telephone wires. In high school, he could kick the ball over a wall about fifty feet beyond the goalposts. At the other end of the field, he could sail it over a fence and onto railroad tracks. He wasn't just a kicker. He led Martins Ferry to the state basketball championship his senior year, and he captained the football, basketball, and baseball teams. He was a surgical technician during the war, and one of his jobs on Okinawa was to dig up bodies buried on the beach and put them in boxes to be sent home. "That was worse than the battle itself," he said.[26] He was twenty-one when he reported to Cleveland's first training camp, wearing his army fatigues and carrying everything he owned in his duffel.

Cleveland won its first seven games, outscoring its opponents 180–34. AAFC owners began grumbling that the Browns were so good they were bad for the rest of the league; some wanted to break up the team. Brown countered that other clubs needed to improve, pointing out that baseball's American League didn't break up the Yankees. The Browns lost twice, first to the 49ers at home as former Stanford great Frankie Albert threw for three touchdowns against Cleveland's league-leading pass defense. The following week, they lost 17–16 to the Dons in Los Angeles, the difference Groza's first missed extra point of the season. Afterward, Brown threatened to cut players and not pay their way home. They protested to Daniell, who told Brown the players thought he was too hard on them. "If you nagged your wife every day at breakfast, lunch, and dinner I'm sure she'd leave you," Daniell told him. Brown demoted him to second string the following week. "Paul never spoke to me again," Daniell said, "except when it was absolutely necessary for him to say something that had a bearing on our games."[27]

Cleveland won its final five games of the regular season, ending with a 66–14 rout of the Brooklyn Dodgers, in which nine different players scored touchdowns. A week before the Browns were to play the New York Yankees for the AAFC championship, Daniell and two other players, Lou Rymkus and Mac Speedie, were arrested following a run-in with two Cleveland patrol officers. Daniell honked his horn at a police car he was following on Euclid Avenue early Sunday morning. Sergeant Joseph Strauss said Daniell "apparently was irked because we weren't running fast enough." The police car stopped for a red light at East 81st Street, and Daniell pulled up beside it and yelled at the officers. Strauss demanded to see Daniell's driver's license and the lineman refused. The officers ordered Daniell, Rymkus, and Speedie out of the car, but they refused. More officers arrived, and the police wrestled the trio into a patrol wagon and took them to the central police station. Rymkus and Speedie were charged with disorderly conduct and Daniell with public intoxication.

When the three reported for practice the next day, Brown told Daniell he no longer was part of the team. Speedie and Rymkus were different matters, he said, and both would play against the Yankees. "So far as Daniell is concerned I've done what I think is best," Brown said. "We run the team on a certain basis and it's up to the players to observe the rules or take the consequences. Daniell is not being made an example. He's simply getting what's coming to him." Brown was done, once and for all, with Daniell and his challenge to authority. "We were a young team and Paul had us in the palm of his hand after that," Graham said. "We thought, if he could do that to Jim Daniell, he'd do it to anyone." For years afterward, veterans told rookies about the day Paul Brown cut Jim Daniell.[28]

The Browns defeated the Yankees 14–9 to win the AAFC title, Graham throwing the winning touchdown to Lavelli in the final minutes. The smallest crowd of the season, just over 40,000, watched the game, but the turnout was blamed on the weather. It snowed all morning and throughout the first half. The players voted Daniell a full share of the game receipts, $931, plus the pen-and-pencil set each member of the team received. Cleveland's seven home games drew more than 400,000 fans, and the Browns outscored their opponents 423–137. They were "as well rounded as a country haircut," an AP writer noted. Players from the NFL and AAFC chose the All-Pro team for the Associated Press, and no Browns made the first team. Motley and Lavelli were chosen to the second team. "I suppose we should consider this a compliment," Brown said. "We won the Western Division without any ball players."

CHAPTER THREE

On the opening day of training camp each season, Paul Brown met with the players for two hours and lectured them on everything from how to practice to proper table manners. "We don't want any butches on this team," he told the players. They ate all meals together. Sports shirts were allowed; T-shirts were not. "Don't eat with your elbows on the table, and don't make noise when you eat," Brown said. "There have been people who failed to make this team simply because they were obnoxious to eat with."[1]

He handed out three-ring binders and demanded the players write down all the rules and, as camp progressed, to diagram every play—not just their assignments, but *everyone's*. He tested them at the beginning of each week. This classroom work, one of his many innovations, became "the very basis of our football system," he said.[2] In 1951 he signed Stan Heath, a standout passer from the University of Nevada, as a potential replacement for Graham at quarterback. Heath didn't take the first written exam seriously and failed to answer a single question correctly. Brown cut him. Some players created cheat sheets. Brown knew it, but let it go. He figured they were learning as they cribbed.

Drinking was discouraged though not banned, but Brown was a stickler on smoking. One day at training camp, defensive end Bill Quinlan spied a trainer's half-smoked cigarette on the lip of an ashtray and took a quick drag on it. "What are you doing, Quinlan?" Brown shouted from behind him. "Trying to ruin my organization?" Whether the story was true, it became part of team lore. The players learned early on it was Brown's way or the highway. "I believed strongly in the things that were necessary for us to win," he wrote in his autobiography, "and I refused to tolerate any exceptions to those beliefs."[3]

He introduced intelligence testing to judge players' capacity to learn, which he associated with the ability to perform under pressure. Among the questions:

—If Mr. Lawson pays $65 a month rent and earns a salary of $3,120 a year, what percent of his salary does he pay for rent?

—What is the opposite of diminutive: distraught, large, inductive or reluctant?

—If lemons sell at three for 10¢, how much will a dozen and a half cost?

The players were given more than 100 questions. Some finished all of them, while others marked only the answers they were sure of. No one ever answered all the questions correctly. "But the test is helpful in appraising the players, particularly the rookies," Brown explained. "[One year] the test showed that one of our rookies would make a fine carpenter. That's exactly what he eventually became."[4] Some players resented the test. Said one, "I don't like somebody giving me a test to find out how smart or dumb I am, when I can't give him one to find out how smart or dumb he is." But no one who wanted to keep his job complained.

Brown valued speed over size and began timing players in the 40-yard dash, an innovation teams at all levels use to this day. He chose 40 yards because he wanted to see how fast his players could sprint downfield to cover a punt. He came up with the face mask on helmets after Graham took an elbow to the mouth in a 1953 game against the 49ers. The quarterback went into the locker room and team doctor Vic Ippolito closed the resulting gash with fifteen stiches. When Graham came out for the second half, a clear piece of plastic across the front of his helmet protected his mouth. The AAFC restricted the number of players a team could carry to thirty-three, so, to add depth, Brown developed a "taxi squad." McBride hired a handful of players to drive cabs and paid them an extra $100 per week to practice with the team. And in the interest of team camaraderie, Brown had the players go to a movie together the night before a game and stay in a hotel before home games. Wives could accompany the players to the movie, but then they had to say good night. "Everything we did together," he explained, "was for the purpose of unity and to remind our players that as a team they faced a very serious business the next day."[5]

The Browns were the first team to use chartered airplanes, and onboard the players ate hot meals, not box lunches like other teams. No alcohol was served, because Brown didn't want anyone becoming drunk and unruly. Players took written exams on the next day's game plan during the flight— "again to emphasize to the players that they were not on a joy ride, but that we were taking them to another city for a very serious business."[6]

He used messenger guards to deliver the play from the sideline to the offensive huddle. Other teams allowed the quarterback to call the play, or at least change to a different play at the line of scrimmage. Brown believed that what he saw from the sideline, and Collier observed from the press box, offered better perspectives. "What does a quarterback see when he makes a handoff? What part of the defense does he see?" he asked. "He doesn't see much. Field level is the worst vantage point in the stadium. Besides, a coach calling plays takes a lot of heat off the quarterback."[7] In this system, the quarterback wasn't in charge of the offense. He was no different than the other players in the huddle; he was given the play and he ran it. Graham didn't like Brown calling the plays, but he accepted it. He did sneak an audible on occasion, but he had to be right. If his call went for a big gain, Brown said nothing. If it didn't work, Graham never heard the end of it. "The rest of the time," Graham said, "Paul called the plays, and the record shows he called them pretty good."[8]

The Browns won the AAFC title again in 1947, and in 1948 they went undefeated, 15–0. They were 26–1–1 during that two-year period. Arch Ward asked Brown to give Graham to the struggling Chicago Rockets to boost their attendance—Graham was from nearby Waukegan, Illinois. Brown responded in character, with one word: no.

The Browns lost for the first time in 1949 in the sixth game of the season. The 49ers beat them in San Francisco. The team stayed on the West Coast to play the Los Angeles Dons the following weekend, and one afternoon the players were scheduled to visit a movie studio. As they awaited their bus, Brown told them that anyone who didn't play better against Los Angeles would be released. None of them thought he was kidding, and none of them boarded the bus. They beat the Dons 61–14.

The Browns were so good they became boring, even to their own followers. They averaged more than 48,000 fans in 1946, becoming the only team in the league to make money. They averaged more than 56,000 in 1947, but attendance dropped to an average of 45,000 in '48, and in '49 they drew an average of only 31,000. The league had just seven teams that season and folded on December 9, 1949. Two days, later Cleveland defeated San Francisco for the league title before 22,550 fans at Municipal Stadium. The Browns, the 49ers, and the Baltimore Colts, who joined the league when the Miami franchise failed (the Seattle Seahawks came much later), were the lone survivors accepted into the NFL.

The NFL's players and coaches looked down on the AAFC and regularly denigrated it in the newspapers. Washington owner George Marshall took a shot at the Browns in 1949. "The worst team in our league could beat the best team in theirs," he said. Paul Brown never commented, but for four years he cut out the stories and posted them on a bulletin board. Cleveland's first game in the NFL was against the defending champion Philadelphia Eagles, who had finished 11–1 the previous season and shut out the Rams, 14–0, in the title game. "This is the best team ever put together," Philadelphia coach Greasy Neale said. "Who is there to beat us?"[9] The game was played before 71,237 fans in Philadelphia.

Cleveland's offense featured timing patterns in which Graham's passes and the receivers arrived at the same place at the same time. It confounded the Eagles. "We just never played against a team that threw to a spot as well as Cleveland," said Philadelphia defensive back Russ Craft.[10] Graham threw touchdowns to Mac Speedie, Dub Jones, and Dante Lavelli, and Cleveland won 35–10.

The Browns lost two games in 1950, both to the New York Giants, then beat the Giants 8–3 in a divisional playoff to earn the right to face Los Angeles for the NFL title game. On a brutally cold Christmas Eve at Municipal Stadium, the Browns beat the Rams before about 30,000 fans. Graham threw four touchdown passes, and Groza kicked a 16-yard field goal in the waning seconds to give Cleveland a 30–28 win. In the locker room afterward, NFL commissioner Bert Bell embraced Brown and told him the Browns were the best team he'd ever seen.

The Browns won division titles each year from 1951 to 1955 and were NFL champions again in 1954 and '55. Graham retired following the 1955 season, having played in ten consecutive title games, winning seven. When Brown negotiated a contract before the season, he figured in the share the player would receive from that year's league championship game. "We always got it," Graham said, "and you could hardly negotiate against it."[11]

The team's success naturally reflected well on Brown, and his system was praised and his methods imitated. But rarely mentioned publicly by the players or sportswriters was the tense relationship between the coach and many of his players. During that first meeting of the season, he told them to call him and his assistants by their first names. "We're all good friends—a happy family," he said. The rookies and newcomers believed him, but the veterans knew differently. They chafed under the restrictions and complained they felt like children. Any questioning of the system met with shunning and, in cases such as Jim Daniell, banishment. War made men of many of the players, but it also taught them to follow orders. "I suppose athletes then were more naïve," Graham said. "Certainly, we still talked about things like sportsmanship, and we didn't question everything. We accepted some things simply because they were."[12]

Brown was intimidating, but he hardly was a physically imposing figure. "I'm 5 feet 11," he testily told a photographer. "I am not a small man." He was carefully groomed and well dressed, and he almost always wore a hat to cover his balding pate. He looked more like an attorney than a football coach, and next to his hulking players he seemed almost frail. But he was effective at motivating by ridicule, and he could be brutal. One game Graham scrambled from the pocket a few times for what he considered valid reasons, including not wanting to get injured. Brown replaced him and within earshot said to one of his assistants, "At least now we have someone in there with the guts to stay in the pocket." Marion Motley said that whenever he made a mistake, the coach would walk over to him and hiss, "Do you know that you are killing our football team?" Motley wanted to choke him. Instead, "I'd go back out there and the first jersey that got in front of me I'd try to kill the guy."[13]

In 1959, the Browns were tied for first place with the Giants and playing the Steelers. Star receiver Ray Renfro caught a team-record three touchdown passes, but Cleveland was trailing by a point late in the game. Quarterback Milt Plum threw a long pass to Renfro, who was running so hard his knee came up and knocked the ball out of his hands. The Browns lost. "I was standing there, and Paul grabbed my arm," Renfro recalled. "He had run down the field to get to me. 'Renfro!' he yelled. 'You're through. You can't make the big play anymore!'

"What shook me up, of course, was this: I was conditioned to believe anything that Paul said. We finished second to the Giants, and I spent all the offseason worrying about being washed up."[14]

Blanton Collier was the perfect assistant for what Brown called "our project," but he was a much gentler man. When he was at Paris, an assistant basketball coach said to him after a big win: "Shake left-handed. It's closer to my heart." It became one of his mottos, and he passed it on to his players. In Collier's biography, Graham said, "I owe more to you than anyone else, and I deeply appreciate all you have done for me. I hope we can always be the best of friends—'whichever hand is up.'"[15]

While Brown ran the organization, he relied on his assistants to coach the techniques, and Collier was the ultimate teacher and scholar of football. During games, he sat in the press box and phoned down observations and suggestions.

His hearing wasn't an issue, because all he had to do was watch and talk. Brown used the information for sending in plays and for adjusting the defense. Brown credited Collier with making the Browns the "greatest third-period team in football." After they lost in 1946 to San Francisco, a game in which 'Niners quarterback Frankie Albert threw three touchdown passes, Collier dissected the game film and devised a different scheme for the second meeting. Cleveland won that one 14–7, San Francisco's only score coming on a fumble return by its defense.

Following each season, Collier took films of Cleveland's games home to Kentucky and went through them frame by frame on a hand-crank projector. He evaluated each player on whether he made or missed his assignment and came up with a percentage grade. He and Brown judged 80 percent as acceptable. Under Brown and Collier, player evaluation no longer was just qualitative; it also was quantitative. You could ask Collier if a particular player had had a good year, recalled Leo Murphy, the team's longtime trainer. "Blanton could tell you."[16] This also allowed the Browns to chart the success of each play over the course of the season. Collier compiled the results into a thick binder that he delivered to Brown in the spring. The coaches drew up a playbook for the upcoming season based on Collier's findings. "Blanton's survey is the most profound study of a football team's performance ever made," Brown said. "I'd have settled for something half as comprehensive when I told him to do the job. But Collier doesn't do things by halves."[17] This provided what football historian Michael MacCambridge called "the most extensive performance analysis done in the history of football to that date."[18]

Brown believed his assistant coaches should be full-time employees. Assistants on most teams essentially were laid off during the offseason and needed additional jobs to make ends meet, same as the players. "There was no dignity in having a man coach our offense for six months and then sell automobiles for six months," he said.[19] With Brown in charge, and with McBride's money, Collier could afford to stay home in Paris and do his research.

Following the 1953 season, Baltimore owner Carroll Rosenbloom was looking for a new coach for the Colts. He heard repeatedly he should hire Collier, but Brown refused to grant Rosenbloom permission to talk with him. He said he'd rather lose his right arm than lose Blanton Collier. Rosenbloom complained to commissioner Bert Bell, who determined he had the right to talk with Collier because the job would be a promotion. But Collier told Rosenbloom he wasn't interested in a head coaching job, and Rosenbloom instead hired another of Paul Brown's assistants, Weeb Ewbank. The Colts owner later said he was puzzled that Collier would turn him down, but what Blanton hadn't told Rosenbloom was that he had an offer from the University of Kentucky to replace Bear Bryant. Brown reluctantly let him go for this opportunity. "I was as close to Blanton as I've ever been to any man," he told reporters. "I shall feel his loss personally as he has been my close friend and confidant. I can understand the move he is making. He has done it in his usual high-class manner. I hope he will enjoy a fine career at Kentucky."[20]

CHAPTER FOUR

Collier walked into what seemed a perfect opportunity at Kentucky. He was coming home to a program he'd long wanted to lead and at a time when it was at its peak. In the previous eight seasons under Paul "Bear" Bryant, Kentucky had played in four bowl games, and following the 1950 season, in which the Wildcats finished 10–1, they faced Oklahoma in the Sugar Bowl. The Sooners had won thirty-one straight games, but Kentucky prevailed, 13–7. Bryant had taken Kentucky to college football's pinnacle. But in Lexington, basketball mattered most, more so even than thoroughbreds and bourbon, and Coach Adolph Rupp was considered a saint, if not God himself. Bryant realized he never would be able to compete with Rupp, and after the 1953 season he resigned and left for Texas A&M. His abrupt departure left Wildcat fans stunned. "The truth is that the University of Kentucky was simply not a big enough stage for Bear Bryant, with or without Adolph Rupp to share it," wrote Bryant biographer Allen Barra.[1]

Enter Blanton Collier. Money wasn't a factor in his decision to leave Cleveland for Kentucky. He was fulfilling a lifelong ambition to be a head coach; that he could return home and lead the Wildcats was a dream come true. Forman endorsed the move by arguing against it, as was her practice throughout her husband's career. "When he was trying to make a decision she would take the opposite side, just to keep him thinking about the pros and cons of both sides," daughter Kay Collier McLaughlin said. The story goes that Blanton listened to Forman and decided to stay in Cleveland instead of going to Kentucky. When he told her she burst into tears. "Whether that's true or apocryphal," daughter Kay said, "I don't know."[2]

Paris, where Forman and Blanton grew up, was less than twenty miles from Lexington. Blanton's father worked for the railroad and farmed. After he died in the early 1940s, his widow let rooms in her house, and among her boarders were people in town for the tobacco market. Forman's father ran the town's drugstore, and its mahogany cabinets with Tiffany glass were a source of pride for the town. Her idyllic life changed when she was twelve:

her sixteen-year-old brother was accidently shot to death by his best friend. Blanton later told the girls their mother suffered a form of survivor's guilt: she needed everything she touched to be perfect; otherwise, what was the value in her being alive while her brother was dead? As an adult, Kay became a professional counselor and agreed with her father's diagnosis, adding, "She was a woman of the South: You dress it up and make it pretty."

The Colliers invested themselves in the university community as well as the football program. Blanton revamped the tutoring system, and Kay and her older sister, Carolyn, tutored the players. Blanton knew some of the boys had been passed on in high school simply because of their athletic ability, and he wanted to make sure they developed basic skills such as writing and note-taking. "It was like we had a bunch of brothers," Kay said. "We loved those guys." The assistant coaches met with Collier in the downstairs den of his home on Ridgeway Road, and after games Forman opened their house to university officials, boosters, and friends and served chili and bourbon. "It was quite a family atmosphere," Kay said. "That's how Mommy and Daddy were."

Blanton's hearing worsened at Kentucky. He wore a hearing aid, but it didn't help much. He became adept at lipreading, and he insisted on eye contact. It bothered him when people didn't look at him when they talked to him, and men with bushy mustaches were a particular problem. The Colliers installed two phone jacks side by side around their house. When he received a call, Forman would plug in the second phone. She'd sit beside him with pencil and paper, listen in, and write down what was said on the other end of the line. The assistant coaches made sure to speak loudly and clearly around him and, with the exception of occasional practical jokes, showed him utmost respect. One day in a coaches' meeting, Collier went around the room asking the assistants their opinions about a particular strategy. Ermal Allen, who had played for Collier with the Browns, said, "You can't tell what the bird eats until the bird shits."[3]

"What was that?" Collier asked as the other coaches cracked up. Blanton laughed too when told what Allen had said.

Bryant had ruled by fear and intimidation, and his practices were physically brutal and laced with profanities. Many of his first players at Kentucky were ex-servicemen, and they were used to such treatment from basic training. "He worked us like we were getting ready to fight the Japanese all over again," said Walt Yaworsky, a lineman from Cleveland. "It was his will against ours for four years."[4] Bryant's first year at Texas A&M became legendary for the preseason camp he ran in the town of Junction. Of 115 players present at the beginning, only 35 survived the ten days of heat and torture. They became known as the "Junction Boys" and were the subject of a book and film.

Collier couldn't have been more different than Bryant. He rarely raised his voice and never swore, and he valued teaching over rough treatment. He quietly explained what he expected from his players, not just on the field but also as people. He wanted young men who exhibited character, poise, and guts. Under Bryant, practices often would end with players going one-on-one in blocking and tackling drills until one or both dropped from exhaustion. Collier's approach was more cerebral. He patiently explained how to tackle and block, as though he and the players were in math class. "You know what force is?" he would ask his linemen. "It's mass times velocity."

Sixty years later, Howard Schnellenberger, who played and coached under Collier at Kentucky, could recite how Blanton taught the drive block: "If you're right-handed, you put your right foot opposite the instep of your left foot. Place your right hand six inches ahead of your left foot. Square your back. Keep your ass as high as your necklace. On the snap take a step that's no more than six inches long and then take a second step that's no longer than six inches. Do this for three steps, with your weight evenly distributed and moving forward like a sprinter coming out of the blocks. Keep your back flat and drive your helmet into the defensive player's sternum."[5]

After the lineman had done this twenty times and mastered it, he'd follow the same process backward, from contact to original stance. In Collier's mind, the blocker had to perfect the technique backward in order to do it forward.

Collier's approach to teaching his daughter Kay to swim is another good example. She was deathly afraid of water, and so instead of starting out by teaching the mechanics of swimming, he explained the dynamics of floating, how the water could hold her up. "The goal of swimming was too far removed from where I was to have meaning for me," she said. "First, my fear had to be dealt with."

He had her hold her nose and duck her face into water, over and over, first in the bathtub and then in a swimming pool. After weeks of that, he had her open her eyes underwater, but only for a moment, and initially in the bathtub. "See how many of your fingers were on the bottom of the tub?" he'd ask. From the tub, they progressed to the swimming pool. She would peer into the water repeatedly, and during breaks she would ride around on his back, arms tight around his neck, as he swam through the water. Next, she stood beside him, waist deep in the shallow end, and leaned forward into his hands, her stomach resting on his palms. First for a count of one, then two, three, gradually longer. Her confidence began to grow. "The long-term goal of swimming seldom, if ever, crossed my mind," she said. "The short-term goals became my obsessions, even as they were his."

Now came time to learn the skills. Again standing in the shallow end, she leaned forward until her face was in the water and practiced strokes, first with him standing behind moving her arms and later with him calling out the rhythm as she practiced on her own. "There was never a reprimand," she recalled, "only steadfast repetition." Success—and newfound confidence—was celebrated with wet hugs.

He taught her the next skill on dry land. She would lie on her bed, her head hanging over the edge, and practice breathing. The head must roll, not bob. Which side should she turn her head? Her choice; whatever's most comfortable. Combine breathing with the stroke. Breathing and stroke practice moved from the bed to the pool, but in a standing position in waist-deep water. "Slowly, so slowly. Adding skill to skill," she said. "One day I kick, a few yards only—to his outstretched hands. . . . Now the stroke is added. Now the breathing. *I am swimming!*"[6]

Most football coaches in that era would have walked their daughters to the end of the dock and thrown them in. Sink or swim. Therein lay the difference between Blanton Collier and other coaches. He was a meticulous teacher of detail. He was patient and compassionate. He instilled confidence.

Collier's manner bewildered the Kentucky players. They couldn't understand why he never yelled at them and wondered if it was because he only had girls and didn't know how to raise boys. "We talked about that a lot," Schnellenberger said.[7] Fans asked the players to compare Collier and Bryant, but they found it difficult because the two men were so different. Bryant was a tyrant, but under him the Wildcats won bowl games and become a national power. The players initially found it hard to make a case for Collier, but they gradually bought into his approach. He unquestionably knew football and effectively imparted his knowledge. He installed the Browns' passing game, and in his first season Kentucky finished 7–3 and defeated rival Tennessee in Knoxville for the first time in twenty years. Collier was named Southeastern Conference Coach of the Year.

For a number of reasons, however, he found it difficult to sustain success. The NCAA suspended Kentucky's basketball program for the 1952 and '53 seasons for recruiting violations. As a result, the university restricted its sports teams from recruiting more than five out-of-state players—a rule that had far more impact on football than basketball. And like all Southeastern Conference schools, Kentucky accepted no black players from anywhere. The state lacked a deep recruiting base of high school players, and Collier couldn't recruit as much as he needed to in the nearby football-rich states of Ohio and Pennsylvania. It created an untenable situation.

Collier also wasn't the aggressive recruiter Bryant was; he was neither a proselytizer nor a salesman. Bryant would take promising recruits on extended car or boat rides or on hunting trips and not return them until they agreed to sign with Kentucky. When Bryant recruited Schnellenberger from Louisville's Flaget High School, he brought along the governor of Kentucky. That failed to sway Schnellenberger's mother, a devout Catholic who told her son he must fulfill his commitment to Indiana University. The next time Bryant came to the Schnellenbergers' house, he brought along the archbishop of the Louisville diocese. Schnellenberger switched to Kentucky, with his mother's blessing.

Collier also was unwilling to bend the rules. When Kentucky's wealthy alums offered him a house and a golf club membership, he turned them down. He didn't want to be beholden to them. They offered to pay for promising recruits—as they had for Bryant—but Collier again said no. Assistant Coach Norm Deeb recalled a conversation in which a booster asked Collier if he wanted a top recruit from Louisville. Collier said he wanted and needed him. The booster said the recruit requested a new car and an addition to his parents' house. The booster waited for Collier to give him the go-ahead. "I'd like to have him, but I'm not going to buy him, and I don't want you to buy him," Collier said, and walked away. The booster's face turned purple with rage.[8]

While Collier worked to build the Kentucky program the right way, Bryant took A&M to its first Southwest Conference title, a 9–0–1 record and Associated Press No. 5 ranking in 1956. At one point in 1957, the Aggies were the top-rated team in the country. Bryant left for Alabama after that season, and the NCAA hit A&M with recruiting violations. That didn't appease Kentucky fans, most of whom gladly would have accepted some cheating if it meant more wins.

Not all of the concepts that worked in Cleveland translated to Kentucky. In 1958, Collier tried to introduce a new blocking scheme to his staff, but his assistants failed to understand it, and he shelved it. "Much too often, at Kentucky, we as a staff rejected ideas of his which we would later see someone introduce as the newest 'wrinkle,'" said Ed Rutledge, who later became a scout for the New York Giants. "But we weren't ready to see it at the time. He was too far ahead of us. And he wanted us to be 100 percent together on whatever he taught."[9]

Collier ran democratic meetings with his assistants. He always made the final decision, but he wanted input beforehand. Whether the other coaches agreed with him wasn't as important as if they could provide complete and detailed reasoning for their opinions. On occasion, he would introduce a new play he knew wouldn't work, but he wanted to know who was willing to stand up to him and reject it. "I want to hear what you really think, what you really believe, what you really see happening," he told them. "Then we'll make a decision in which we all believe, and when we all believe it, we can all go out and teach it. But every individual has to stand up and be counted." During lunch he would lecture through the meal, trying to get his assistants to understand what he'd introduced at practice. "He would talk you into submission," Schnellenberger said. "Jesus Christ, he'd wear you out."[10]

Collier continued grading players based on film study. His assistant Bill Arnsparger called it "the greatest contribution he made to football." "When you grade, you look at each technique or movement. Nothing slips by unnoticed," Arnsparger said. "Blanton graded each player on every move, and out of this came the realization of what must be taught, and how it could be taught—step by step and skill by skill."[11]

The Wildcats finished 6-3-1 in Collier's second season, again beat Tennessee, and the Associated Press ranked them seventeenth in the nation at the end of the season. They lost the first two games, and in the fourth Auburn shut them out. On the Monday following that game Collier replaced the usual walk-through with a physical, grueling practice run by two assistants—likely Allen and Buckshot Underwood, holdovers from the Bryant regime. That night, Collier gathered the team and apologized. He said that in his disappointment over the Auburn loss, he'd let others plan the practice. It wasn't in keeping with the kind of program he wanted to run, and it wouldn't happen again. "I already respected him tremendously," said Jim Miller, a sophomore guard, "but I respected him twice as much after that."[12] Kentucky won its next five games but lost the finale to Tennessee.

In 1961, the team finished 5-5, coming on the heels of 5-4-1 and 4-6 seasons. The boosters lost their patience and wrote letters to the university administration calling for Collier and his aides to be fired. One morning Kay, then in high school, awoke to find her father hung in effigy on a branch outside her bedroom window. The family felt betrayed. "There would be people who came and ate our chili and drank our bourbon," Kay said, "and were knifing him in the back."[13]

Forman was a partner in her husband's career, and a nurturer. She treated the assistants and the players as family—Schnellenberger called her "a blessing."[14] As the losses mounted and the pressure built on her husband, she experienced what today are termed anxiety attacks. Life in Lexington became unbearable. She loved to socialize and entertain, but she gave it up. "It just became uncomfortable to see people, even some of our friends," Kay said. Forman suffered stomach pains and took tranquilizers. She didn't go downtown all fall and winter, and she wouldn't have anything to do with anyone who hurt her husband or daughters. "It was painful," Kay said. "You're watching the work people are putting in. You see the hours and dedication, and you just want to lash out at people, and say, 'What's wrong with you?'" Through it all, Forman remained stubborn and loyal to her husband. One day, a disconsolate Kay dropped her chin to her chest, and her mother took her by the collar and said, "Get your head up. Don't ever do that." After Forman died, her daughters discovered letters written between her and Blanton. "We had always seen Daddy as the strength," Kay said. "When we read those letters we realized what a real partnership it was. They each had strengths. She very much made him the focus; everything was planned around him."[15]

On January 3, 1962, Kentucky bought out Collier's contract, which had three years remaining and was worth $50,000. Charlie Bradshaw, who had been an assistant under Bryant and was then at Alabama, replaced him. At the first team meeting, Bradshaw promised the players he planned to make changes. "We're going to find inner toughness and there will be sacrifice," he said. "It will be the hardest work you've ever done and it will require complete dedication and discipline." He was following the model Bryant had used at Texas A&M, and he became notorious for his brutal methods. By the end of the season, the squad had shrunk from eighty-eight players to thirty. "Bradshaw said we should play football like he killed Japs during World War II," said a former army officer who played for Collier and Bradshaw. "He destroyed me as a player. I don't watch football anymore."[16] Over the next seven seasons, Bradshaw's teams won twenty-five games and lost forty-one.

Collier won forty-one games over eight seasons at Kentucky, and although the Wildcats lost to Tennessee in 1961, his final year, he had the best record against the rival Vols of any Kentucky coach: 5–2–1. Only one other coach has won as many games as Collier at Kentucky since—Frank Curci's teams won forty-seven games over nine seasons in the 1970s and '80s.

Much has been written about Paul Brown's coaching legacy, his "coaching tree," but Collier's Kentucky tree is impressive in its own right. The men who worked under him as assistants included, among others, Don Shula, an NFL Hall of Famer and coach of the undefeated 1972 Miami Dolphins; Schnellenberger, who built the University of Miami into a national champion; Arnsparger, architect of the '72 Dolphins' "No-Name Defense" and head coach of the New York Giants; Rutledge, an NFL assistant and scout, including with Shula's Baltimore Colts; Allen, an assistant coach with the Dallas Cowboys; John North, head coach of the New Orleans Saints; Leeman Bennett, head coach of the Atlanta Falcons; and Chuck Knox, head coach of the Seattle Seahawks, Los Angeles Rams, and Buffalo Bills.

A decade later, *Sports Illustrated* wrote a story about Collier's final coaching staff at Kentucky, all of whom were gone the following year, and all of whom went on to success in pro football. "Fired anybody else lately, Kentucky?" the magazine asked.[17]

"This was a sensational man, a sensational coach," Schnellenberger said. "His problem was he came in behind Bryant."[18]

CHAPTER FIVE

Paul Brown not only achieved his goal of creating the professional football equivalent of baseball's Yankees, he did them one better. Between 1946 and 1955, the Yankees won six World Series championships. The Browns won seven titles in that span—four in the All-America Football Conference and three in the NFL. The Yankees failed to win the American League pennant three times; the Browns played in their conference championship game every year. Tom Landry, later head coach of the Dallas Cowboys, played and coached against the Browns for the New York Giants in the '50s. In his autobiography, he wrote: "What Sir Edmund Hillary must have felt in 1953 looking up at Mount Everest, I felt in 1954 looking at the seemingly insurmountable Cleveland Browns."[1] Forty-five years later, the authors of *The NFL Century* wrote that the Browns of the 1940s and '50s "might have been the greatest football team of all time."[2]

The game had evolved from leather helmets and the single-wing Red Grange and Jim Thorpe played to a more wide-open passing game using the T formation, and Paul Brown and Blanton Collier were at the forefront of that evolution. The Browns "took offensive football from the rough-draft stage and created the final blueprint for the foundations of the game as we know it today," Landry wrote. "For the first time football became a game of finesse. Not that the Brown teams weren't strong or tough; they were. But they never beat you with brute strength; they used precision." Teams like the Steelers, Eagles, and Lions resorted to pokes in the eyes, stomps on ankles, and whacks to the head. Their opponents wore extra padding to protect themselves but still ended up bruised and battered—and more often than not winners. "In contrast, teams would go into Cleveland, lose by three or four touchdowns," Landry wrote, "and wake up Monday morning feeling as if they had taken Sunday afternoon off."[3]

Otto Graham quarterbacked the Browns to the NFL title in 1955 and retired after the season, leaving a gaping hole in the offense in both talent and leadership. Three different players started at quarterback in 1956, and the Browns finished 5–7, their worst season under Brown. The upside was that Cleveland would choose relatively high in the draft of college players. Since teams picked in reverse order of how well they'd finished the previous season, all those years of winning had resulted in Cleveland regularly picking near or at the end of the first round. Green Bay, Pittsburgh, and the Browns all finished with 5–7 records in 1956, and they flipped a coin to determine the order of picks. The Packers won the first toss, and Pittsburgh and Cleveland then flipped. The Steelers won, meaning the Browns would choose sixth overall.

In those days the draft included a "bonus pick"—basically, a lottery. The teams put their names in a hat, and the winner received the first overall pick. The Packers won and chose Paul Hornung, Notre Dame's "Golden Boy" and Heisman Trophy winner. The Los Angeles Rams chose second and picked "Jaguar" Jon Arnett, an All-American running back from Southern Cal and an L.A. hometown hero. Paul Brown, desperate for a quarterback to replace Graham, coveted Stanford's John Brodie, but San Francisco chose him with the third pick. The Packers, with the choice they'd won in the coin toss, took Michigan end Ron Kramer. Brown wanted Purdue quarterback Len Dawson, a native of Alliance, Ohio, but so did the Steelers, and they snatched him with the fifth pick. One of the reasons Cleveland and Pittsburgh both needed a quarterback was they'd whiffed on Johnny Unitas the previous season. Pittsburgh had drafted him in the ninth round and cut him without giving him much of a chance. Unitas reached out to Cleveland, but Brown felt confident in his quarterbacking because Graham was still "perking along." He told Unitas to call back in a year. Unitas called Baltimore instead.

Cleveland chose next. Brown considered the draft the only way to build a firm foundation of talent, and he took it seriously before other teams did. In the early '50s, teams would show up with a football magazine as research for picking players. Cleveland's coaches arrived with notebooks containing rankings of players at every position. Brown preferred to take the best available player, not choose for need. The exception was quarterback. Even when he had Graham, he tried to draft another one. "If there was an outstanding candidate on the board when it came our time to select, I thought long and hard about choosing him, even if we already had a great one on our team," he said. "A quarterback is a unique property in professional football."[4]

The top quarterback prospects were gone, so Brown scanned his charts for the best of the rest. Some of Cleveland's scouts lobbied for Clarence Peaks, a running back from Michigan State. Peaks was a versatile back, and that he'd played in the Big Ten fit Cleveland's bias toward midwestern players. But Brown was worried about Peaks's health; he'd missed part of a season with a gimpy knee. After some debate, Cleveland chose Jim Brown of Syracuse—"strictly because he was the best player available," Paul Brown wrote in his autobiography.

In retrospect, it seems odd Jim Brown would last as long as he did, but a couple of factors were at play. In the 1950s, football in the East was considered inferior to the rest of the country, especially if one looked beyond the military academies. Teams such as Pittsburgh, Penn State, and West Virginia would occasionally make it into the final wire-service rankings, but the strongest teams were in the Midwest, on the West Coast, and in the Southwest. During his time at Syracuse, Brown had amassed impressive numbers in and against some fine teams, but the Orangemen's schedule regularly included the likes of Fordham and Cornell. In his final regular season game, he set an NCAA scoring record with forty-three points, but it came against Colgate. No other player from the East was taken in the '57 draft until Cleveland chose Penn State quarterback Milt Plum in the second round. Also, unlike today, the NFL draft was conducted near the end of the season and before the colleges had played their bowl games. Jim Brown was an All-American, but he had yet to showcase his talents before a wide audience. Compared to Hornung and Arnett he was relatively untested.

Jim Brown was born February 17, 1936, on St. Simons Island off the Georgia coast. His father, Swinton "Sweet Sue" Brown, a sometime prizefighter, golf caddy, and oft-time gambler, left the family shortly after his son's birth. Jimmy's mother, Theresa, moved to New York's Long Island to work as a domestic when he was two, leaving him behind to be raised by his great-grandmother, whom he called "Mama"; his grandmother; and an aunt. At age eight or nine (accounts differ), he was handed a box lunch and packed off on a train to join his mother. The two initially lived in a room of the Great Neck house she cleaned but later moved to their own house in Manhasset Valley. Sweet Sue lived nearby and occasionally stopped in, but when he did he and Theresa fought violently, while their son sat in a corner and watched wordlessly. Theresa sometimes brought dates home, which confused and irritated Jimmy, and this led to arguments so heated Theresa would kick her son out of the house, leaving him to walk the streets at night. He eventually moved in with his girlfriend's family in a neighboring village. Biographer Mike Freeman wrote that Brown's childhood instilled "a lasting feeling of abandonment and insecurity that would haunt Brown for much of his life."[5] He developed a hair-trigger temper and responded to taunts and insults with his fists. He coldcocked a seventh-grade classmate who called him a "dirty nigger" during a basketball game. A week later, his coach received a call from the kid's mother. "She said she didn't particularly agree with her son's sentiments," the coach said, "but she wondered how another boy her son's age could hit him so hard that he would be laid up in bed for a whole week."[6]

Brown channeled his rage into sports, complementing it with a drive to dominate others who had slighted him or might do so. He challenged the fastest kids in the neighborhood to races, and if they surged past him he'd grab them by the shoulders and yank them back. "It wasn't fun for me—it was serious," he said. "People who knew me then would sometimes get scared."[7] He won thirteen varsity letters in five sports at Manhasset High School and during his senior year was named all-state in football, track, and basketball, averaging thirty-eight points per game. He received scholarship offers from more than forty colleges, and his high school football coach, Ed Walsh, believed he should go to Ohio State. "You have a special talent," Walsh told him. "I think you ought to play against the best."[8]

Kenneth Molloy, a Manhasset attorney and Syracuse alumnus, was an amateur recruiter for his alma mater. He had befriended Jimmy and became a mentor to him—Brown later described him as one of his best friends. Molloy argued that Syracuse was a program on the rise, and it was close to home. If he encountered problems, Molloy would be nearby to help him. The last point sold Brown. He'd been shuttled from St. Simons to his mother, and from one house to another on Long Island. "Ohio State seemed like the other side of the country to me," he said. "I'd never been to the Midwest. . . . The prospect of being yanked up again and deposited way out in Columbus with no friends worried me."[9]

There was one hitch: Syracuse hadn't offered him a scholarship. Its coaches hadn't even recruited him. In the early '50s, an outstanding athlete named Avatus Stone became Syracuse's first black star. He was a triple threat for the Orangemen—quarterback, defensive back, and punter—but he also dated a white cheerleader and was showy and outspoken. He didn't exhibit the humility and subservience young black males were expected to in the 1950s. Brown didn't know him, but he later heard much about him. "He was a new kind of Negro in the old-style Negro time," Brown said.

Syracuse head coach Ben Schwartzwalder told Walsh, "I'm not prejudiced but I never want another colored person on my team at Syracuse. Never again. They are too much trouble." He said he'd take a chance on Brown as long as Walsh assured him the young man would follow a set of rules, including no dating of white women. Walsh refused, unless Schwartzwalder made all the Syracuse players and coaches follow the same rules. And so Syracuse declined to offer Brown a scholarship.[10]

Undeterred, Molloy sent a letter to prominent members of the Manhasset community soliciting money to pay for Brown's first semester, with the idea he'd quickly earn a scholarship. "Several of us have joined to see what can be done to give Jimmy Brown his big chance," Molloy wrote. "We think this will be one of Manhasset's soundest investments."[11] Forty-four men—from a bank president to the village clerk—pitched in. All of this was unbeknownst to Brown, who thought he'd been granted a scholarship. He didn't find out the truth until after he'd graduated.

Unaware he'd been foisted on the Syracuse coaches, he was surprised and angered by the hostility he encountered, racial and otherwise. He was third-string on the freshmen team and rarely played. The coaches tried to convince him he should move to end. He was so frustrated that one afternoon at practice he simply lay on his back and stared at the sky. The coaches ignored him. At the end of his first semester, he came home and declared to Walsh he was done. Walsh told him he had to go back in order to prove the Syracuse coaches were wrong. Brown agreed to return, and he told himself he'd never again let anybody tell him what he could and couldn't do.

Brown's talent was too much for even the most racist and stubborn of Syracuse coaches to ignore. He was awarded a scholarship and in his sophomore year lettered in football, basketball, lacrosse, and track. Before his arrival, Syracuse's football program was mediocre and unheralded—it lost to Cornell his sophomore year—but his senior year he led the Orangemen to a 7–1 record and the Lambert Trophy as the East's best college team. He finished fifth in the Heisman Trophy voting.

Cleveland was eager to sign him to a rookie contract, but Molloy advised Brown to hold off until after Syracuse met Texas Christian in the Cotton Bowl. Jimmy would be playing against a strong team from the Southwest and before a national television audience, and Molloy figured it would be an opportunity for him to show his true worth. "You'll have a big day and then you'll be in position to ask for good money," Molloy said. Brown wasn't as confident. Syracuse's last bowl appearance, in the Orange Bowl in 1953, had resulted in a 61–6 loss to Alabama. But he agreed to wait. "I had to follow any advice this man gave me," he said. "He'd always had my best interests at heart."[12] Brown scored three touchdowns and kicked three extra points, but Syracuse lost 28–27. The game would have ended in a tie but Brown's final extra point attempt was blocked. He was named Cotton Bowl MVP.

Brown checked with other college seniors who were expecting to sign contracts and figured he'd be fortunate to get $10,000. The Browns claimed they'd never gone higher than $9,000 for a rookie contract. Molloy used the Canadian Football League as a negotiating chip, which wasn't much, though some good players had gone north, among them Alex Webster, who later starred for the New York Giants, and Bill Glass, Brown's future Cleveland teammate. Molloy had studied NFL salaries and was a shrewd negotiator, and he convinced Paul Brown to pay $12,000, plus a $3,000 signing bonus. Jimmy used his bonus money to buy a new red-and-white Pontiac Bonneville convertible with white leather interior. One afternoon before a lacrosse game, he picked up his white girlfriend, drove her to the field, and walked her to the stands. After the game, he went into the stands, took her by the hand, and the two of them drove away in his convertible. No one was going to tell Jim Brown what he could and couldn't do.

That spring he scored forty-three goals in lacrosse, tied for most in the nation. The Syracuse Nationals of the National Basketball Association drafted him, even though he hadn't played basketball his senior year. "He could have made it, too," said Vincent Cohen, an All-American teammate at Syracuse.[13] He was an average student—above average, considering all the time he spent playing sports—and graduated in four years. Instead of a cap and gown, he wore his ROTC uniform to graduation and received his lieutenant's bars. He left Syracuse as the school's most accomplished athlete and arguably as the greatest college athlete of all time, later inducted into both the college football and lacrosse halls of fame. He also left a changed man. "He was different after Syracuse," said childhood friend Ed Corley. "I think he wanted to be a great football player, but I think he also wanted to change society. He was going to do whatever it took to make things better for his people."[14]

Paul Brown discouraged his players from driving flashy cars, but when his rookie fullback arrived at training camp in his new Pontiac, the coach didn't say a word. Even he wouldn't cut his first-round draft choice over a car. But the rookie learned early on from his teammates not to question the head coach. Veteran lineman Len Ford, a future Hall of Famer and one of the few black players on the team, pulled him aside and offered some advice: When running a play in practice, don't jog a few steps and flip the ball back. "The Man doesn't like that," Ford said. "Run hard for 20 yards, even if you feel silly. He likes to see that." Also, Ford told him, keep your mouth shut and run the play the way he tells you. "If you have an idea for improving the play, keep it to yourself. Suggestions make the Man mad."[15] He also learned the Man's rules were colorblind. Paul Brown preached there was no black or white, just Browns, and he applied his rules to all equally. Egos, opinions, hard living, lack of commitment were dealt with harshly; this discouraged cliques and racial divisiveness. All the strictures were fine with Jimmy Brown. He was a loner, preferring to keep quiet and distant from both the staff and his teammates. Plus, the head coach initially greeted him with a smile and went out of his way to compliment him. At one of the first practices, the coach pointed at his rookie running back and said, "There is the best draft choice we ever made. Can you think of a better football player we've drafted?" In the second exhibition game, Jimmy ran 40 yards for a touchdown against the Steelers. As he came to the sideline, Paul called him over. "You're my fullback," he said. Jim Brown later said it was the greatest moment of his career.

Others weren't so accommodating. The incumbent fullback, Ed Modzelewski, was popular among his teammates, and they pounded the rookie in practice, hoping to break him down. He took the hits, broke tackles, said nothing, and quickly gained his teammates' respect. "You could almost see them thinking, 'Maybe he'll help us to a championship,'" Modzelewski said. "The writing was on the wall for me, so I became his number-one rooter. You know, I doubt Jim ever knew the guys were hitting him extra hard."[16]

Brown stood 6-foot-2 and weighed 230 pounds. He had a 32-inch waist, 17-inch biceps, and a 46-inch chest—"a gorgeous hunk of man," a *Los Angeles Times* writer gushed. He clocked faster in the 40-yard dash than any Cleveland player before him, running 4.5 seconds in full uniform and starting from a three-point stance. "I remember running sprints on the first day of practice," Modzelewski said. "I'd always had a quick start, but when the whistle blew, I looked to the side and Jim was three steps ahead of me already."[17] At training camp the next year he raced rookie teammate Bobby Mitchell, who'd set a world record for the indoor hurdles while at the University of Illinois. Brown outweighed Mitchell by nearly forty pounds but could beat him in the 40-yard dash—not always, but at least half the time. The races attracted their teammates, who had front-row seats to the two fastest men in football. "We always said Jimmy could keep up with Bobby for forty yards," said quarterback Jim Ninowski, "but if they went past forty it was all Bobby."[18]

Brown quickly established himself as the best running back in the NFL. He rushed for nearly 1,000 yards in 1957, and various news organizations named him Rookie of the Year, All-NFL, and the league's most valuable player. Willie Davis, a teammate of Brown's that season and later a Hall of Fame defensive end for Green Bay, said Brown "came in the league and took command quicker than any football player ever."[19]

He wore no hip pads, and his thigh pads were stripped to bare plastic. He toted the ball in one hand like a loaf of bread, and he could slash, overpower, and outrun defenders. In a November game against the Rams, he carried thirty-one times, set an NFL record with 237 yards rushing, and scored four touchdowns. Afterward, Los Angeles coach Sid Gillman said, "If he carries the ball that much in many more games, he'll wind up either punch drunk or a basket case." But he seemed impervious to injury. He believed if "the enemy" hurt him they would defeat him mentally as well as physically. No matter how hard they hit him, he'd hit back as hard, if not harder. He used his free arm as a weapon, leading with a stiff-arm, and when needed he'd throw an elbow or drop his shoulder. Bill Glass, who played against Brown while with Detroit, recalled taking a shot to the head from Brown's forearm; it felt like he'd been struck with a lead pipe. "Some of the biggest, toughest guys in the NFL got pretty scared when they saw Jim swinging that arm of his," Glass said. But Brown didn't just run over and through defenders. He relied on his moves and balance as well. "That's why it was so hard for one defender to bring him down," Glass said. "He made it almost impossible for you to get a clean shot at him."[20]

Brown rose slowly after each play and took his time going back to the huddle. It was a mental as well as physical ploy. He might be hurting—and he sometimes was—or maybe not; the defenders never knew. Opposing defenses were stacked against him, but as the game wore on he crushed their will. In order to stop him, said one opponent, "give each guy in the line an ax."[21]

In a game against New York his rookie season, he and the Giants' second-year linebacker, Sam Huff, collided head-on. Huff's helmet crashed down onto the bridge of his nose, gashing and breaking it, and his teeth slammed together so hard they shattered. He was out cold. "I always took great pride in those teeth; in fact, people always used to tease me about my nice, big smile," Huff said. "Well, it wasn't so nice anymore."[22]

Cleveland rode its rookie to the Eastern Conference title, finishing 9–2–1. Detroit overwhelmed the Browns in the title game 59–14—the latter's number one and two quarterbacks were hobbled and ineffective—but it seemed the franchise was returning to its place of prominence. Much of the old guard from the championship teams of the 1950s was aging or gone, but the 1957 roster included twelve rookies and five second-year players. Changes were coming to the rest of the NFL as well, changes that would spell the demise of Paul Brown in Cleveland.

CHAPTER SIX

In 1954, the year Blanton Collier left for Kentucky, Paul Brown lost another of his top lieutenants when Weeb Ewbank was hired as head coach of the Baltimore Colts. At the same time, the New York Giants were building a staff unrivaled in the NFL. Jim Lee Howell, an end on the Giants' teams that won NFL titles in the 1930s and '40s, took over from longtime coach Steve Owen. Howell didn't know much about football tactics, but he was smart enough to delegate control of the offense to a new assistant from Army, Vince Lombardi, and control of the defense to player/coach Tom Landry. "I can remember walking down our dormitory at training camp in St. Michael's, Vermont," recalled Giants receiver Kyle Rote, "and I'd look to the left and see Lombardi in a room running the projector for his plays, and I'd look to the right and I'd see Landry running his plays, and then on down the hall I'd look in Jim Lee's room and see him reading the newspaper."[1] The players joked that Howell's job was to decide what time the team bus would leave and to call roll once the players were on the bus. Howell was fine with it. He often joked that he just inflated the footballs and kept order.

The Giants had finished 3-9 in 1953, and they hadn't won a conference title since 1944 or an NFL title since 1938. But the team was about to be reborn. On offense, Lombardi inherited Frank Gifford, who would become a Hall of Fame halfback; Charlie Conerly, a veteran quarterback; and Rote, a talented multipurpose receiver/running back. A year later, fullback Alex Webster joined the team from Canada, providing Lombardi with a formidable backfield. He instituted a power sweep and a halfback option play in which Gifford could run or pass. Such plays opened up the passing game for Conerly and then for Y. A. Tittle after he joined the team in 1961.

Landry devised a new defense—the four-three. It was especially effective at stopping the run, which was imperative in those days, because teams ran more than they passed. And after Jim Brown joined Cleveland it was the only way to defeat the Browns. Instead of using five defensive linemen, Landry moved the nose tackle from over center to a stand-up position in the middle of the scrum. This "middle linebacker" could play the pass as well as the run. The success of the four-three depended on the front four linemen holding their ground, thus freeing the middle linebacker and defensive backs to come up and make tackles. Landry had the personnel he needed to make it work. The front four consisted of Rosie Grier, Andy Robustelli, Jim Katcavage, and Dick "Little Mo" Modzelewski, Big Ed's little brother—all of whom were named All-Pro at some point in their careers. Sam Huff, drafted in 1956 out of West Virginia, where he was a lineman, was installed as middle linebacker. When the Giants played Cleveland, he was assigned to shadow Jim Brown.

The Giants posted winning seasons in 1954 and '55, finishing third in the Eastern Conference both years, and in 1956 Gifford was named the league's MVP and the Giants won the NFL championship, pounding the Bears 47–7 in the title game. Having a championship team in New York was good for the entire NFL. The city was the media capital of the nation, and stars such as Gifford, Conerly, and Huff became national celebrities. Gifford posed for magazine layouts and appeared in television commercials, and the ruggedly handsome Conerly portrayed the Marlboro Man in cigarette ads. In 1960, CBS aired the first documentary about a professional football player, *The Violent World of Sam Huff*. Narrated by Walter Cronkite, and with Huff wired for sound, the half-hour show took viewers onto the field and inside the locker room, providing a behind-the-scenes look at professional football. Cronkite's narration was presented in second person: "If you were the middle linebacker of the New York Giants . . ." You, the viewer, were part of the action. "It's a rough game," Huff intoned at the conclusion. "It's for the men, not the boys, but I've got no complaints. Pro football has been real good to me." Huff had been a football star; now he was a household name.

The Giants' archenemy was the Cleveland Browns. The city of New York's distaste for the Browns dated to the beginning of the All-America Conference, when the Browns and Yankees developed an immediate rivalry, playing for the title in the league's first two years. When the Browns joined the NFL in 1950, the only team to beat them was the Giants, by a score of 6–0, the first shutout loss in Cleveland history. Both teams finished with two defeats, and the Browns won a playoff for the division title. After that, Cleveland had New York's number, culminating in a 42–14 win in the final game of the 1953 regular season, Owen's last as Giants coach. "The New York media became frenzied and emotional," Paul Brown said, "because they weren't used to seeing their teams beaten with such regularity by a new, college-like team from Middle America.

"As a result, we suddenly became the 'big, bad Browns.'"[2]

In 1958 Jim Brown carried Cleveland's offense, breaking the NFL single-season rushing and touchdown records by the eighth game. In total he ran for 1,527 yards and seventeen touchdowns and again was named All-NFL. Cleveland was the most prolific running team in the NFL—the Browns led the league in rushing and were third in total offense. They hadn't found a replacement for Otto Graham, but so what? They had Jim Brown. The Browns were 5–0 when they met the Giants for the first time that season, in Cleveland. New York was 3–2. The Browns led 17–7, Brown running 58 yards for one of the scores. But second-year quarterback Milt Plum was ineffective, and rookie halfback Bobby Mitchell fumbled three times. New York won 21–17.

The teams met again at Yankee Stadium in the final game of the year. The Browns were 9–2, the Giants 8–3. A Cleveland win or a tie, and the Browns were conference champs. Cleveland led 10–3 late in the third quarter and faced a fourth and four on the New York 16-yard line. Lou Groza had missed two field goals earlier in the game in the swirling wind and snow, but he'd made one from 33 yards, the same distance he now faced. Brown called a timeout to discuss a fake. The players were stunned. Despite the weather and the sloppy field, they believed in Groza. The Giants saw the Browns debating on the sidelines, and when the teams lined up they yelled, "Watch the fake! Watch the fake!" The holder, Bobby Freeman, took the snap and began running. The Giants threw him for a loss. When Freeman came off the field Brown glared at him and said, "You've lost some of your agility."[3]

The Giants tied the game in the fourth quarter, 10–10, but it appeared the Browns had sewn up the title when Gifford caught a pass near midfield and fumbled as he was falling to the ground. Cleveland's Walt Michaels picked up the ball and started running the other way for what seemed a sure touchdown.

Charles Berry, the official closest to the play, paused, looking to the other refs for a cue. When none responded, he slowly waved his arms in front of him: incomplete pass. Paul Brown believed Berry hesitated because he hoped one of the other officials would get the message and help him out. The Cleveland bench protested vehemently, but the call stood. A few plays later, and with a little more than two minutes left, Howell sent Pat Summerall out to try a 49-yard field goal. Everyone was surprised, including Summerall. He'd already missed from 35 yards, and now he was kicking into a swirling wind with snowflakes the size of half dollars. "You couldn't see the yard lines," he said later. "Nobody was sure how far it was." But somehow he made it. The columnist Red Smith compared the kick to Bobby Thomson's "Shot Heard

'Round the World" to win the 1951 pennant for the baseball Giants. *Sports Illustrated*'s Tex Maule wrote that it was "as dramatic an ending for a football game as any script writer could devise."[4]

As upset as the Cleveland players were with the officiating, they were just as angry with their coach. They couldn't understand why he had called the fake field goal, and they were bitter that he blamed Freeman. "That damn fake field goal," guard Gene Hickerson said. "I hate to say it, but Paul Brown cost us that game."[5]

The New York win forced a playoff for the Eastern Conference title the following week, again at Yankee Stadium. "Our hearts had been ripped from us by losing to the Giants that way," Paul Brown wrote in his autobiography, "and there was a hollow feeling within all of us, having to prepare for another game in New York that shouldn't have been played."[6] Even with the conference title on the line, the team played down to its coach's low expectations. "It was like we weren't supposed to win," linebacker Galen Fiss said. "We took the field that day with a lot of baggage."[7] Jim Brown rushed seven times for 8 yards, a career low, and they lost 10–0.

Contemporary accounts credited the play of Sam Huff—his mano a mano rivalry with Jim Brown is among the NFL's enduring legends—but in reality it was defensive coordinator Landry's game plan that made the difference. It seemed as though the Giants knew where Brown was going every time he carried the ball. And, in fact, they might have. Much like Blanton Collier, Landry was a student of the game. He broke down game films looking for the other team's offensive tendencies. He determined how often a team would run a certain play in a given situation and a particular formation. He was especially adept at figuring what Cleveland would run, because Paul Brown's offense was becoming predictable—"stereotyped" was the word most often used to describe it. Landry's understanding of the technical details of playing defense had surpassed Paul Brown's once-sophisticated offense. The Cleveland head coach was either unable or unwilling to keep up. "After a while, Tom could predict almost exactly what Jim was going to do," Frank Gifford said. "In certain situations—first and ten, second and short, second and long, etc.—Tom would tell you [Brown] was going to carry the ball off right tackle, around end, or a quick trap. . . . At times it must have seemed as if we had their huddle tapped."[8]

New York played the Baltimore Colts for the title and lost in overtime in what is considered the greatest NFL game ever played. Paul Brown was asked whether the game would have garnered the same attention and had the same impact if Cleveland had played the Colts. "That question can never be answered," he said, "but one thing is for certain: The popularity of the Browns, and their great rivalry with the Giants, were very responsible for the great surge of popularity that finally brought the nation's attention to pro football."[9]

As heartbreaking as 1958 was, at least the Browns were in the chase; that wasn't so in 1959. Cleveland started the season 6–2, and *Sports Illustrated* published a story headlined "Why the Browns Will Win," Tex Maule predicting they would finish atop the Eastern Conference. Maule, formerly a press agent for the Los Angeles Rams, joined *Sports Illustrated* in 1956, two years after the magazine's founding, and he'd become a leading authority on professional football—"intrigued as many fans with the point and counterpoint of gridiron strategy," according to Michael MacCambridge. In its early years, *SI* regularly covered such sports as bowling, polo, and sailing, but it soon began treating professional football with a seriousness it didn't receive in newspapers. With Maule as its lead football writer, the magazine helped "change the perception of the games themselves."[10] In "Why the Browns Will Win," he touted Paul Brown's "tactical brilliance" and called him "one of the best analysts in football."[11]

Cleveland dropped its next three games and finished the season 7–5. The low point came in the next-to-last game, a 48–7 drubbing by the Giants. Yankee Stadium was a huge cocktail party, and with a couple of minutes remaining a thousand or more drunk and frenzied fans stormed the field. They tore down the goalposts and milled around behind both benches. "I took one look at their eyes and was stunned at what I saw," Gifford said. "I had never seen so many crazed expressions. I think we were all wondering how many of us would get out alive. It was the closest I've ever been—or want to be—to mob hysteria."[12] The players fought their way off the field and headed for the locker rooms. The pockets were torn from Paul Brown's overcoat as he fled. The Giants were undressing when word came that Brown demanded the game be called a forfeit unless it was finished. It was a dangerous move on his part, considering the tenor of the crowd, but a smart one: It gave Cleveland a chance at victory.

Spectators trotted along with the players as they came back onto the field. The teams lined up near the New York goal line with people in coats and hats milling around them. Police tried to disperse them, but it was impossible. Mob rule reigned. Twenty or so people lined up in the Cleveland backfield, while dozens more took three-point stances in a long line up-front. On the other side, about a hundred fans had lined up with the Giants. Milt Plum called two running plays. It was the first—and last—time he called plays under Paul Brown.

The finish was a metaphor for everything going wrong for Cleveland. In the locker room afterward, some of the New York players told writer Jimmy Cannon that football seemed to have passed by Paul Brown. "You got to let men think," Gifford said. "You got to let the man on the field choose the plays. I don't know why Brown tries to do it." Cannon asked Andy Robustelli why the Giants beat the Browns so soundly. "Tom Landry knows how to whip Paul Brown," he said.[13]

The game also was a turning point in Paul Brown's relationship with his superstar fullback. On the first play from scrimmage Jim Brown was kicked in the head and suffered a concussion. He stayed in the game but couldn't remember the plays. He asked Plum to tell him where to go. After a few plays, Plum called time-out and asked Paul Brown to take him out. He sat out the second quarter and at halftime was lying on his back in the locker room. The coach looked down at him and said, "Well, Triplett got hurt and he's back in there," referring to New York fullback Mel Triplett.

Brown played the second half, having regained his senses somewhat, but the New York defenders were surprised to see him back in the game. They even helped him up after tackling him. "That guy's crazy," Huff said. "He should get you out of here."

The running back didn't fault Paul Brown for leaving him in the game. He often played hurt and, in fact, hadn't missed a game in his three years with Cleveland, despite a myriad of nicks and bruises. But he bitterly resented the coach's halftime remark, which made it seem as though he was a malingerer, or worse, soft. In *Off My Chest,* he wrote:

> As a consequence of Paul's words that day in New York, his big brute arrived at a policy-making decision. . . . During the season, he paid my salary, I played his game. Winter, however, would be a time for speaking up, a time for needling Paul. . . . In short, if he regarded me as nothing more than a means to his end, a weapon for victory, I thought of him now as nothing more than a means to my end—more cash. I was willing to die for the dear old Browns, but I would take a lot of their banknotes with me.[14]

"Jim was not going to score touchdowns and get beat up physically and then stay quiet and say nothing once the game was over," Bobby Mitchell said. "He found the notion offensive that he was supposed to be this quiet brute. Jim was anything but quiet. Jim was opinionated. Under Paul, players were not supposed to be opinionated. You were supposed to just shut up and play."[15]

New York won the Eastern Conference again, marking the first time since Cleveland joined the NFL in 1950 that a team other than the Browns won back-to-back Eastern Conference titles. To his own players, Paul Brown seemed intimidated by the Giants. The offensive players were especially frustrated, even humiliated. The Cleveland defense also was failing to evolve. Philadelphia quarterback Norm Van Brocklin said, "Whenever I came up to the line of scrimmage I knew exactly what I'd see when I looked at the Cleveland defense. I liked it that way. It made my job easier." Paul Brown had shipped off some of his best defenders. He convinced Green Bay to hire Lombardi after the 1958 season—he wanted him off New York's staff—and then traded defensive linemen Henry Jordan, Bill Quinlan, and Willie Davis to the Packers for little in return. They became three-quarters of Green Bay's champion defensive line. "I thought I could have played for Paul Brown," Jordan said, "but who am I to say? *He's* a genius." Jordan weighed 235 pounds, small for a defensive lineman, but he played with a slashing style that made him difficult to block. "At Cleveland," Jordan said, "Paul Brown has big guys and has them just stand there."[16]

Many of Cleveland's players thought their coach was living in the past. If Plum hung onto the ball too long, Brown would remind him how Graham always put the ball in the receiver's hands as he made his cut. He urged the players to adopt their predecessors' attitudes, to be more like Dante Lavelli and Bill Willis. "No doubt Paul meant to inspire them," Jim Brown said, "but they were men living in their own time and they grew weary of ghosts from Paul's past."[17] The coach applied the same psychology he'd used on those who'd played for him earlier, but the new breed didn't bend as easily to his will. Bernie Parrish, a defensive back from Florida who considered himself a "revolutionary," believed the coach picked on meeker players and left alone the more assertive, such as himself and Jim Brown. "I grew to hate him," Parrish said. "I felt like a heart attack would be too good for him."[18]

The Browns finished second in the Eastern Conference in 1960 and following the season faced West runner-up Detroit in the inaugural Playoff Bowl in Miami. The purpose of the game was to provide television exposure to the next-best NFL teams at a time when the championship was the only playoff game contested, and it also was a charity event for the league's pension fund. It was more of a chore than a prize for the players, but the Lions approached it as a vacation. Their practices were short, leaving time for relaxing on the beach, and with no curfew they were free to carouse at night. Paul Brown maintained his restrictions on smoking, drinking, and hours, and the team practiced and attended meetings the same as it did during the regular season. The two teams met one night at a Miami Beach hotel for a banquet. The Lions drank beer as their cigarette smoke wafted above them, while across the room the Browns sat stiffly and drank water with their meals. "Over there in that clear area, I could make out those guys in blazers—made you feel like a bum," one of the Lions said. "But you could see from the guys' faces looking at us, like pleading, how much they wanted to sit with us and cadge a drink, maybe a smoke."[19] Detroit won the game 17–16. The Playoff Bowl was Cleveland's last postseason game under Paul Brown.

CHAPTER SEVEN

The syndicate that owned the Cleveland Browns put the team up for sale following the 1960 season. It was an attractive franchise. Pro football's history and tradition ran deep in the region, and the Browns were popular nationally because of their sustained success, their rivalry with the Giants, and because they had the Browns—Paul and Jim. Cleveland businessman Dave Jones, who'd bought the team from Mickey McBride in 1953, headed the syndicate. The major stockholders were wealthy Clevelanders—Nationwide Insurance held 30 percent of the shares—and they collected their money and left the football to the coach. "[They] were nice fellows who occasionally would show up at a banquet and shake my hand and pat me on the back," Jim Brown said, "but so far as I know, exerted no influence in the operation of the club."[1]

Jones offered a finder's fee to Fred "Curly" Morrison, a former Browns fullback and head of sports sales for CBS. Morrison pitched his boss, CBS president William Paley, who agreed to buy the team. Professional football was becoming increasingly popular, with stadiums filled to capacity on Sunday afternoons and television networks paying higher and higher fees for broadcasting rights. The television / pro football relationship was about to create a windfall for everyone involved, and Paley surely saw it coming. But he worried the Federal Communications Commission would deem his buying the Browns a conflict of interest because CBS aired some of their games. He pulled out of the deal.

Morrison called a New York theatrical agent he knew, Vinnie Andrews, who recommended Art Modell, a friend and client. A thirty-five-year-old advertising executive, Modell was a rabid football fan and Giants season-ticket holder. He wanted in. He sold both a television production company he owned and his partnership in an advertising firm to raise the $500,000 down payment and went looking for other investors. Rudy Schaefer, head of the Schaefer Brewing Company, bought in, as did others, including Dave Jones. The syndicate agreed to take $3.925 million, then a record price for an NFL franchise. The paperwork was completed in March 1961. Modell liked to say he bought the Browns without a nickel in his pocket, but in truth he was majority owner, controlling about 50 percent of the stock. He was chairman of the board, and after one year he took over from Jones as president.

Modell was born and raised in Brooklyn, and among his closest and longtime friends was comedian Buddy Hackett. He grew up a football fan, and as a boy he had walked with two of his cousins three miles to Ebbets Field to watch the Brooklyn Dodgers of the NFL. They brought their lunch to save money and paid a quarter to sit in a special section for public school students. Modell's father and an uncle owned a chain of radio stores, some of the first in America, and they made good money. His father owned a Packard limousine, and he regularly took the family to the shore for vacations. Then came the Depression, and the business went bust. Modell's father became a traveling wine salesman. "To go from eleven stores to working for someone else and selling wine out of a suitcase, it was horrendous," Modell said.[2]

When Modell was fourteen, his father died in an Austin, Texas, hotel room. He reportedly had spent the night with a woman, whose identity remained a mystery. The death was tainted with scandal and left the family devastated. "He was handsome, a wonderful, wonderful father," Modell said. "I loved him dearly."[3] Modell promised his mother he'd never leave her to marry and, in fact, remained a bachelor well into middle age, marrying actress Patricia Breslin in 1969.

Modell dropped out of high school at fifteen and worked at Bethlehem Steel Shipyards, cleaning the hulls of ships for eighty-seven cents an hour. "I went to the school of hard knocks," he said later. "I worked my ass off for what I got today. I didn't have anything handed to me."[4] He joined the Army Air Corps in 1943 at age eighteen and after the war returned to New York, where he attended the American Theatre Wing, an organization that promoted theater and educated veterans under the GI Bill. Modell and another student formed a production company and decided to try their hand at the television industry. "I knew nothing about it," Modell said. "But it was so new, neither did anybody else. Therefore, why not start in a business where almost no one has experience?"[5]

The number of American households with television sets exploded following World War II, and by 1955 half of all U.S. homes had one. No new invention had entered American homes faster than black-and-white television sets.

Modell came up with an idea for a two-hour daytime show aimed at women shoppers. It was filled with tips on cooking, decorating, and shopping, plus interviews and music. He and his partner, Charles Harburuck, landed a contract with ABC, which began airing *Market Melodies* in 1949. Televisions were installed in the aisles of Grand Union supermarkets, and *Market Melodies* broadcast for twelve hours a week. Modell supplied the television sets and programming, ABC aired the show, the sales of advertising paid for it all, and Grand Union expected to benefit by selling more groceries. It was, as one reviewer described it, "twelve hours of solid commercials, uninterrupted by entertainment." The idea of airing *Market Melodies* in the supermarkets didn't work, because the televisions lost their signal when subway trains roared by. Nonetheless, the grocery chain was impressed with Modell and hired him as its account executive. "This guy was a wonder," Grand Union's advertising director said. "He always got along. He always had an angle."[6] The Grand Union account led Modell to partnerships at big advertising firms, first L. H. Hartman Co., and later Kastor, Hilton, Chesley, Clifford & Atherton—the kind of firms later portrayed in the television series *Mad Men*.

Modell had never been to Cleveland before attending a Browns game while considering buying the team. "I was a New York guy, never wanted to live anywhere else," he said. "You know what they used to say, 'Anything outside of New York was Bridgeport.' That was my attitude until I had a chance to buy the Browns."[7] Much of the appeal to owning the team was the opportunity to work with Paul Brown. "We will be consulting frequently," he said. "We'll be partners in the Browns' operation."[8] Or so he thought.

Modell learned, to his surprise, that Brown was general manager as well as coach, and his contract gave him authority to sign the players and to pay them what he decided. The *Washington Post*'s Shirley Povich wrote that Modell "was just another salaried figure on the team's payroll."[9] But Brown had cashed in almost a half-million dollars' worth of stock when Modell bought the team, and he was beholden to the new owner, regardless of whether he acknowledged it. Brown had an eight-year contract worth about $50,000 annually, and Modell approved a ten-year extension, calling for Brown to be paid $82,500 per year. If he thought Brown's subservience could be bought, he was badly mistaken.

Modell moved into Brown's office at team headquarters and showed up for work every morning at 7:30. He wanted to be to be part of the team, and prior to a game early in the 1961 season he went into the locker room and sat on a duffel bag in the back. As the players were filing out after Brown's pregame speech, the coach came over to him. "You don't belong here," he said, "and can't come back."[10]

Modell insisted he wasn't an owner-*coach*—as Brown described him with disgust. "I'm an owner-*promoter*," he said. "You hire football talent just as you hire television talent. You put it together, put on a show, look for the biggest audience possible."[11] Modell tried to promote Paul Brown—"I could make him the idol of America!"—but Brown would have none of it.[12] No one promoted Paul Brown, or his team, but Paul Brown.

Shunned from the practice field and the locker room, Modell went to work applying his talents to building his new franchise. He attended his first game as Cleveland Browns owner—an exhibition against Detroit—on September 9, 1961, at Municipal Stadium. The fans' rowdiness took him aback. He was used to raucous crowds at Yankee Stadium, but this was a different level of unruliness. Afterward, he checked the police blotter. "There were riots in the bleachers, fights in the stands and other incidents that were shameful," he said.[13] The major trouble spots were the bleachers, where fans fought over balls kicked their way on extra points and field goals, and in sections with Detroit fans. The club was paying Cleveland's uniformed police officers to serve as security, but Modell discovered there weren't enough of them and they weren't assigned where they were most needed. This was a situation he neither expected nor wanted. Going to a Browns game should be a mark of social status, not an excuse to brawl. He boosted the security force by 50 percent and posted more officers in the visitors' sections. He reduced the number of seats in the bleachers and sold them all as reserved. He also hired plainclothes officers to patrol the restrooms. By 1964, Cleveland was spending more on security than any other team in the league.

Modell also began working to advance the NFL. He believed television would elevate professional football over baseball as the national sport, if it hadn't already. Advertisers could fit commercials into timeouts, halftime, and at the end of quarters, and the play on the field translated well to the TV screen. "It has action, sometimes more action than the cameras can handle," he said. "Television only emphasizes baseball's slowness, lack of action."[14]

In 1951 the NFL eliminated competition between television and ticket sales by imposing a blackout: games couldn't be televised within seventy-five miles of the home stadium. Challenged in federal court, the restriction was upheld. "We don't compete with ourselves at the gate," Modell said, "and television has given us mass appeal because it's a football medium."[15]

The relationship between pro football and television dated to October 22, 1939, when NBC broadcast the Brooklyn Dodgers–Philadelphia Eagles game from Ebbets Field. A crowd of about 13,000 saw the Dodgers defeat the Eagles 23–14, but, more importantly, hundreds more watched it on monitors at the RCA Pavilion at the World's Fair in Queens. The fair's theme was "The World of Tomorrow."

Modell was among a group of young executives changing the face of professional football: Lamar Hunt, instrumental in forming the American Football League, which began playing in 1960; Dan Rooney, who was taking a more active role than his father, Art, in running the Pittsburgh Steelers; and Pete Rozelle, who became NFL commissioner a year before Modell bought the Browns. Rozelle replaced Bert Bell, who'd held the position since 1946 and had died of a heart attack while watching an Eagles game the previous fall. Rozelle was thirty-three, the general manager of the Rams, and a compromise choice after the owners considered a dozen other candidates. A chain smoker like Modell, he recognized the power of television and moved headquarters from a Philadelphia suburb to 1 Rockefeller Plaza in New York to help the league establish better ties to the television and advertising industries.

Modell knew the players in television—the producers and network bosses—and his fellow owners named him chairman of the league's broadcast committee in 1962. He insisted they work in partnership with television executives, not try to shortchange them; that way, everyone would benefit. The strategy paid off. When Rozelle became commissioner in 1960, the NFL's annual income from television was less than $2 million. The next year, Congress voted to exempt the NFL from antitrust laws and allow sports leagues to negotiate their own television contracts. In 1962, the NFL signed a two-year deal with CBS to televise all of its regular-season games for nearly $4.7 million per year. In 1964, Rozelle negotiated a television-rights package worth $14 million per year. The revenue was to be shared among all NFL teams, ensuring each was financially stable and competitive. Modell figured the league was only as strong as its weakest link. A small-market franchise such as Green Bay was now on equal footing with clubs in Los Angeles and New York. "Modell has brought imagination to this league," said Cowboys general manager Tex Schramm, "and that has to be good for everyone. Some of the owners have been staid. They've done pretty well with what they had and they've made no effort to improve their product. But Modell has shown them a few things, and he'll probably show them more."[16]

Cleveland's newest and most eligible bachelor dressed immaculately, and his black, wavy hair gleamed. If his life were a movie, a reporter said, he'd be played by Tony Curtis. In public appearances he chose his words carefully, but he also could be refreshingly candid, which made him popular with reporters. When excited, he spoke rapid-fire, sometimes transposing words. He once introduced Indians general manager Gabe Paul as a "real shoot-straighter." He seemed too eager to impress at times, and could come off as brash and glib. He was part-owner of a horse stable and bemoaned the horses' diet. "It's terrible," he said. "You know what the horses are eating now? Dietetic food. Imports only! Before you know it, they'll want their teeth capped."[17] Because he was a New Yorker, many in Cleveland didn't trust him. That he was Jewish was a strike against him with some as well. "Every time I wrote a nice story about him, I got a couple of 'Dirty Jew' letters," said Hal Lebovitz of the *Plain Dealer*. "That was always there for Modell."[18]

He moved into an apartment on Cleveland's Gold Coast, a neighborhood of high-rise condos and apartment towers west of downtown and overlooking Lake Erie. A few years into Modell's tenure with the Browns, Lebovitz sent reporter Jane Artale to his apartment to interview him. A sheathed sword and a pair of brass gladiator helmets hung on one wall. A china plate hung above the kitchen sink, inscribed: "Bless this lousy apartment."

"Do you like music?" he asked Artale. "Want to hear some of my collection? I'm nuts about bullfight music. I'm thinking about putting on real bullfights between the halves of the Browns games sometime. Everything but the killing. The real thing, you know, the matadors, the picadors, live bulls from Mexico." He pondered the idea for a moment and grinned. "Say, we could keep the bull in the bullpen. How about that?"

Artale asked him about his hobbies. He mentioned music (he wanted to learn to play the guitar), true crime stories ("I gobble them up"), and golf (he'd joined Beechmont Country Club). "But best of all I like the Browns," he said. "They're not only my business but my No. 1 hobby."[19]

Nothing ever came of the bullfights, but prior to the 1962 season Modell hatched the idea of a football doubleheader. The Browns would play one of their Eastern Conference rivals, and two Western Conference teams would play, giving Cleveland fans a chance to watch teams they wouldn't see during the regular season. Since preseason attendance was down and player salaries were up, a doubleheader would attract more customers, and thus more money for the clubs. It also would get people excited about football earlier in the season, thus boosting season-ticket sales. He pitched his plan at a league meeting, and only the Chicago Bears' George Halas and the Steelers' Rooney supported him. Most of the owners looked at him "as though he'd been sniffing glue," the *Los Angeles Times* reported. But Modell was a born salesman—and Halas and Rooney were powerful allies—and the event became a reality.

The first doubleheader was played at Municipal Stadium during the 1962 exhibition season. The Browns faced the Steelers in one game, and the Dallas Cowboys and the Detroit Lions met in the other. His plan worked; attendance was 77,683, a record for a preseason game in Cleveland. The two contests were played in little more than five hours—with a fifteen-minute intermission between—and most of the fans stayed for both. Modell had guaranteed each club $30,000, but afterward he threw in another $5,000 for each. The preseason doubleheaders lasted for ten years and became much more than a pair of football games. They were an event—the circus and football in one—and they sold out weeks in advance. Modell framed tickets from the first one and hung them in his office. "My pride and joy," he said.[20]

Modell was indeed the owner-promoter he claimed to be. His first season in Cleveland, the team sold 16,846 season tickets; it sold nearly twice that number in 1964. Those who owned season tickets were hanging onto them and often willed them to their descendants. "The big difficulty now is trying to satisfy a longtime customer who wants to buy tickets alongside his for his growing family," Modell said. "We try to make adjustments, but really what can we do?"[21]

CHAPTER EIGHT

All those years with Otto Graham at quarterback had spoiled the Cleveland Browns and their fans. Graham retired after the 1955 season, and the team struggled to find a capable replacement. Paul Brown tried three different quarterbacks in 1956—Tommy O'Connell, George Ratterman, and Babe Parilli—with little success. They combined for eight touchdown passes and eighteen interceptions, and the Browns scored 167 points, compared to 394 the previous season with Graham. In 1957, Brown brought thirteen quarterback prospects to training camp, more than he ever had, and he settled on O'Connell and Milt Plum, the second-round draft pick from Penn State. Brown later described Plum as a "competent, no-frills guy who had reasonable mobility and size and seemed to be mistake-free during a game."[1] Compared to his later comments, this was a glowing appraisal.

O'Connell, a 5-foot-11 scrambler from the University of Illinois, quarterbacked the Browns to the Eastern Conference title. He threw only 110 passes, but, more importantly, he was adept at handing the ball to Jim Brown. O'Connell started the title game against Detroit, but he was playing on a broken leg and was ineffective. Plum replaced him, but he was suffering from a severe hamstring pull. Each threw two interceptions, and the Browns lost 59–14, one of the most lopsided defeats in Cleveland history.

O'Connell retired after the season, leaving Plum as the incumbent quarterback. For backup, Brown drafted Jim Ninowski from Michigan State in the fourth round. Ninowski had started three years for the Spartans, and during that time Michigan State was one of the top teams in the country, twice finishing third in the Associated Press poll. He played in three all-star games following his senior season and was named MVP of all three, including the College All-Star game, in which he engineered an upset of the champion Lions. He stood 6-foot-1 and weighed 210 pounds and played defensive back as well as quarterback. Some scouts said his legs were too big, but he countered that he didn't throw with his legs. He played two seasons for Cleveland but couldn't beat out Plum. Brown thought he was "too jittery." He wasn't tall enough to see over the defensive line and fled the pocket too soon. After obtaining Len Dawson from Pittsburgh, Brown traded him to Detroit before the 1960 season. But Dawson didn't work out, either—"Len's arm was never strong enough to suit me," Brown said.[2] Dawson threw twenty-eight passes in two seasons as Plum's backup and was released. (He went on to lead the Kansas City Chiefs to a Super Bowl title. The Browns and Steelers whiffed on not one Hall of Fame quarterback, but two.)

Plum blossomed into an All-Pro in 1960. He began the season throwing sixteen touchdown passes without an interception—an NFL record that stood until Peyton Manning tied it in 2013. He finished with twenty-one TD passes, most in the league, and just five interceptions. His passer rating of 110.4 set an NFL record that stood until Joe Montana broke it in 1989. He also led the league in completion percentage and yards per completion. Cleveland topped the NFL in scoring and total offense (Jim Brown rushed for a league-leading 1,257 yards) and finished second in the Eastern Conference behind Philadelphia. It appeared the Browns finally had found a replacement for Graham, as well as a complement to Jim Brown's running.

In 1961, Plum again threw for more than 2,000 yards, and he was named to the Pro Bowl for the second straight year. But Cleveland underachieved—in the minds of the players as well as the fans—and finished 8–5–1 and in third place in the East. Among the defeats was a 49–17 thumping by Vince Lombardi's Packers, the worst home defeat of Paul Brown's career. The loss demoralized the players and marked another turning point in the coach's control over the team. The veterans became tired of his know-it-all approach and his habit of blaming players when things went poorly. He still called all the plays, but they didn't work as often or as well as they had in the past. Younger players who hadn't won a championship under him questioned why he was considered such a genius.

Following the season, Plum told reporters that Brown was stifling the players. They had no input in game plans; on Fridays they were asked for suggestions, and that was the last they'd hear of them. They felt like cogs in a machine, like robots, and as a result played with little emotion. They believed they could beat anyone if their head coach would simply loosen up. "The team is in a rut," Plum said. "We don't get up for the big games most of the time and often have to struggle with the not so strong teams."[3]

Plum said he initially had welcomed Brown calling the plays because it made his job easier. But as he became more experienced and better at recognizing defenses, he began second-guessing some of the coach's calls. When defenses switched their formation to counter the play sent in from the bench, he was helpless to do anything about it. He wasn't asking for a drastic change, just a bit more leeway. "Any time I don't like what the coach sends in I can call my own play," he told attendees at a postseason banquet. "The only catch is, that'll be my last game with the Cleveland Browns." He said he expressed his unhappiness because as quarterback he was supposed to be a leader—"although it's tough when you never get a chance to lead."[4]

The press asked Graham, then coach at the Coast Guard Academy, what he thought of Plum's remarks. He said he understood the young quarterback's frustration and sympathized with him. "That was the only real bone of contention between Paul and me," Graham said. "It's the only thing in which all players disagree with Paul. I believe check-offs are good. I argued for them as a player and I feel the same way as a coach." Then came the dagger: "Paul says that a quarterback gets stereotyped in his play calling. But he fails to realize that he himself can become stereotyped."[5]

Players had been grumbling among themselves for years about Brown, but no one had gone public until now. Plum's comments provided fans with a behind-the-curtain look at the unrest within the Cleveland organization. His insubordination was going to come with a price (see Daniell, Jim); there was no way Paul Brown would stand for it. Knowing this, Edwin Anderson, Detroit's general manager, called Brown and asked if he was interested in trading Plum for Ninowski. Brown said sure, he'd make the deal, and Anderson told his staff. They couldn't believe it. Ninowksi had shown potential with the Lions, but he was prone to throwing interceptions, one of the reasons Plum beat him out for the starting job in Cleveland. When Brown told *his* coaches, they threw a fit. He called Anderson back and said he would need more than Ninowski. Cleveland received defensive end Bill Glass and running back Howard "Hopalong" Cassady in exchange for Plum, linebacker Dave Lloyd, and halfback Tommy Watkins. As it turned out, Glass was the centerpiece of the deal; he would be a key member of Cleveland's defense for a half-dozen years.

Trading Plum wasn't enough to appease Brown. He held a grudge and nursed it publicly. He told Tex Maule that Plum couldn't scramble and lacked Otto Graham's peripheral vision. He wasn't patient enough to wait for his receivers to break open at the one-second intervals Brown prescribed and as a result completed only short passes (two years earlier Maule had touted Plum's patience and quoted Brown as saying the quarterback was mastering the skill of looking for his secondary receivers). The other problem was Bobby Mitchell, the fifth-year halfback from Illinois. He fumbled when he ran into the line, so Brown believed he could only use him on sweeps. As a result, opposing teams knew Plum couldn't throw deep and Mitchell couldn't run inside, so they could assign a linebacker to cover Jim Brown wherever he went. The Giants were especially successful at this, siccing Sam Huff on him, Maule explained, and that's why they throttled Cleveland's offense. Cleveland's front office issued a press release with statistics showing 70 percent of Plum's passes traveled 7 yards or less, proof of his inability to throw long. That didn't set well with the players. "All of us on the team knew that (a) Paul called the pass plays, and (b) one of our frequent plays was a short flare pass behind the line of scrimmage," Jim Brown said.[6]

Nearly twenty years later, in his autobiography, Paul Brown continued to excoriate Plum. He blamed him for the team's failures to win championships in the late '50s. He wrote that Plum choked in big games: the players "had begun to lose faith in Plum's ability to play under stress, reducing their confidence in their offense." The players also became frustrated with him because of his weak arm and inability to throw downfield—"he lost credibility with our players when we lost too many games because of it." In the end, he wrote, it turned out Plum was "a very average quarterback without a strong arm [who] could have carried us farther down the road if he had only recognized his limitations and been satisfied to work within the scope of the offense we had prepared for him."[7] In other words, if he'd simply shut up and run the plays Brown called, things would have turned out much better.

Plum wasn't Otto Graham, but he wasn't the weak-armed, big-game choker Brown described either. During the four years he played for Cleveland, the team's record when he started was 33–16–2. He set an NFL record, since broken, of 208 consecutive passes without an interception. And, contrary to Paul Brown's claims, he was effective throwing downfield, averaging 14.2 yards per completion.

When Brown told Ninowski he'd traded for him, Nino was livid. Detroit was his hometown, he'd won the starting job there, and the Lions had finished second both years he played with them. He lived ten minutes from training camp and had established a business. He said he'd rather retire than play for Cleveland. "You've screwed up my whole life," he told Brown. The coach was in a difficult position. Plum was gone, and now Ninowski didn't want to come back. Ninowski said he wanted to call the plays, and Brown relented. "I had him over a barrel," Nino said, "and I took advantage of it."[8]

Brown told reporters he was going to allow Ninowski to call his own plays because Nino was a good runner as well as passer, and Brown wanted to take advantage of his skills. "We will start the changes in our signal calling right here," he said. "We have a different style quarterback in Jim Ninowski."[9]

Unloading Plum failed to quell the unrest building within the team. Jim Brown told reporters that Plum's complaints reflected the attitude of many of the players. "They feel they're playing under wraps all the time," he said. Worst of all, they believed their coach no longer cared about winning championships but "merely . . . having a good season, one that did not disgrace his name."[10] It later was revealed that some of the veterans considered quitting unless changes were made. "That's true," captain Mike McCormack said. "Some of us just felt that we weren't going anyplace. It wasn't the money we were worrying about, either. There was a matter of pride."[11]

Modell complicated matters by arranging for Plum and Jim Brown to host their own radio shows, and both men criticized the offense in general and the messenger-guard system specifically. Paul Brown believed the shows undermined his authority and hurt team morale, but Modell thought they would help attract fans and sell tickets. Modell also fraternized with players. He bought them drinks and dinners and chatted them up, asking them what they thought of the coach and his play-calling. He tried to find them off-season jobs, offered tax advice, and helped with personal problems. It made good business sense. "I think all employers try to give their employees peace of mind, so they can devote their full energies to work," he said. "Yes, I'm guilty of that."[12] Underlying it all, at least in Brown's mind, was Modell's intention to push him out and to become the franchise's ultimate authority. "The player-coach relationship became progressively more intolerable," Brown said, "to the point where I was no longer able to call the shots, no longer in a position to demand from all our players all the things which make or break a successful football team. That had never happened to me before in all my years in football."[13]

During the offseason, Brown overhauled the offense. He unloaded ten players, in addition to Plum, for eight players from other teams. His biggest move—one that raised eyebrows across the league—was to send Bobby Mitchell and first-round pick Leroy Jackson to Washington for Heisman Trophy winner Ernie Davis of Syracuse. Mitchell never seemed to satisfy his coach, despite his world-class speed and big-play ability. In the third game of his rookie season, he ran for 147 yards on just eleven carries. After five games, the Browns were undefeated, Jim Brown led the league in rushing, and

Mitchell was second. But in the sixth game, against the Giants, Mitchell fumbled three times in the second half, and though the Browns recovered all three, he was benched. For the rest of the season, Mitchell primarily was used as a kick returner. At times over the next three seasons, he was sensational. He averaged more than 5 yards per carry and during his time in Cleveland scored thirty-eight touchdowns: sixteen on the ground, sixteen on receptions, three on kickoffs, and three on punt returns.

Jim Brown said later that the coach was jealous of the two running backs receiving so much credit for the team's success, which rings true. He also said Paul Brown was uncomfortable having two black stars, but that doesn't make as much sense. He used whomever he could to help him win, regardless of race, dating to the days of Marion Motley and Bill Willis. In any case, Mitchell became expendable. "Paul was running a business, he may have been motivated by economics," Jim Brown said. "Whatever, I hated what Paul did to Bobby."[14]

Paul Brown's rationale—other than Mitchell's fumblitis—was that he wanted another big back to team with Jim Brown, to emulate what Vince Lombardi was doing with great success in Green Bay with Paul Hornung and Jim Taylor. Ernie Davis stood 6-foot-2 and weighed 220 pounds and was the first African American awarded the Heisman Trophy. Jim Brown had helped recruit him to Syracuse, and Davis wore Jim's number 44. He also broke most of Brown's rushing and scoring records. Publicly, Paul Brown said Davis was to team with Jim Brown, but he also expected him to serve as his successor. He'd learned his lesson with Otto Graham. He wasn't going to allow his best player to leave without a suitable replacement.

Davis was one of the most heralded players in college football history. President John F. Kennedy was in New York when Davis was there to accept the Heisman, and he invited him to his hotel for a chat. The Redskins picked him first in the NFL draft, as did the Buffalo Bills of the American Football League. Washington owner George Marshall didn't want to engage in a bidding war with the Bills, and he accepted Paul Brown's offer. Mitchell thus became the Redskins' first black player and went on to a Hall of Fame career, and Washington became the final NFL team to integrate.

Brown made the trade on draft day without consulting Modell, and when Marshall asked the Cleveland owner what he thought of the deal, Modell asked, "What trade?" Marshall responded, "Aren't you running that franchise? Don't ever let that happen again. You are the owner. You own the franchise. It's *yours*."[15]

A bidding war did ensue between Cleveland and Buffalo, and Davis signed a three-year, $80,000 contract with the Browns. It included a $15,000 signing bonus and was the richest contract ever signed by an NFL rookie.

When Jim Brown heard about the trade, he asked Paul if he was going to be traded. The coach assured him he wasn't. But Jim Brown was covering his bases anyway. His two-year contract worth $65,000 was up, and he intimated he wanted $50,000 per year, the same as Elgin Baylor was making playing for the NBA's Los Angeles Lakers. He told reporters he was overworked and might quit. "It was my feeling last season that I was asked to do more than my share," he said. "I have never objected to doing my bit, but I don't care to take the burden to help a trading scheme on the part of the club."[16] He said he wanted to live in New York in order to concentrate more on his marketing job with Pepsi Cola and would consider playing, but only with a New York team. Whether he was serious or simply posturing for a better deal for 1962, it worked. He signed a one-year, $45,000 contract, with a $5,000 bonus if the Browns won the East, making him the highest-paid player in the NFL.

With the trades of Mitchell and Plum, Cleveland was without its second-leading rusher and its starting quarterback from the previous season. In July 1962, while in Chicago for the College All-Star game, Davis was admitted to a hospital with a fever and swollen glands. Doctors ran tests and discovered he was suffering from acute monocytic leukemia, a form of blood cancer. A week later Modell gathered reporters and told them Davis had a year to live. He vowed them to secrecy, and they reported only that he was suffering from a "blood disorder." Cleveland suddenly found itself without a running back to pair with Jim Brown.

On the eve of training camp, Paul Brown traded defensive end Larry Stephens and two draft choices to the Rams for running back "Touchdown Tommy" Wilson and quarterback Frank Ryan. Wilson, a seven-year veteran, had rushed more than 2,000 yards in his career, third best in Rams history. As a rookie in 1956, he'd set the NFL single-game rushing record with 223 yards against the Packers. Wilson provided insurance in case Davis couldn't play. Ryan became expendable when the Rams drafted Roman Gabriel. They also had Zeke Bratkowski, which made Ryan, in essence, third string. Still, Cleveland needed *someone* to back up Ninowski. Before trading for Ryan, Paul Brown had given Ninowski a list of quarterbacks and asked whom he thought would be worth trading for. The list included Ryan, Bratkowski, and Ryan's old Rice teammate King Hill, who was playing for Philadelphia. Ninowski remembered Ryan playing well for Los Angeles against Detroit in 1960 and recommended him. Forever after he joked, "Like my wife says, 'Me and my big mouth.'"[17]

Brown's final move in rebuilding his offense was rehiring Blanton Collier. After his dismissal by Kentucky, Collier said he wanted to remain in football—"[it] has been my life"—but planned to take time off and relax before making any decisions about his future. Less than two weeks later, Brown announced Collier had rejoined him in Cleveland as offensive coordinator. Blanton had one requirement: none of the other assistants would be fired to make room for him. That was no problem for Brown. "I'm tickled to death to have him back on the staff and know he'll be a tremendous help to us," he said. "I have a lot of confidence in his ideas."[18] Collier said he was grateful Brown took him back, adding that his happiest days coaching had been with the Browns. He was coming home—again. Brown put him in charge of the offense, but he didn't give him an office in the team's Municipal Stadium headquarters. Instead, Collier worked in the film room and from a desk in a hallway. He didn't complain. He was loyal to Paul Brown, and he was thankful for the opportunity to continue teaching football.

CHAPTER NINE

Two weeks before the opening of the 1962 season training camp, Tex Maule visited Paul Brown at his home in Shaker Heights. Katy Brown made them dinner, and afterward they went for a walk in the neighborhood. Maule was reporting for a lengthy profile of the Cleveland coach to be published in *SI* in September. Brown walked briskly, Maule recounted, and as always was well groomed. During the season, Maule noted, Brown was "cold as a Comptometer [an early calculator]." But during the offseason he was warm and gregarious, fond of music, gin rummy, golf, and small children.[1]

Maule's finished profile, "A Man for This Season," described the coach in glowing terms. Although he was a journalist, Maule was in a sense a member of the old-school NFL establishment. The man who'd replaced him as press agent with the Rams was Pete Rozelle, now the league's commissioner. Maule wasn't looking to stir up controversy, and he wasn't about to turn on Paul Brown, who as much as anyone represented the league's history and tradition. He laid out the reasons for Cleveland's recent problems on offense as though they were facts, but he clearly was parroting Brown. The trouble wasn't the coach's play-calling; it was the team's personnel: Plum couldn't throw long, Mitchell fumbled too much. Maule wrote that Brown still was considered an innovator and a genius—at least outside of Cleveland, where "followers often think of him as a loser." Maule also pointed out that Brown had won more games in the past five years than any other coach and in the past sixteen years more championships than anyone else. He acknowledged that the "suave, keen-eyed" Brown no longer seemed as imposing as he once had and that some, including his own players, considered his offense stereotyped. But he remained "as inventive as any coach in the game today and is responsible for originating ideas about offense that changed the face of defensive football." (Brown's critics would argue Maule was focusing too much on the past and that Brown was living and coaching in the past.)

"[He], apparently, has listened to at least some of his critics," Maule noted. "After he had seen [Jim] Ninowski in practice, he announced: 'I'm going to let Ninowski call the signals for himself at the beginning of the game.'" To assure those around him that he hadn't really gone soft, Brown added a lengthy explanation:

> I still think a coach can do a better job, for several reasons. One, the defenses change so many times before the ball is snapped that, when the quarterback guesses with the defensive signal-caller, he has to change two or three times at the line of scrimmage and has as much chance to be wrong as I do from the sideline, and with less information. Also, when I call the play from the sideline, I have two coaches on a telephone hookup in the stands who know what the play is, watch the players in their bailiwick and can tell me how they performed. If the quarterback called the signal, we wouldn't know what the play was and wouldn't know what each player should have done . . .
>
> But there is one thing that a quarterback can do by calling his own signals. He can infect the team with his personality and give you a certain exuberance. I think Ninowski can do that for us. That's why he'll call the signals, at least part of the time.

Brown seemed confident in his current squad—"and he certainly has good reason," Maule wrote. He still had Jim Brown, and the Eastern Conference looked weaker than usual, because the Giants were beginning to show their age. "Reasonably enough, as this season approaches, Cleveland is appearing more and more often as the choice in the Eastern Division in the opinions of experts," Maule wrote. "Brown would rather be the underdog, but he isn't exactly displeased with the way things have been going for his team in training. You won't hear that from him now and, if he wins, he won't crow either. Paul Brown will let his record speak for him. As in the past, it should speak eloquently."[2]

Blanton Collier had his colleague and old friend's blessing to retool the offense, and it became more diversified. He let the quarterback change the play at the line of scrimmage, and he installed a variety of formations not used before. The players were delighted. They had heard about this genius who'd helped build the Cleveland dynasty, and now they had the chance to learn from him. With all the changes, the team seemed loose and confident and on the verge of regaining its dominance. The players also noticed Paul Brown had mellowed with Collier's return. "Brown wasn't doing it by himself anymore," Mike McCormack said. "Collier was the only man Brown would listen to."[3]

Cleveland won all its exhibition games for the first time since joining the NFL in 1950, and writers from Scripps-Howard papers across the country picked the Browns to win the East. Despite the success the changes brought, Brown sensed his absolute control—of his franchise, his team, his opponents, even his assistant coaches—was slipping away. Modell was trying to overthrow him. The players were happy, but it was hard to say for how long, especially if they started losing. Collier was not only taking control of the offense, he was receiving credit for its improvement, and his growing popularity and influence were proving yet another threat, and an unexpected one.

Brown had always been a bit paranoid, but he was becoming more so. He saw a car parked near the practice field at League Park, and he sent trainer Leo Murphy over to check it out. It was a salesman, and he was napping. "I had to wake him up and tell him that Paul Brown didn't want him watching practice," Murphy recalled. "The guy thought I was nuts."[4] When helicopters flew over the field, Brown suspected scouts from opposing teams were taking photos, and he stopped practice. He had a seven-foot canvas fence installed around the field, and he periodically walked the perimeter and checked for peepholes. One day, telephone repairmen raised a cherry picker on the opposite side of the fence and had an unobstructed view of the field. Brown halted practice and walked over to them. "Don't try to kid me," he shouted up to them. "I know what you're up to—from *Baltimore*, aren't you?" The repairmen looked down at him too puzzled to speak, and one of them spun his finger near his head and pointed at him.[5]

During the preseason, Collier and Jim Brown conferred on the field before games, Collier asking what plays he thought would work against that day's opponent. Collier then made sure those plays were run. "It worked—it really worked—because Jim *knew* what he could do," guard John Wooten said. "He trusted and respected Blanton's judgment. Blanton trusted and respected Jim's."[6]

A friend of Paul Brown's read an article in the *Atlanta Constitution* headlined "Collier's Back, the Browns Are Winning Again." Some of the players believed the story made Brown so jealous he demoted Collier; others couldn't believe the head coach could be so petty. In any case, Brown reasserted himself as sole commander of the offense. He sought little input from Collier at practices, and the players sensed tension between the two old friends. Brown later said it was a misunderstanding caused by Collier's hearing problems: "Not always being able to hear everything that was said, he imagined after a while that I was ignoring him." Brown also believed Collier's experience at Kentucky led him to develop an attitude of "either get or get gotten," and as a result he made himself inconspicuous as the rift grew between Brown and Modell. "He gradually withdrew from associating with the other coaches and said less and less at our meetings."[7] Brown's explanation of his estrangement from Collier took the onus off him and put it on his assistant, but anyone who knew Blanton Collier knew he wouldn't—couldn't—be so conniving. It simply wasn't in his nature. Collier's daughter Kay wrote in her biography of her father, "Paul had gone back to his old ways because he could not accept the fact that someone other than himself was receiving the credit."[8] It's hard to say how much of that is a daughter defending her father, but it rings true. It seemed inconceivable that Paul Brown, a man so organized, so in control, would allow jealousy and paranoia to bring down what he'd built, but it was happening.

Ninowksi and Paul Brown met before the season opener against New York and went over ten plays Brown had scripted to start the game. Ninowski ran one of the plays and then began calling his own. "It rejuvenated the guys in the huddle," he said. "Someone was standing up to Paul Brown."[9] (The coach continued to alternate guards so that it looked as though he was in charge. He told Ninowski, "It will protect you, and it will protect me.")[10] Nino called a flea flicker he'd used while playing for Detroit. He pitched the ball to Jim Brown, who handed to flanker Ray Renfro coming on a reverse. Renfro flipped it to Ninowski, who threw a 27-yard touchdown pass to Rich Kreitling. It wasn't in Paul Brown's playbook, nor the kind of play he normally would run, and afterward he instructed Nino to tell reporters "*we* called it."[11] Ninowski was irked, but he didn't expect much different from Brown. And anyway, Cleveland had beaten the Giants, 17–7.

The coaches and quarterbacks met at Shaker Heights Country Club early each week during the season, and, as usual, Brown ordered everyone's meals. Ninowski told the waitress he wanted something different. Afterward Brown asked, "Why did you do that to me?" Nino explained he didn't like what Brown had ordered for him. Brown let it go. "A lot of guys feared him," Ninowski said. "If you stood up to Paul he appreciated that and you had a better relationship with him."[12]

Modell sensed the team was looser than in previous years, a result of it being less "stereotyped" (there was that word again; Brown must have cringed every time he heard it). Lou Groza credited Collier's presence with changing the team's attitude. "I think this year the fellows are more relaxed, more effervescent," he said. "Blanton helped. He's someone Paul can talk to."[13] McCormack, who, like Groza, had played on Cleveland's last two championship teams, said the squad was more united than it had been the previous few seasons. There was no whining, no finger-pointing. "There is an old-time unity on this team," he said. "It reminds me of the years when we were winning."[14] He credited Ninowski and the new play-calling policy as the major reasons for the improved morale.

The following week Cleveland lost 17–16 to the Redskins. Washington's first score came when Jim Brown, hemmed in by the defense, tried lateralling to Ninowski. A Redskin defender intercepted and ran in for a touchdown. To Paul Brown, the play epitomized Modell's negative influence on his players. They were becoming too independent, too freewheeling. Such a play never would have happened in the past. "My relationship with the team had greatly changed," he wrote in his autobiography. "The complete control and authority I had once held over them had worn dangerously thin."[15] To make matters worse, Bobby Mitchell scored Washington's winning touchdown on a 50-yard pass reception.

Brown responded by returning to using the guards to shuttle in plays *he* called. A week later, Cleveland lost to Philadelphia 35–7. In the first three games of the season, the Browns had scored just forty points. Attendance dropped from 81,115 for the opener to 44,040 for a 19–10 win over the Cowboys in the fourth game. Fans booed the team more than they'd booed the sixth-place Indians that summer, and that was saying something. Ninowski was a particular target of their ire, as was the head coach for leaving him in. After a promising start, Nino was bitten by his old bugaboo. Over a three-game span, he threw five interceptions and just one touchdown pass.

The vaunted Cleveland rushing attack didn't provide much help. After running for 134 yards in the opener, Jim Brown failed to rush for 100 yards again until the last game of the season. Unbeknownst to the public and to Cleveland's opponents, he had suffered a badly sprained left wrist in the fourth game of the season. He could barely carry the ball, but he kept playing. The day after the Colts shellacked the Browns 36–14, a game in which Brown carried fourteen times for 11 yards and fumbled three times, Frank Gibbons of the *Press* wrote, "No Browns team, with the exception of that of 1956 [when the Browns finished 5–7], has ever seemed as disorganized and lacking in poise."[16]

As if responding to Gibbons, the Browns routed St. Louis 34–7, proof of their ability when motivated. Ninowski played his best game of the season, passing for 339 yards and three touchdowns, with no interceptions. The following week against Pittsburgh, however, it all came crashing down, in the form of Gene "Big Daddy" Lipscomb. Ninowski suffered a broken clavicle and dislocated shoulder when Lipscomb, all 6-foot-6 and 306 pounds of him, landed on him in the second quarter. He was done for the season.

In came Frank Ryan. The fans had been calling for Ninowski to be replaced, but they hadn't thought much about who was next in line. Few had heard of Ryan before he joined the team during the preseason, and they didn't know what to expect from him. He made a first good impression, completing eleven of eighteen passes for 144 yards and two scores in a 41–14 Cleveland victory. Los Angeles had drafted Ryan in the fifth round in 1958, one round after Cleveland took Ninowski, and he'd made only a handful of starts in his four years with the Rams. He often seemed on the verge of stardom but never quite clicked. He was a good scrambler, but his critics said he was indecisive and held onto the ball too long, resulting in sacks.

Despite their troubles, the Browns were 4–3 and in third place after the Pittsburgh game. But two weeks later they scored just nine points in a loss to the Redskins. The *Plain Dealer*'s Gordon Cobbledick took them to task for whining about officiating. The real problem, he wrote, was an inability to move the ball because of unimaginative play-calling. "When grandstand regulars can predict three times out of four what play will be called in any given situation—and they can and do—it must be assumed that the opposition can predict it accurately something like nine times out of 10."[17] Cobbledick didn't use the word "stereotyped"; he did worse. He succinctly voiced what critics considered the Browns' greatest obstacle to winning a championship: Paul Brown and his play-calling.

Modell visited Washington owner George Marshall during the week leading up to the Redskins game. They were chatting during a practice and when the Washington offense began running plays, Modell began to leave, believing his presence unwarranted and a distraction. Marshall wouldn't let him go. "Oh, come on, if you did catch our plays and gave them to Paul Brown he wouldn't believe you," Marshall chided him.

Modell replied, "How can I give Brown any information? He won't talk to me."[18]

During the game, Modell pounded the table in the press box and shouted, "Oh, come on, let's get organized!"

Paul Brown, unorganized?

He also was overheard to say, "I've got to get rid of this man."[19]

Ryan's emergence provided one bright spot. In the tenth game of the season, the Browns beat the Cardinals 38–14. Ryan completed fifteen of twenty-one passes for 241 yards and a score and didn't throw an interception. Afterward, Paul Brown said, "The most encouraging part of today's game was that it looks like Ryan is settling down. This was the first time he's really looked like that." Gary Collins, a 6-foot-4 rookie from Maryland, replaced Ray Renfro, who was injured in the first quarter, and caught six passes for 88 yards and the touchdown. He'd caught only two passes in the previous nine games. The following week the Browns beat the Steelers 35–14, and Ryan threw for 284 yards and three scores. "If he continues to improve, that deal with Los Angeles could dwarf all the others," Brown said. "I don't want to build this thing out of proportion, but the more I see of him, the more I like him."[20]

Ryan grew up in Fort Worth, Texas, in an extended family of high achievers. His grandfather on his mother's side, Dr. Frank Beall, was a surgeon and a scholar. John Ryan, his paternal grandfather, developed Ryan Place, a neighborhood of homes on Fort Worth's south side with marble columns, beveled-glass doors, and underground ballrooms. Ryan's father, Robert W. Ryan, and three uncles attended Yale, as did his older brother. His father was a fine athlete, and an especially good tennis player, captaining the Yale tennis team. But he suffered from diabetes and alcoholism. He tried buying and selling oil lots but was unsuccessful, and he moved his family from Mississippi to Ryan Place when Frank was in grade school. The Depression had taken its toll on Ryan Place, and by the time Frank moved there it no longer was in its heyday, though it still was an upper-class neighborhood.

Two of Ryan's uncles lived nearby, and they contributed money to help the family. "My father was a total loss," Ryan said. "He was not a happy person at all." Ryan witnessed his father's unraveling, and though he was too young to fully comprehend what was happening, it did instill in him an intense desire to succeed. "That gives a person a chance to decide what you want to be," he said. "I didn't want to be like my father. That was an attitude that was front and center in my teens."[21]

Ryan's cousin Eddie, who lived across the street, taught him how to throw a football. Eddie was four years older and had played football at a prep school back East and at Yale. He showed Ryan the proper grip and taught him to throw over the top instead of sidearm. "He was my great teacher," Ryan said.

Ryan hung a tire on a hedge and threw the ball at it, perfecting a spiral and his accuracy. He was fascinated, he said, with "the sense of making that awkward object go in a beautiful way."[22]

Ryan attended Paschal High School, which boasted a strong football program. He failed to make the cut as a sophomore, and one of the coaches saw him crying. The coach recognized how much it meant to him and told him he could play. He grew to over 6 feet and developed into a fine athlete, though he didn't start at quarterback until his senior year, and then only because another boy quit football to concentrate on basketball. "We looked around and picked Ryan," his coach, Bill Allen, said.[23]

Ryan always downplayed his abilities. He claimed he couldn't hit a baseball or dribble a basketball. "I pick up a dart and people start running," he said.[24] But he excelled in Paschal's Split-T offense. The Split T was the predecessor of the wishbone and veer offenses and required a quarterback who was a good runner. If he could pass well, so much the better. Ryan would take the snap and move parallel to the line of scrimmage. He could hand the ball to a halfback on a dive into the line, he could pitch to a trailing halfback, or he could keep it himself. "I kept it a lot," he said later, laughing.[25] He also was a fine passer because of how he applied his fascination with the dynamics of a twirling leather ellipsoid. A high school physics teacher told him he'd studied the shape of the football and calculated a person could throw it no farther than 50 yards. Ryan and the teacher went to a field and Ryan launched the ball. They measured the distance it covered on the fly. Seventy-three yards.

Because Ryan was such a good runner, Paschal's coach alternated him and another player at quarterback and halfback. Ryan ran for 93 yards against Amarillo one week and passed for 188 yards the next week against Pampa. He made all-state and was chosen to play in the Greenbelt Bowl in Childress the summer after graduating. One of the coaches was "Slingin'" Sammy Baugh, a Texas football legend and at the time an assistant at Hardin-Simmons. "He throws like he's roping a calf," Baugh said. "Just puts the ball up by his ear, flips it, and it's happened."[26]

Ryan considered attending Yale—his older brother already was there— and was recruited by a number of football powers, including Oklahoma, a perennial national title contender under the legendary coach Bud Wilkinson. The Sooners had perfected the Split T and would lose just one game during the next four years. Ryan made two visits to Oklahoma. On the first, he met a quarterback who'd been an outstanding passer in high school but wasn't playing much because he wasn't a good runner. On his second visit, he met the starting quarterback, who'd suffered separations of both shoulders running the ball. Ryan decided Oklahoma wasn't for him. He'd watched the state championship game at Rice Stadium in Houston when he was a senior, and he loved the stadium, which was built in 1950, the year after Rice Institute won the Southwest Conference. Rice's offense emphasized passing as well as running in its version of the Split T, and that appealed to Ryan; so did the school's rigorous academics, which were close to Yale's, if not quite on par. He wanted to study physics.

It became apparent early on that football was going to interfere with his schoolwork, and he asked the Rice coaches to allow him to miss practice twice a week to attend physics labs. They agreed. Head coach Jess Neely said Ryan and classmate King Hill of Freeport were the best quarterbacks ever to enroll at Rice. Ryan stood 6-foot-2 and weighed 195 pounds, and Hill was 6-foot-3, 205 pounds. "He couldn't throw the football as well as me," Ryan said, "but he was a superior athlete to me in all other ways."[27] Neely initially didn't like Ryan's rope-a-calf delivery, and he told the backfield coach to change it, but the assistant said it worked and they should leave it alone. "Ryan has about convinced me that he's right and everybody else is wrong," Neely said.[28] In those days, college athletes played both offense and defense. Ryan injured his knee as a sophomore and was unable to play defense, opening the door for Hill to become Rice's starting quarterback. Hill would go on to become an All-American and the first player taken in the 1958 NFL draft.

During a preseason scrimmage their junior year Ryan gained 134 yards rushing, scored twice, completed six of thirteen passes, punted, and kicked two extra points. A *Star-Telegram* writer called him "a new Walter Fondren." An All-American at Texas, Fondren had played halfback, quarterback, and punted. Ryan had matured into a rangy, fast, and skilled athlete. He passed for four touchdowns that season and rushed for three scores. Hill played quarterback, halfback, and caught passes from Ryan. Before their senior season, a sportswriter described Ryan as the best passer in the Southwest Conference. "Hill sort of lays the ball in there, and it's easy to catch," end Buddy Dial said. "But you had better be ready when Ryan throws. He gets the ball to you quick, especially on the buttonhook plays. He doesn't want anybody intercepting, and he takes advantage of the quick openings."[29]

College rules at the time allowed a player to substitute into the game only once per quarter. Rice employed a consistent strategy: Hill started, Ryan replaced him at some point each quarter, and Hill finished up. Despite sharing time, the two became good friends and roomed together on the road. Rice won the Southwest Conference championship their senior year after starting the season with a 3–3 record. They upset twelfth-ranked Arkansas in the seventh game and the next Saturday faced undefeated and number-one ranked Texas A&M, coached by Bear Bryant and led by Heisman Trophy winner John David Crow. The game was played at Rice Stadium before a crowd of 72,000, the largest in school history. Late in the first quarter, Ryan moved the Owls 70 yards to the 6-yard line, half of the yards coming on his runs, and he tried to carry it in on the last play of the quarter. He spun off tackle and stiff-armed Crow—"really sprang his neck back," Hill recalled—but fumbled at the goal line. The Owls recovered, and Hill replaced Ryan to start the second quarter. He scored two plays later and kicked the extra point. Rice won 7–6. Hill received the accolades, but he pointed out Ryan made his touchdown possible. "You just gotta like a guy like that," he said.[30] Ninth-ranked Rice played eighth-ranked Navy in the Cotton Bowl in Dallas following the season and lost 21–7. The Owls fell behind early and tried to pass their way back into it with Ryan at quarterback and King as receiver. "It was a good system," Ryan said in his understated way. "They got some good use out of me."[31]

In March of his senior year Ryan and Joan Busby, a Rice coed and English literature major from Houston, were married. Slim and blond, she was described as a ringer for the actress Celeste Holm. She and Frank met at a picnic their freshman year. She recently had broken up with her high school boyfriend and was, in her words, "looking to play the field." Frank still was seeing his high school sweetheart, and they didn't begin dating immediately. Joan was chosen to represent Rice at the Cotton Bowl parade their junior year. Each Southwest Conference school was represented, and the champion school's delegate was chosen queen. As she wrote later, she figured she was a shoe-in to become queen. "My boyfriend was quarterback of the mighty Owls and I was as confident of wearing the ermine as Richard III. Let others twirl their batons, I sniffed. My sights were set on a scepter."[32] It didn't work out that way—Rice finished 4–6 that season—but she did participate in the parade. "She was a very energetic person," Frank said, "and absolutely captivated me from the beginning."[33]

Ryan earned a degree in physics and, following the advice of his Rice professors, planned to attend graduate school. He considered MIT and Princeton, among other schools. Sid Gillman, head coach of the Rams, recognized his passing ability, despite his limited playing time in college, and picked him in the fifth round of the NFL draft. "Guess what?" Frank told Joan, breathless. "I've just been drafted!"

"As a bride-to-be," she said later, "I had imagined early married life, at the worst, in terms of dingy graduate school housing; at the best, nightly candle-lit dinners and weekly gifts of flowers." But now her husband, apparently, was headed into the military. "Not the *Army* draft," he said. "The *NFL* draft!"[34]

He initially decided to stick with his plan to attend graduate school, but his desire to continue playing football won out. He also needed the money to support his family, and he wanted the challenge. "I really thought I could throw a football just about better than anybody," he said. "So there was a sort of feeling that I could prove myself, show I really could do it. The allure was that of performing in the very best circles and showing I could cut the mustard."[35]

Ryan told the Rams he wouldn't sign unless he could attend graduate school at the same time (he had been accepted at UCLA), and Gillman agreed. "Ryan is the better bet [than King Hill]," Gillman said. "He would have been drafted sooner, only no one believes he'll try pro ball. The kid is a nuclear physics genius." That likely was the first of many times the press would describe Ryan as a genius, though he never had any proof he tested at genius level. Ryan signed in March, and, after traveling to Houston to sign him, Gillman said he would "fit in beautifully." Gillman knew a good quarterback when he saw one. He was instrumental in developing the pass-oriented West Coast offense and was inducted into the Pro Football Hall of Fame. "This is the longest trip I have made this year to sign a boy," he said. "Most of the time I send my assistants, but this was a very special trip.

"Frank's ambition is to be a physicist and we're going to cooperate so he can realize that ambition."[36]

Ryan attended morning classes at UCLA and was at team meetings by 10 or 10:30. Mathematics was his focus, and on long road trips he worked on complicated problems. Math and football complemented each other for him. "One of the great things about football is that it involves a lot of brinkmanship. You're always getting out on a limb, getting into situations where you have to do something that will make or break you," he said. "I sort of like a situation like that, where nothing is absolutely certain and you have to extemporize to get the job done. You don't find that in mathematics."[37]

With Rams' star quarterback Norm Van Brocklin retired, Ryan competed with Billy Wade for the starting spot. He played a total of nineteen minutes his rookie season. The following year, the Rams finished 2–10, and he continued as Wade's backup. Gillman left the Rams for San Diego of the American Football League after Ryan's second year, and former Cleveland Rams quarterback Bob Waterfield took over as coach. Ryan never had an abundance of confidence, in large part because he had played in King Hill's shadow at Rice, and his experience in Los Angeles reinforced his feeling of inadequacy. Whenever he made a mistake, he found himself on the bench. In 1960, the Rams were winless after four games, and Waterfield decided to start Ryan against Chicago. He played well, and the Rams tied the Bears 24–24. Waterfield started him again the next week against Detroit. He threw for a touchdown to put Los Angeles ahead 7–0 in the first quarter, and in the second quarter he threw a pass to Jon Arnett, who lateraled it back to him and he ran 37 yards for a score.[38] He threw another touchdown pass shortly before halftime to put the Rams up by ten. Ryan's opportunity finally had come, and he was making the most of it and feeling confident. On the second series of the second half he threw an interception, and Waterfield pulled him for Wade.

The following week, Los Angeles played at Dallas, and Ryan was the starter. He was on top of the world, returning home as a starting NFL quarterback. In the first quarter, he threw a 61-yard touchdown pass to a streaking Red Phillips to put the Rams ahead 7–3. He connected with Phillips for another score in the second quarter, and Los Angeles led 24–13 at halftime. "Oh, boy," he thought to himself, "I feel great!" Early in the second quarter he badly overthrew a wide-open Arnett, and Waterfield again replaced him with Wade. Ryan didn't understand why Waterfield was jerking him around, and his new-found confidence drained away.

In the third game of the 1961 season, he came off the bench to lead the Rams over the Steelers, connecting with Ollie Matson on a 96-yard scoring pass that won the game in the final minute. But he rode the bench the final four games, now playing behind Zeke Bratkowski. The Rams finished 4–10, and after a season-ending loss to Green Bay Ryan stormed into the locker room and demanded to be traded. "What the Rams did to their quarterbacks, it took them all a long time to get over," said Joan. "It's like being at sea and when you're back on land you still think you're rocking. He'll always be a little insecure because of the Rams."[39]

Frank and Joan were miserable in Los Angeles. They had no social network outside of a few players and their families. The city's celebrity culture was well established, and the Ryans were relatively naïve and unsophisticated—Joan later described herself as an "innocent abroad." She was at a Rams game at the Coliseum and thought she spotted someone she knew from Houston. "I waved like a good southern girl should," she said. "I soon realized I had waved at Ozzie Nelson." She blushed and turned back toward the field.[40]

The Ryans moved to an apartment in Burbank with a view of the Los Angeles County Flood Control channel. "That is California for 'ditch,'" Joan said dryly.[41] When it rained, it flooded. For entertainment, the players' wives took their children to the windows of their apartments and pointed out the chairs and other debris flowing by. The Ryans' two oldest boys were born by then: Frank Jr., known as Pancho, Frank's nickname as a boy; and Michael. When the channel was dry, the boys threw their toys into it, and Joan had to pay teenagers from the neighborhood to climb down and retrieve them. The family returned to Houston in the off-season, and Frank took classes at Rice with the goal of earning a doctorate.

The Rams obliged his demand to be traded and sent him to the Browns—"neither to think nor to play," the writer Roger Kahn noted. Under Paul Brown he wasn't expected to do much thinking, and he wasn't expected to play much as backup to Ninowski. The trade came on Ryan's twenty-sixth birthday.

Ryan considered Gillman a great coach, but he and Waterfield never connected. "At L.A. I was never coached on the safety valve or alternate receivers," he said. "If I was told to throw to the flanker, say, and he was covered I had to take the loss."[42] Playing in Paul Brown's offense in 1962 was an epiphany. Like Plum in his early years, Ryan welcomed having the coach call the plays because he had one less thing to worry about. And Brown's calls often were something he hadn't thought of. "I was terribly impressed with him," Ryan said.[43]

Joan's only impression of Paul Brown that year came at the airport following a late-season game. The team had lost, but the players were laughing and patting Ryan on the back as they entered the terminal. She asked Frank what everyone was so happy about. He grinned and told her he'd accidentally cleated Paul Brown in the pregame warmup. The players were hopeful Brown might miss the next game because of the injury.

After beating Pittsburgh, Cleveland was in second place with a 6–4–1 record and had a chance to make the Playoff Bowl. But the Browns lost their next two games, 45–21 to Tom Landry's Cowboys and 17–13 to the Giants at Yankee Stadium. On the flight home from New York, Bernie Parrish slipped into the seat beside Jim Brown. He said he'd had enough. Other players joined the conversation. "Soon we had a regular huddle going around my seat," Brown said. The players decided a committee should meet with the coach and try to persuade him to open up the offense and to loosen up in general. The committee consisted of Parrish, Brown, McCormack, and veteran offensive lineman Jim Ray Smith. "We were simply going to state our grievances to Paul, and request that he seriously consider their possible merits," Jim Brown said. Someone suggested they talk to Paul right then, but they nixed the idea. They figured he'd say they were just upset because they'd lost the game. They decided to wait until the following week in San Francisco and talk to him in his hotel room. Modell got wind of their plan and told them to hold off. They agreed but told the owner that unless the head coach agreed to make some changes they would insist on being traded, or they would quit.[44]

The Browns practiced at League Park in a snowstorm the day they were scheduled to depart for San Francisco. The snow was up to their knees, and Brown sat in his car 20 yards behind the offensive huddle. Equipment manager Morrie Kono ran over to the car and Brown rolled down the window and told him what play to run. Kono then ran back to the huddle and relayed the play. It was a new take on the messenger system, and it showed how far removed Paul had become from his team. The man who'd preferred midwestern players because they could handle nasty weather couldn't be bothered to join them on the field in a snowstorm. "It was so out of character for him that, to this day, I don't understand it," linebacker Jim Houston told Terry Pluto years later.[45]

The team flight to San Francisco was diverted to Sacramento because of fog, and during the layover Modell bought drinks in the airport bar for some of the players. He asked them what they thought of Brown and of Collier. Brown's absolute control was kaput, and he knew it. "The last vestige of anything I had ever stood for was destroyed," he wrote in his autobiography. "Player was set against player; the loyalty of my coaching staff was questioned, and attempts were made to find out which ones were 'Paul Brown men'; public criticism of my coaching was encouraged through the media; discipline and control were torn apart by flagrant disregard for team rules."

Modell and Paul Brown met at team headquarters in Cleveland Municipal Stadium on Monday, January 7, 1963. The owner told Brown that key players were threatening to quit if he remained as coach. Modell said he could stay, but as vice president—not coach, not general manager. He no longer was in charge. The stunned Brown stormed out of Modell's office and sat in his car in the parking lot. "I couldn't believe what had just happened; I had never imagined that anything like this could ever happen to me," he later wrote. "I had never felt so hopelessly alone in all my life as at that moment."[46]

Jim Brown later said Modell had manipulated the players, making it seem as though they were the reason for his need to make the move. What he wanted was to run the team himself. "Art didn't create the situation, he didn't tell us to be unhappy with the offense, but he utilized it, from a business standpoint, beautifully," Brown said. "When Art fired Paul he knew there was player unrest, as did everyone else. Art took that fact, used it skillfully with the media, diverted the glare from himself onto us, and smoothed his transition into power.... In their awe of Paul, a lot of folks failed to see [Modell was a force himself]. Art understood business and money, had the ego to take on Paul Brown."[47]

Whatever his motivation, Modell took full responsibility for Paul Brown's demotion. "I spent three weeks of soul searching," he said. "I talked to all the board members. I talked with a friend of mine from New York.... The decision was mine from start to finish."[48]

An expected flood of protest failed to materialize. The Browns received about twenty-five phone calls the first day and about a dozen the next. Reporters sought out reaction and found it mixed. Some fans praised Modell for having the guts to stand up to Brown; others said Modell was a bum and the demotion was a dirty deal.

"It's Art Modell's business but I don't like it," said Dr. Myron Weitz of Parkland Drive. "Paul Brown gave a great deal to this league, and he has more to give."[49]

Joe Woods, superintendent of the St. Clair Recreation Center, echoed what the players had contended: "Paul Brown felt his importance too strongly. I feel that he was bored with his job."[50]

City Council president Jack Russell steered the politically neutral path: "I've heard so many reports that conflict, I don't know what to say!"[51]

Parrish checked with his teammates and was "virtually certain they were 100 percent in favor of the change," he told reporters. "I know that five, and maybe seven of them, would have retired rather than play for Brown next year. I was one of them."[52]

John Morrow, Cleveland's All-Pro center, summed up the attitude of many of the players. He said he felt sorry for Paul, but the firing was good for everyone involved, including the coach. "He had problems of his own, and everybody was working overtime trying to figure out what was wrong with us,"

Morrow said. "All I know is that it wasn't a relaxed team. There were too many mixed-up feelings."[53]

Some players were quoted anonymously, and they were harsh. One said Brown was an egomaniac who'd become unbalanced by all the praise and adulation heaped on him over the years. Another said he tried too hard to live up to his self-image as the all-knowing coach, and he quit trying to learn and quit listening to his assistants (that certainly applied to Collier). A young player described an encounter with a longtime veteran—"one of the most highly respected ever to play for the Browns"—not long after joining the team. "I see you really like that guy, kid," the veteran said. "Can't understand that. I hate the sight of him."[54]

A handful of Browns played in the Pro Bowl under New York's Allie Sherman following the 1962 season. They said they appreciated Sherman's upbeat approach. "I threw a good block and Allie almost kissed me," McCormack said. "He patted me on the back and praised me and I felt real good. I like to be congratulated. Paul never did anything like that."[55]

All the criticism, especially about Brown's predictability on offense, was somewhat overstated. In order for change to occur, it probably needed to be. But under his leadership, the Browns were always a formidable team; they just weren't champions every year, and certainly not as good as they had been in the past. Jim Brown wrote that if the coach had given the quarterback "a slight amount of authority—if Paul had called, say, 90 percent of the plays instead of 100 percent—the messenger system would have been fine. But under his absolute hand, problems arose that were maddening."[56]

And therein lay the problem. Paul Brown tried to maintain *absolute* control. He wouldn't bend at all, and in the end it proved his downfall. After a period of stunned silence, he responded. He maintained he was coach and general manager, and his contract made no mention of any other duties. "My position in this thing is simple," he said. "Art Modell, in my mind, has changed the contract which I have. My status is that the matter is in the hands of the lawyers. It may take a few days or weeks to resolve."[57]

Modell countered that there had been no breach of contract. He had offered to terminate Brown's contract, but Brown had turned him down. So he made him vice president. Brown retired to La Jolla, California, where he devoted time to his golf game and collected his salary. Someone pointed out that the only two people making more money playing golf were Jack Nicklaus and Arnold Palmer.

CHAPTER TEN

By 1963, football had replaced baseball as America's most popular sport. Baseball still was considered the national pastime, and it still could draw large crowds, but the baseball season lasted for more than six months, and games were played day after day. One game didn't make or break a team's fortunes, at least not until the season's final days. But a football season lasted only four months, and games were played once a week, each an event—live at the stadium or at home on television. (The Browns' total attendance topped the 1 million mark for the first time in 1963.) Fueled by television revenue, the sport was expanding. The NFL added the Dallas Cowboys in 1960 and the Minnesota Vikings in 1961. Each team now played fourteen games instead of twelve. The American Football League, begun in 1960, had eight teams, stretching from Boston to San Diego, and its games were televised on ABC.

Christian Century magazine declared professional football a "folk religion," its "missionary zeal" spread by television. Its "sacrificial sufferers" were willing to spend their Sunday afternoons in front of their television sets or to endure subfreezing temperatures in stadiums. Baseball, though, had become too slow and was putting its viewers to sleep. *Christian Century* blamed the pitchers. "They indulge in Zen reverie, contemplate their navels, whirl the resin bag like a prayer wheel, and in general conform more to the norms of a post-Buddhist society than to a post-Christian one." A sure sign of football's emergence was the recent dedication of a $600,000 Hall of Fame in Canton, Ohio—"a pilgrimage chapel for those who wish to pay homage to pro football's pantheon."[1]

Baseball's Hall of Fame had opened in 1939 in Cooperstown, New York, and it only made sense football should have one too. Canton was a logical site for a number of reasons. First of all, football was in the DNA of northeastern Ohio. Paul Wiggin, the Browns defensive end, grew up in California and never saw fans as passionate as those in Ohio. On Friday nights he and some teammates would travel south to Massillon and Canton to watch high school games. He was amazed how deeply ingrained the game was in the communities. "Trust me, time and place, there were no fans like those in Cleveland," he said. "It's a culture there. Football is paramount."²

Canton couldn't lay claim to being the birthplace of professional football— William "Pudge" Heffelfinger was the first player to be paid, when he accepted $500 from the Allegheny Athletic Association of Pittsburgh in 1892—but it certainly was at the heart of the pro game. The Canton Bulldogs were an early powerhouse, before and after the establishment of the NFL, and their rivalry with the Massillon Tigers dated to the early 1890s. The American Professional Football Association, the forerunner of the NFL, was born in Canton in 1920 at a meeting in Ralph Hay's Hupmobile showroom. Just as important, the citizens of Canton lobbied to bring the Hall of Fame to their city and provided the funding to make it possible.

The *Canton Repository* launched a campaign in 1960 under the headline "Pro Football Needs a Hall of Fame and Logical Site Is Here." The next day, Henry H. Timken Jr., chairman of the Timken Roller Bearing Company, called the paper and offered his support, pledging $250,000. Timken wasn't a rabid football fan, but he did want to do something to change Canton's image as a wide-open town where gangsters from Detroit and Cleveland came to lie low.

W. R. "Tim" Timken Jr., Henry's nephew and a longtime member of the hall's board of trustees, had attended prep school in the East as a young man and regularly took the train from Canton to New York's Penn Station. From there he'd catch a cab to Grand Central Station and trains heading to New England. The cabbies would ask him where he was from. "Canton, Ohio," he'd say, and invariably they'd respond, "That's where the gangs and crooks are, right?"

"It seemed like every New York cabdriver knew the bad parts of Canton," Timken said. "I can guarantee you today that if I were in New York and I got a cab and the driver said, 'Where are you from?' and you say, 'Canton, Ohio,' he'd say, 'Ah, Pro Football Hall of Fame.'"³

Ground was broken in 1962, and the "modernistic" building with its football-shaped dome and adjacent theater was completed a few weeks before its dedication and the first induction ceremony. Seventeen charter members were enshrined on September 7, 1963, a Saturday afternoon, among them Jim Thorpe, who'd played for the Canton Bulldogs, and George Halas, the Chicago Bears' founder and coach. Both men had been present when the league was established in Ralph Hay's auto showroom.

Pete Rozelle was so impressed with the festivities he instructed his PR man to send a message via teletype to all the league's owners and general managers, instructing them to watch the televised highlights and the next day's exhibition between the Browns and Steelers in Canton's Fawcett Stadium. CBS televised the game, and at halftime it showed clips from the dedication ceremony. Sportscaster Chris Schenkel served as host for a tour of pro football's pantheon.

Fortune magazine stated that professional football had become "a real business"—in other words, it was profitable. Eleven of the fourteen teams would make money in 1963; the most profitable, the New York Giants, would earn about $500,000. In 1950, the Browns' first season in the NFL, the league's gate receipts totaled less than $5 million and included little television revenue. In 1964, the NFL teams were expected to gross about $18 million at the gate, not including exhibitions, and another $16 million in television revenue.

One reason for the sport's growing popularity, according to *Fortune,* was that it was "wonderfully attuned to the pace and style of American life in the 1960's." "In a time of mass education, it is an educated man's game; no other physical sport has so many elaborate and sophisticated strategies or requires such precise coordination of so many specialized skills." Baseball devotees would dismiss that notion out of hand; they considered football violent and crass, while every pitch in baseball was replete with nuances, plots, and subplots. *Fortune* supported that argument in a way, noting that football mirrored the uncertainties of the atomic age. "It may or may not be significant that fans refer to the long pass as 'the bomb,'" the magazine noted.[4]

But most significant, football was ideally suited for television, and the windfall it created astonished old-timers. "I can remember when we had to *pay* radio to broadcast our games," said the Steelers' Art Rooney.[5] A one-minute commercial for an NFL telecast cost roughly $75,000, making it the highest-priced minute in the history of daytime television. The rationale for the high cost was the audience—predominantly male, well educated, and financially comfortable, all of which made advertising attractive for manufacturers of big-ticket items such as automobiles. The Ford Motor Company was the biggest single sponsor.

Fortune noted that in millions of American households, the most noticeable consequence of football's growing popularity was "a total lapse in whatever it is the headman used to do on Sunday afternoon, as he now spends his time peering raptly at the television set."[6] (This consequence later would result in the term "football widow" to describe the headman's significant other.) If his team's home game was blacked out, and if he had failed to obtain a ticket, he would drive seventy-five miles or farther to watch it on television. Browns' home games were televised on stations throughout the state—in Cincinnati, Columbus, Dayton, Lima, and Zanesville—and in Erie, Pennsylvania, and as far away as Lexington, Kentucky.

The NFL reportedly was considering allowing theaters to show games in home cities, and the inevitable next step, some surmised, would be games available in homes on pay TV—a kind of NFL Network. "I envision the time when the league will be the exhibitor, the operator, the promoter," Modell said. "We'll hire banquet halls and meeting rooms for screening the games ourselves."[7]

The confluence of television's ubiquity and the game's growing popularity sent the value of franchises upward. Modell and his partners set a record when they bought the Browns in 1960 for just less than $4 million. Now, three years later, William Ford reportedly had offered $6 million for the Detroit Lions. When he bought out his partners during the offseason, Dan Reeves said the Rams were worth $7.1 million. "Where will it all end?" asked the *Plain Dealer*'s Gordon Cobbledick.

Pro football was riding high on the eve of the 1963 season, but Cleveland's storied franchise was at a turning point. What would become of it now that Paul Brown was gone? What was the team going to be called, the Cleveland Modells? The owner assured all that the name would remain the same. Charles Heaton of the *Plain Dealer* figured the Browns to finish third in the Eastern Conference, behind the Giants and Cowboys, and Tex Maule picked them sixth, ahead of only Washington. "Few NFL teams have started a season with as many unanswered questions as Cleveland," he wrote.[8]

First of all, could Blanton Collier replace Paul Brown? If he tried to maintain absolute control, as Brown had, the players surely would revolt against him. But if he was too easygoing they might walk all over him. To many, it seemed Modell had been forced to make a choice between the two Browns, Paul and Jim, and had sided with the fullback. Some people considered the players brats who'd thrown a fit to get their way. A fan from Euclid wrote to the *Press*: "Now we see the reason of Modell getting rid of Paul Brown. It was a case of the Jim Brown cry babies."[9] Loren Tibbals of the *Akron Beacon Journal* figured Collier was in for trouble. "If I were Blanton Collier, I would be mighty wary of the Jim Browns and all the other rebels," Tibbals wrote. Collier should offer them as trade bait, "and ship 'em off in baby carriages at the first opportunity."[10]

Who would quarterback the team? It's an axiom in football that a team with more than one starting quarterback has no starting quarterback. That appeared the case with the Browns heading into 1963. Ryan had shown promise in 1962, throwing for more than 1,500 yards and ten touchdowns against seven interceptions. His passer rating was fourth best in the league, better than John Brodie's and John Unitas's, but neither he nor Jim Ninowski had proven himself championship caliber. They certainly weren't the next Otto Graham, probably not even the next Milt Plum.

Could the Browns find a running back to pair with Jim Brown? The team's second-leading rusher in 1962 had been Ryan, and that wasn't by design. He rushed for 242 yards, more than 100 more than "Touchdown Tommy" Wilson. One possibility was second-year back Ernie Green, who'd come from Green Bay in exchange for a seventh-round pick prior to the 1962 season; another was Charley Scales, the team's third-leading rusher in '62, but neither prompted much excitement.

Ernie Davis, of whom so much was expected, had died during the offseason. He underwent three months of treatment with a chemotherapy drug called 6-MP—Modell paid his medical bills and salary—and in October 1962 his doctors said his leukemia was in remission. They weren't hopeful for a long-term recovery, but they said he was fit to play. He began training with the Browns at League Park, even though Paul Brown thought he shouldn't play. Modell argued that Davis would serve as an inspiration to others with leukemia—not to mention a huge gate. When Davis was introduced and walked across the field at the doubleheader in August, the crowd of nearly 80,000 stood and cheered.

Later, after his death, sportswriters speculated Paul Brown's firing had to do with the disagreement over playing Davis. Modell said that had nothing to do with it, which is likely. Despite their differences and faults, both men acted honorably in regard to Davis. "Our disagreement on the matter was an honest one," Modell said, "and I'll repeat myself, it had nothing whatsoever to do with Brown's dismissal."[11]

Davis stopped by team headquarters in the middle of May 1963 to talk with Modell, Collier, and other Cleveland officials. He was headed to Lakeside Hospital for treatment. His neck was noticeably swollen, but he said he was suffering from a sore throat and would be out of the hospital in a few days. "We all knew what it meant," Modell said. "He was coming by to say good-bye."[12]

Davis died Saturday, May 18, 1963, two days after entering the hospital. He was twenty-three. His funeral and burial were in his hometown of Elmira, New York. Nearly 10,000 people filed by his casket at Neighborhood House, a community gymnasium where he had played basketball as a boy. Honorary pallbearers included Jim Brown and their Syracuse coach, Ben Schwartzwalder. About thirty Cleveland players and coaches attended the funeral. Modell later announced that the number 45, which Davis wore in photographs, would never again be worn by a Cleveland player.

Who would block for Brown and whoever else carried the ball? The core of the offensive line from the championship years was gone. Lou Groza had retired after the 1959 season because of an ailing back, and when he decided to return in 1961 he no longer could play tackle and was limited to kicking. Right tackle Mike McCormack retired after the '62 season, and guard Jim Ray Smith stuck to his vow that he would retire rather than play for Cleveland and was traded to Dallas for tackle Monte Clark. The team had emerging stars in guard Gene Hickerson and tackle Dick Schafrath and other promising young players in guard John Wooten and center John Morrow. But was this unit capable of replacing the old stars and clearing the way for Brown?

The team also was dealing with the death of popular teammate Don Fleming. He'd joined the Browns in 1960 and started at safety, lining up on the left side behind cornerback and best friend Bernie Parrish. The two had roomed together at the University of Florida, where they excelled in baseball and football, and became inseparable. Parrish, from Long Beach, California, was an All-American second baseman and left Florida after his junior year, when the Cincinnati Reds offered him a $90,000 signing bonus. Fleming, from Shadyside, Ohio, was among the many Ohio River "Valley Boys" to make it in pro sports, including his Cleveland teammates Groza and Bob Gain. He played end at Florida and was chosen in the twenty-eighth round of the 1959 draft by the lowly Chicago Cardinals. He decided to pass on pro football.

The Browns chose Parrish in the ninth round of the 1958 draft—he would have gone higher but for his interest in baseball—and after a year of pro baseball, he decided to switch to football. He wrote Brown a letter that began, "Being drafted by the Browns was the greatest honor I ever received in football. I don't know you, but you have the best record against the best competition in the world, and that's all I need to know." He went on to detail his credentials as a running back, placekicker, and punter but said he believed his best position was defensive back. He ended, "Baseball had been a disappointment to me, and I'd like to give pro football a try"[13] He repaid the Reds half his signing bonus, and on the first day of training camp in 1959 Paul Brown made him the starting left cornerback.

Parrish urged the Browns to sign his old buddy Fleming, and Cleveland agreed to give Chicago a draft pick if Fleming made the team. Parrish and Fleming worked together in Florida before the 1960 season, and it paid off: Fleming became the starting left safety and intercepted five passes, one fewer than Parrish. Fastest of the team's defensive backs and a sure tackler, he was named All-NFL by the *Sporting News* following the 1962 season.

In June 1963, just a few weeks before the beginning of training camp, Fleming was foreman on a construction project in Orlando, Florida. He was helping one of his crew when a crane hit a 12,000-volt power line. Both Fleming and his coworker were electrocuted. Earlier that day, Modell had announced Fleming's signing of a new contract for the upcoming season. His death stunned his teammates and devastated Parrish. "We were like brothers," he said. "We were so close. It's a terrible loss for me."[14]

Despite the departure of Paul Brown, nothing seemed to have changed much when the Browns reported for training camp at Hiram College. The small liberal arts school about forty miles southeast of Cleveland had been the team's summer headquarters since 1952. The coaches, except for Paul Brown, were essentially the same. Fritz Heisler, in charge of the offensive line, was starting his eighteenth season with Cleveland. The defensive coordinator, Howard Brinker, was in his twelfth season. The one change in the staff was the addition of Dub Jones as offensive coordinator. He replaced Paul Bixler, who became head of player personnel. Jones had played for the Browns from 1948 to 1955, and he was running a building materials business in Louisiana. He said he'd had other offers to coach over the years but the opportunity to work with Collier drew him back to the Browns.

On the first day, the new head coach addressed the team from the front of a classroom. "This is the most challenging experience any of us have faced," he said. "We're being watched by the entire football world. You might think that they are watching me more than you, but I doubt that.

"There's only one basis on which we will be judged, and that is by wins and losses. There is no other basis for it. I ask no quarter and give none."[15]

To illustrate his point, he told a story from his Kentucky days. The Wildcats had beaten archrival Tennessee, and a drunk alumnus shook his hand. "You're the greatest coach today," the drunk said, "but if you lose to Tennessee next year I'll be against you." That's the way of the world, Collier told his players.

The coach's message resonated with his players. They wanted to show the football world they were good enough to be champions, and not just because they'd played in Paul Brown's system. They saw it as a challenge, and it united them. "We all had a common goal," Ninowski said. "Since Paul was gone, we wanted to prove we could win without him."[16]

Collier told them he wasn't going to discuss the past. He'd had some wonderful experiences with the Browns, but those were behind him. All that mattered was the here and now. He was a sore loser; maybe he wouldn't show it outwardly, but he didn't take defeat well. He wasn't going to try to imitate anyone (he didn't have to say who); he was going to do what he thought was best to win. He told them he thought about football all morning and all afternoon and dreamed about it at night. But, he added, he and the other coaches were open to suggestions. "If you have an idea for a play, or if you have an idea that will improve a play, tell us," he said. "I won't guarantee we'll use your idea, but we'll listen."[17]

Here was the freedom and opportunity the players had been craving. It seemed possible that under the new regime they no longer would be robots, following orders without emotion. Along those lines, Collier said he wanted more enthusiasm. "This club has been too quiet. Let's hear some noise on that bench. Help each other out, whether it's in practice or in game or wherever . . . we don't want a collection of men who are satisfied to go through their own little routine and call it a day."[18]

Collier eliminated the intelligence test; he said he already knew his veterans and wasn't interested in testing the rookies. "We hope to find out things on the field," he said. When the rookies took the field for their first practice, they wore full gear instead of the usual T-shirts and shorts, and the thud of their hitting resounded across the field. "I had to establish that we want to play aggressive football," Collier explained to reporters afterward. "Some of the newcomers may not understand how the game is played in the National Football League. They might just as well face up to it right now."[19]

After the full team's first day of practice at Hiram, Collier met with reporters, and they asked him about play-calling. He answered with his characteristic patience and detail. It would be a cooperative effort. He and Dub Jones would come up with the game plan, and then they'd let the players run it. He still planned to send in plays, but it would be up to the quarterback whether to use them. "Emotion plays a big part in this game," he said. "I think the boys like to feel they have a part in running the thing. And if this helps morale, I guess it's pretty good."[20]

He recalled a play from his earlier days in Cleveland to illustrate his point. The Browns were on the 1-yard line, and he phoned down the play to the sideline: Motley off tackle. Instead, Graham scored on a quarterback sneak.

When Graham returned to the sideline he got on the phone with Collier. He apologized, but he said the guys refused to leave the huddle unless he agreed to run a sneak. "To this day I believe our call was the right one and theirs the wrong one," Collier said, "but theirs scored the touchdown. Belief in yourself counts for something. They just picked up that whole defensive line and pushed it into the end zone."[21]

Such words were exactly what the players wanted to hear, but they couldn't help but be somewhat skeptical. They were used to doing what they were told, and Collier had been a disciple of Paul Brown's, the *foremost* disciple. But early on, they discovered things truly would be different. They ran a play in which the guard, in this case John Wooten, was supposed to allow the defensive tackle to go where he wanted and to block him in that direction. Wooten was struggling with the concept, and rookie Jim Kanicki repeatedly was knocking him into the backfield. "A guard's helpless on this play," Wooten told Collier—something he never would have said to Paul Brown.

"You can handle him," Collier responded. "Pick out one spot on him, maybe his right knee, or anything else. Just pick out a target and keep your eye on that spot and drive your shoulder into it regardless of where that spot goes."

Two days later, Wooten came into the locker room and told Jim Brown, "You know that block Blanton was showing me the other day? I'll be doggoned if it doesn't work. I've been trying it on Kanicki all day. It's such a small thing, but it's a helluva thing."[22]

This was the essence of Blanton Collier. He didn't harangue, he taught. And he listened. Regardless who made a suggestion, he considered it. If it didn't work, so be it. Move on. This was a fresh approach, and a welcome one.

True to his word, Collier had his hand in all aspects of the game. He worked with everyone from the quarterbacks to the defensive linemen. One afternoon after practice he stopped Wiggin as he was leaving the field. Collier had noticed that Dallas defensive end George Andrie started off in his stance with his heel on the ground, while most ends, including Wiggin, started with their heel slightly raised. Collier discussed the physics of whether a lineman could start faster with his heel down or up, and he had Wiggin give it a try. After fifteen minutes Collier decided Andrie simply was a unique player, and he didn't make Wiggin do it. He'd just wanted him to try it.

In his never-ending quest to find an edge, Collier introduced his team to different psychological concepts, to help them become better players and better men. He read books on hypnosis in hopes of overcoming problems inherent in an inability to sustain concentration. He read *The Power of Positive Thinking* by Norman Vincent Peale and *The Magic of Thinking Big* by David J. Schwartz, both of which taught techniques for achieving success and personal satisfaction. About the time he returned to Cleveland, he came upon a book titled *Psycho-Cybernetics: A New Way to Get More Living Out of Life*. A plastic surgeon named Maxwell Maltz recognized that through plastic surgery he had given his patients a new and positive self-image. Maltz believed people had inner scars just as they had scars on their skin, and those inner scars created negative self-images that prevented them from getting what they wanted out of life. "It was as if personality itself had a 'face,'" he wrote. "This non-physical 'face of personality' seemed to be the real key to personality change." If someone learned to remove those negative thoughts—if this "face of personality" could be reconstructed—then he or she had a better chance of succeeding. The way to reconstruct personality was by removing negative thoughts and habits and focusing on past successes.[23] Collier kept a copy of the book by his bedside.

Collier shared what he'd learned with his players, though not always explicitly, because such thinking was new to athletics. He and defensive end Bill Glass, a devout Christian, talked philosophy and psychology for hours, read every book they could find, and even consulted psychologists. "Of course, we kept this very confidential," Glass said, "because people would think that, especially in those days, extremely weird."[24]

Other players bought into it, including Jim Brown, Dick Schafrath, and Monte Clark. It became part of their regular training regimen. They performed mental repetitions, just as they worked on physical reps. They would find quiet places to meditate, often with soft music playing. They closed their eyes and pictured themselves perfecting their techniques against their opponents. "I'm talking about visualizing every little detail of every play," Schafrath said. How he stood in the huddle while awaiting the quarterback to call the play. Jogging to the line of scrimmage. Getting into his stance. Exploding into his opponent. "For me, this type of concentration and picturing gave better results than I had ever experienced before," Schafrath said.[25]

Sometimes the offensive linemen gathered together and followed prompts from a record or a hypnotherapist. "Visualize yourself down in your stance. The defensive lineman is coming across the line on the count. You're going to beat him to the punch because you're going to hit him with your right hand up under his pad. Picture yourself putting him on his back. And our fullback is running right by him. Doesn't that feel good?"

"Yeah."

"OK, now the next play he's going to rush you on the pass. Your head's up. Your eyes are open. Move your feet."[26]

They would meditate in the dressing room, on the field, in their homes. Brown sat in front of his locker before games staring into space. His teammates asked what he was doing. "I'm picturing myself running," he said.

Not all the players bought into it. Ryan was too analytical. He always was trying to figure out what he needed to do to perform better, but closing his eyes and picturing it was a waste of time. Hickerson thought it was a joke at best, voodoo at worst. He joined his line mates in the meditation sessions but quickly fell asleep.

Collier also introduced the concept of zero defects. He adopted the idea from industry; it was designed to instill pride in every member of the work force by eliminating defects before they occurred. Three ingredients were necessary for its success: relationships, involvements, and commitments. With the Browns, the message began on Tuesday, when the players gathered for their first meeting after the previous game.

"We have to develop the discipline and habit of doing the job right the *first time*, of not making the first mistake," he explained. "The people who win on Sunday are the ones who make the fewest mistakes, and who completely understand what their responsibilities are." Collier could accept players being beaten physically, he said, because sometimes they were overmatched. What he could not accept was a player being unprepared mentally. "There is *no* excuse for leaving the huddle and not knowing what you're supposed to do," he said. "If you don't know, *ask* somebody!"[27]

As popular as Collier was with the Browns, he remained a nonentity elsewhere in the country, even within the NFL. Cleveland opened its preseason against the Lions, and George Plimpton described in his book *Paper Lion* how Detroit coach George Wilson kept mentioning Paul Brown as if he still was the Cleveland coach. Wilson emphasized to his players the game would show how their relaxed approach was superior to Brown's dictatorial one. The Lions won 24–10, Cleveland's only touchdown coming on a Vince Costello interception return.

The Browns stumbled through their exhibition season, losing to the Colts 21–7 in the nightcap of the doubleheader. The two games attracted a then-record crowd for a Browns game in Cleveland: 83,218. The Browns' lone score came on a 1-yard run by Jim Brown after Cleveland recovered a John Unitas fumble. The fans booed Ninowski, who started and gave way to Ryan in the second half. Some disgruntled fans began calling for Paul Brown's return, but what they didn't understand was that Collier was substituting freely, interested less in winning than in assessing his personnel. The Browns were rebuilding.

He reinstituted the messenger system, but not to take control of the play-calling. Instead, he wanted the quarterbacks to get an idea of what the coaches wanted. "I thought we were awfully tight, and I thought we were playing too conservatively," he explained. "Pro football can't be played conservatively, and I don't want my team to play that way."[28]

Cleveland won its third and fourth exhibitions, and both Ryan and Ninowski played well. Collier told his two quarterbacks that whoever started the final exhibition, the Hall of Fame game against Pittsburgh, would be the regular-season starter. Ninowski was named starter, and Ryan came up to him before the game, congratulated him, and shook his hand. The Browns laid an egg, losing 16–7. The offense crossed midfield just twice and managed only 41 yards on the ground. "On a weekend dedicated to remembering great football players of the past, the Browns played a game they would just as soon forget," Heaton wrote in the *Plain Dealer*. One wag noted that Cleveland couldn't be counted out of the title chase, at least not yet, because the regular season didn't start for another week. Collier looked pained afterward and admitted the team was flat. "I don't know whether they just thought of this as just another exhibition game or not," he said. "You just don't know how kids are going to think."[29] His statements didn't instill much confidence in the Cleveland faithful.

Ryan's performance was the only bright spot. He completed sixteen of nineteen passes, including thirteen in a row, and the only score came on his 30-yard pass to rookie tight end Tom Hutchinson. After the game, a group of players went to Collier's Aurora house to talk about the upcoming season. Collier told Ryan he was the starting quarterback. Ninowski had gone home to Detroit for a few days after the game, and on his drive back to Cleveland he stopped at a restaurant on the Ohio Turnpike for breakfast. He read in a newspaper that Ryan had won the starting job because of his performance in the Pittsburgh game. Nino was angry, but he decided against making an issue of it. He understood how much pressure was on Collier.

CHAPTER ELEVEN

Two days before the season opener, Collier addressed about 1,500 people at the team's kickoff luncheon at the Sheraton Cleveland Hotel. He peered at the crowd from behind horn-rimmed glasses, his lips pursed. In preparation, he'd taken copious notes on three-by-five cards, and he glanced down at them periodically. He was an inveterate storyteller, and this wasn't the first time he'd spoken to a banquet of Browns fans, but none had been bigger, in terms of both numbers and pressure. He said he'd heard the team was picked sixth by one writer and third by another. "I don't think we're a sixth place team or a third place team, either," he said. "We started with the idea we'd be contenders. I'll be very unhappy if we're not."[1]

The crowd wanted to know about Jim Brown. How did Collier plan to use him? How was their relationship? (Unspoken was whether he was up to the challenge of coaching the recalcitrant running back). Brown was coming off one of the worst years of his career. He failed to rush for 1,000 yards only twice: his rookie season and in 1962. To many, his impact off the field had been more significant than what he'd accomplished on it. Collier defended his fullback, explaining that his relatively poor year was the result of a sprained wrist. It hurt so much he couldn't tie his shoes. (Equipment manager Morrie Kono tied them for him, but Brown never wanted anyone to see, even his teammates, because he didn't want them to know he was hurting.) He could only carry the ball with his right hand, Collier explained, but he had refused to sit. He never missed a practice. Only three other backs carried the ball more times than he did in '62. "Jim is a very proud man, too proud to use the wrist as an alibi," he said. "But that same pride will drive him to prove what doesn't need proving at all—that he's one of the greatest power runners ever to play pro football." Another coach might have downplayed his star's importance or challenged him publicly, but true to his nature, Collier heaped praise.[2]

The new head coach switched the talk to the defense. He undoubtedly was tired of answering questions about Paul Brown, about who would start at quarterback, about who would be calling the plays. He said he was excited about the team's pass rush. Paul Wiggin and Bill Glass gave Cleveland two imposing defensive ends. Glass, obtained in the trade for Milt Plum, was quickly becoming one of Collier's favorite players. He had "the physical equipment to be a pass rusher like Gino Marchetti," the coach said. That was high praise. Baltimore's Marchetti was considered the game's best defensive end, arguably the best ever. Glass wasn't on Marchetti's level, but he definitely was one of the league's best, chosen to the Pro Bowl in 1962.

Collier singled out Jim Houston, the former Ohio State All-American, as "one of the fastest big men in football." Houston was the little brother of Cleveland Brown original Lin Houston. He won a state championship at Massillon and a national championship with the Buckeyes. He stood 6-foot-3 and weighed 240 pounds. Paul Brown had played him at defensive end, but he was stuck behind Glass and Wiggin. Collier wanted him in the lineup and moved him to linebacker, where he became the prototype of the modern outside linebacker: big enough to stop the run, capable of dropping back into pass coverage, and fast enough to come off the edge and rush the quarterback. (He would be named first team All-NFL and make the Pro Bowl in 1964.)

Bernie Parrish was "one of the toughest players on the squad," Collier said. "He's mean about it and I like it."[3] Parrish had butted heads with Paul Brown, but Collier welcomed his input. Parrish carried a notebook with more than three hundred pages of notes. He calculated plays on graph paper, each square representing a yard. He would berate other defensive players who didn't live up to his standards. One afternoon, he and linebacker Vince Costello were walking down the hallway and passed Wiggin. Parrish was telling Costello he'd have him cut if he didn't shape up. He looked at Wiggin and said, "The same goes for you." Wiggin spun around and kicked the notebook out of Parrish's hands. "He came down the assembly line with a chip on his shoulder," Wiggin said. But he also "was one of the most dedicated players I've been around."[4]

As for fan favorite Lou Groza, well, he was in excellent shape, Collier said. His teammates said this was "the first time in three years he can see the football over his stomach."[5] Groza was no joke. He no longer was the intimidating left tackle he'd been in the franchise's first dozen years, protecting Graham's blind side and opening holes for Marion Motley and Jim Brown. But now, at age thirty-nine, Groza said he was a better kicker than ever. He believed it was a simple matter of attitude, whether kicking a football or playing a violin.

The Browns opened at home against the Redskins, to whom they'd suffered two humiliating defeats the previous season. They were slight favorites, but they needed to play better than they had in Canton. Opening the post–Paul Brown era with a loss would be a public-relations fiasco. If they lost, Heaton wrote, Collier and Modell would need to find a bridge from which to leap. Even a win would fail to satisfy some skeptics; they'd claim it was because of the foundation Brown had laid. The *Plain Dealer*'s Gordon Cobbledick said the future of professional football in Cleveland depended on the game's outcome. "[Collier's] a man on the spot—an uncommonly hot spot," he wrote.[6]

The game plan called for Brown to run wide against the Redskins with sweeps and pitches. Cleveland had struggled running inside against Washington in the past, and Collier wanted to better utilize Brown's speed. The first play set the tone for the afternoon: a sweep around end with Brown gaining 14 yards. He ended the day with 162 yards rushing on fifteen carries, an average of nearly 11 yards, and he caught three passes for another 100 yards. His 262 total yards were the fourth most in NFL history. He also scored three times: on an 83-yard screen pass, an 80-yard pitch to the right, and a 10-yard sweep to the left. On the screen pass, six Washington defenders took a shot at him but couldn't bring him down. "What do you say when a guy runs right through you?" one of them asked. The Browns won 37–14 and compiled 543 total yards, nearly twice as many as Washington.

The players awarded game balls to Frank Ryan, who passed for 334 yards and two scores; Brown; and Collier. Brown rarely said much in the locker room, but on this day he thanked his blockers. "You keep knocking people down," he said, "and I'll keep running harder than ever."[7]

Afterward, a reporter asked Collier who called the plays. He laughed. "Are you going to start that all over again?" he asked. The reporter persisted. "Just say, I thought Ryan called an excellent game and we got some good information from our coaches upstairs," Collier answered. He said the play-calling discussion reminded him of something his grade-school teacher told him back in Paris. "You can do anything you set your mind to do as long as you don't try to get credit for it." Collier then did something Paul Brown never did: He spread credit around. He pointed out that Dub Jones and Fritz Heisler drew up a key third-down completion from Ryan to Tom Hutchinson. Later in the week, at a team meeting, he pointed out that Jim Ninowski called two of the plays that resulted in scores. "Those were Nino's plays," he said.[8] It helped ease some of Ninowski's sting from not starting.

Collier addressed the Sigma Delta Chi luncheon at the Manger Hotel that week, and, as always, Paul Brown's name came up. Asked if he'd heard from him, Collier snapped. "I pass." His impatience was understandable. Everything he and the players had been advocating for finally had come to fruition. The rout of the Redskins vindicated them. No one could blame Collier for being angry, but after the luncheon he sought out the questioner. "I didn't mean to put you off," he said. "The answer is no, but we're still friends."[9]

Key to the success of the running game was a new scheme Collier had implemented during training camp: option blocking. Under Paul Brown, Cleveland had relied on symmetrical line play, with each blocker battling head to head against the man in front of him. The blockers tried to push the defenders out of the way of a predesignated, numbered hole. For example, a running play into the five hole called for left tackle Schafrath to block the defensive end out of the way to the left. Left guard John Wooten was to block the defensive tackle out of the way to the right. The running back rushed forward behind them into the five hole. The defensive linemen simply tried to hold their ground. It was hand-to-hand combat. This approach to blocking had worked in the past because the Browns had so many strong blockers, men like Willis, Groza, and McCormack. But defenses had become more sophisticated in recent years. They stunted, shooting into gaps in anticipation of the offensive play, in essence running their own plays. This forced the offensive lineman to step back and reposition himself in order to move the defensive lineman out of the hole.

In Collier's mind, the old method caused plays to develop too slowly. The running back was forced to hesitate while waiting for an opening. With option blocking, the offensive lineman allowed his opponent to go wherever he wanted and used his momentum against him. For example, if the defensive end tried looping outside, the tackle pushed him that way, even if the play called for the running back to run outside. If the end tried crashing inside, the tackle pushed him aside and let the blocking back take him on. The tackle would then head upfield looking for someone to block, much like a pulling guard on a sweep. It kept the defenders off-balance—and out of the way. The running back no longer needed to be cautious. He could slash to an opening instead of to a designated spot.

The key to option blocking was getting off the ball quickly. The offensive linemen had to beat the defense to the punch. If the defense penetrated into the backfield, the play would be disrupted. Cleveland's offensive linemen practiced every day against a seven-man sled, firing out into the padded dummies in unison again and again. Collier broke it down to his players simply: make sure the runner gets to the line of scrimmage untouched, and then everybody use your discretion.

Vince Lombardi was having great success with the scheme in Green Bay, where he coined it "run to daylight." Players such as fullback Jim Taylor (the league's MVP in 1962), halfback Paul Hornung, and guard Jerry Kramer were becoming famous because of it. Collier had tried to install it in 1962, but Paul Brown had nixed it. Now he held the reins. "I don't think anyone could teach that but Blanton," Schafrath said. "He would teach it daily, daily, daily."[10]

Jim Brown was the ideal running back for option blocking. He was labeled a fullback, but that was a misnomer. Fullbacks traditionally were bruisers, big men like Marion Motley and Bronko Nagurski who crashed into the middle of the line and bent it backward. But while Brown could pound like a fullback, he also was elusive and deceptive, and in that way more like smaller and speedier halfbacks. In the option-blocking scheme, he ran instinctively, spotted the hole and roared through it, then accelerated into the defensive backfield, where he ran over smaller defenders. He would finish the 1963 season with a career high 1,863 rushing yards, more than all but two teams, and he would average more than 6 yards per carry. "This was run to daylight taken to its highest level," Wooten said.[11]

Option blocking required linemen who were hard-nosed and strong, but, more importantly, quick off the ball and fast enough to get upfield ahead of Brown, no small feat. Tex Maule and others had questioned the effectiveness of Cleveland's rebuilt line prior to the 1963 season, but, in fact, the pieces already were in place for what would be one of the league's best units. Paul Brown might have become predictable in his play-calling, but he remained adept at recognizing talent. In 1957, the year he drafted Jim Brown in the first round, he took guard Gene Hickerson of Mississippi in the seventh. In 1959, he selected Schafrath from Ohio State in the second round and Wooten from Colorado in the fifth.

Hickerson initially was a messenger guard, alternating with Chuck Noll, the future Steelers coach. He was a 225-pound fullback in high school, and when he arrived at the University of Mississippi he asked for a new position. The coaches suggested end. "I want a position where I don't have to run as much," he said. They asked what he had in mind. "Make me an offensive guard or a defensive end," he said. "Let me play somewhere that I don't have to run in all this Lord-awful heat."[12] By his sophomore year he weighed 260 pounds and still could run like a fullback.

Brown chose Hickerson with a future pick after his junior year, which demonstrated his foresight, because Hickerson became an All-American as a senior and likely would have been a first-round pick. He was among Cleveland's quirkiest players. He would regularly show up at training camp out of shape and ten pounds overweight. "The heaviest thing he ever lifted was a glass of Cutty Sark," said linebacker Dale Lindsey.[13] Before games he would lean against the goalpost while his teammates stretched and did calisthenics, uninterested in wasting time and energy warming up. Yet other than the 1961 season, during which he was sidelined with a broken leg, he never missed a game in fifteen years and was elected to the Pro Football Hall of Fame.

Wooten played offensive and defensive tackle at Colorado, where he became the first Buffalo lineman named All-American. He was a backup his first two seasons with the Browns but took over as starting right guard when Hickerson was injured in 1961. He weighed 265 pounds, and he, too, could run like a fullback. In 1963, Collier moved him to left guard in place of the traded Jim Ray Smith, beside Schafrath.

Collier had recruited Schafrath while at Kentucky, and Schafrath's decision came down to the Wildcats, Ohio State, and Notre Dame. Raised on a farm outside Wooster, he was enamored with Kentucky's horse country, but in the end he chose the Buckeyes. While visiting Lexington, however, he learned the George theory from Collier, and it stuck with him: "Don't let George do it, you do it."

Schafrath was a preseason All-American his senior year as a tackle, but Woody Hayes moved him to tight end shortly before the season, when the starting end was injured. The Buckeyes had three outstanding tackles—future All-Pros Jim Tyer and Jim Marshall, in addition to Schafrath—and Schafrath was the logical choice to switch to end because of his speed and athleticism. He weighed 220 pounds, and Hayes said he was the best-conditioned player he'd ever coached and the best downfield blocker. The Buckeyes didn't pass much—only three things could happen on a pass play, according to Hayes, and two of them were bad—and Schafrath caught only a handful of passes. Nonetheless, he was selected to play in the College All-Star Game, and the Browns picked him in the second round of the 1959 draft.

He worked for a construction company in Wooster during the summer before his rookie season, and, knowing he needed to put on weight if he was to play the line, he had his coworkers fashion him an iron jockstrap, which he held up by suspenders under his T-shirt. He tied it to his legs to keep it snug. At his initial physical with the Browns he weighed in at 252 pounds, much to the surprise—and skepticism—of Paul Brown, who discovered the iron jock. Brown tried him at a number of positions his rookie year, including offensive end, guard, and defensive tackle. "I had no idea where I fit in," he said. The coaches told him he could play tackle or center, but only if he added weight. He already was a weightlifter, a practice he began as a youngster after seeing ads for Charles Atlas. His father helped him cement weights onto a tractor axle, and he lay on a tree stump to perform bench presses. Weightlifting was a relatively unused training technique at the time, but he continued it through college and into the pros. He supplemented his workouts with prodigious eating and drinking, devouring dozens of White Castle hamburgers at a sitting and washing them down with cases of soda pop and beer. He and some teammates were having dinner at the Kon Tiki one night, and the waiter brought them steamed napkins. Schafrath dipped his in mustard and started gnawing on it. He entered eating contests around the state, both to consume food and to earn money. "I'd eat to win," he said. By 1960 he was up to 250 pounds and had replaced Groza as starter at left tackle.

Schafrath lived a few blocks away from Collier in the Cleveland suburb of Aurora, and at night the two of them watched film in the Colliers' den. Blanton would stop the projector, and he and Schafrath would stand up and the coach would show him the proper stance—not too much weight forward, not too much back—and they'd walk through the proper footwork, over and over and over. Then they'd turn off the lights and switch on the projector. "I watched so much film I felt like I was a part of the family," Schafrath said.[14] Afterward, he'd go home and practice some more.

Even with the added weight, he still possessed good speed, and the sight of number 77 roaring downfield ahead of number 32 became commonplace—and frightening for linebackers and defensive backs. "I could run side by side with Wooten," he said. "We all could run, and we all played in this option blocking together."[15]

Collier also taught Schafrath how to avoid injury. He stopped the film after a play involving an injury and pointed out that someone had rolled up on the player's leg after the whistle. "Let me tell you, Dick," Collier said, "90 percent of the injuries happen within two seconds after the whistle blows." From then on, Schafrath always stayed on the move. "When I was going down or I was in a pile, if the whistle was blowing, or even if it wasn't, I kept running for two seconds," he said. "If I was ten yards down the field, then I was fifteen or twenty after the whistle blew. So I never got hurt in my thirteen years."[16]

The Browns began the season with six straight wins, the first time they'd accomplished that since 1953 and only the second time since joining the NFL. The city of Cleveland was aglow. People who brought up the growing conflict in Vietnam were met with blank stares. All conversations revolved around the Browns and their star running back. One fan was heard to say that if his grandchildren ever questioned who was the greatest fullback ever he'd tell them, "Anybody who never saw Jim Brown never saw a running back."[17]

Not everyone was sold. Skeptics were unimpressed with Cleveland's early-season wins over Washington, Dallas, and Los Angeles, none of which were strong teams, and they expected Pittsburgh to bring the Browns back down to earth in the fourth game. A Saturday night showdown against the unbeaten Steelers at Municipal Stadium drew 84,684, the largest crowd in Cleveland football history to that point. The Steelers had allowed only 254 yards total on the ground in their three games, but Brown ran around and through them for 175 yards and a touchdown. The defense twice stopped the Steelers on the 1-yard line to force field goals, and the Browns won 35–23. Ryan threw three touchdown passes, two to Gary Collins and the clinching score to Rich Kreitling late in the fourth quarter. He also ran 13 yards for a score on a play he had suggested, a keeper after faking a handoff to Brown. Pittsburgh coach Frank Parker said Ryan was the best running quarterback in the league. "In fact," he said, "a couple of times he looked better than most of the halfbacks I've seen."[18] The *Press* ran a photo of Ryan and Collier embracing after Ryan's touchdown run. "Paul Brown never indulged in this messy kid stuff," the paper's Frank Gibbons wrote.[19]

Next up were the defending Eastern Conference champion New York Giants, at 3–1, having lost to the Steelers in the second game of the year. This was the most important contest between the two rivals since the conference playoff game in 1958, and the Giants were four-point favorites. To the remaining doubters, the Browns still hadn't proven anything and wouldn't, unless they beat their old nemesis.

Yankee Stadium was filled with 63,000 fans, and others perched on a water tank on the roof of a nearby building. Ryan threw an interception in the opening minutes and Dick Lynch returned it 47 yards for a touchdown. On the Browns' first possession of the second half, down 17–14, Ryan tossed Brown a screen pass that went for 72 yards and a touchdown. Later in the third quarter, Brown weaved through the Giants for 32 yards and another score. He had his best day ever against New York. He rushed twenty-three times for 123 yards, caught four passes for 86 yards and scored three touchdowns. The Browns won 35–24. So much for the Giants.

The reinvigorated rivalry between the NFL's best-known franchises, and that the game was in New York, attracted a television audience of millions and more reporters than usual. Brown was a revelation to those who hadn't seen him before. His combination of speed, power, and instinct was unique in pro football. The writers flocked to him in the Cleveland locker room. He looked like a boxer who'd just gone fifteen rounds—a mouse under his right eye and gouges around his left. His face mask consisted of two bars that ran in front of his mouth, leaving much of his face exposed, and from the beginning of the game the Giant defenders had stabbed at his eyes. They also kicked him in the head twice. From the first quarter on, he saw the field as though peering through a sheer curtain. He didn't say anything to his teammates or his coaches during the game, but now in the locker room it was clear the Giants had done everything they could to hurt and intimidate him, but to no avail. They weren't playing dirty, Brown told the reporters. "I guess they were just a bit anxious out there."

Brown apologized to his teammates for the media throng following him around the dressing room. "Imagine that, Jim apologizing after the way he played," linebacker Galen Fiss said. "He didn't want the rest of the team to think he was taking credit for the win. I've never seen him with a better attitude or spirit."[20]

Jim Brown was, in fact, a changed football player. The suppression and constant tension he'd felt playing for Paul Brown were gone. Under Collier he could express himself; there was a give-and-take of ideas. Years later, he related to Collier's daughter Kay the effect her father had on him.

> I was prepared for his genius—but I wasn't prepared for his humanity. People used to worry about whether Blanton was tough enough. Those people don't know what it is to play for someone you like, someone you respect. I relate to Blanton as a sanctuary of mine—one of the men that I hold above all other men because he treated me with respect as a human being, dealt with my mentality, and enabled me to further my life in a positive manner. That's just about the highest praise I can give anybody.

Brown stayed behind in New York, where he gave a speech to the Pro Football Quarterback luncheon. He said the Browns were playing to win for themselves, not to spite Paul Brown. He noted that Collier had retained many of Paul Brown's ideas. "But he also added a few things—like compassion," Brown said. "We all feel we're part of a team now." The quarterback could now call plays; even Brown was calling a few, something he'd never dared before. "I never opened my mouth," he said. "Everybody is helping everybody else."[21]

Free to be himself, Brown became more assertive and more of a team leader. He'd always been pensive and quiet, and he remained so, but he became a better teammate, which in turn engendered more respect. In the second game of the season, in Dallas against Tom Landry's Cowboys and on a 100-degree day, he rushed for 232 yards and two touchdowns. Late in the game, he was asked whether he wanted to go back in to break his single-game record of 237 yards. He declined. He told the coaches to give Charley Scales some carries. "When you're as good as Jim Brown," Wiggin said, "so much of your leadership is what you do. There's a lot of leadership that comes from your presence, and Jim's presence became more prominent."[22]

Collier's philosophy and calm demeanor created a new confidence throughout the team. The day after the Dallas game, Ryan spoke to the Touchdown Club at the Pick-Carter Hotel. He said Collier provided him with a better grasp of the fundamentals of quarterbacking than he'd ever had. He noted that after each of the two interceptions he threw against the Cowboys, Collier called him over and explained what he'd done wrong.

In Los Angeles, Ryan never felt comfortable—"always felt hurried, jittery, rushed in execution. And no one ever told me what to do about it," he said. But Collier helped him to think things through, to analyze why certain aspects of the game worked and why others didn't. "There are several, logically connected moves to think of, and when I throw a bad pass I can reflect on the one thing I did to ruin the pass," Ryan explained. This, he said, was the key in his evolution from "a young journeyman quarterback to an effective pro quarterback."[23]

The *Plain Dealer*'s Cobbledick noted the team's growing confidence in Ryan: "The Browns haven't believed completely in any quarterback since Otto Graham, undoubtedly because they knew or sensed that the coaching staff didn't believe. But Ryan has earned the confidence of Collier and his assistants, and that confidence is reflected in the team's performance."[24]

The Browns routed Philadelphia 37–7 for their sixth straight win. They were the only undefeated team in the NFL and held a two-game lead on New

York and St. Louis, which were tied for second place. Their domination of the Eagles showed how far they'd come since the previous season. The defense, minus three injured starters, held Philadelphia to 161 total yards. The offense amassed the most yards of the season, 500. Brown ran for 144 yards and in the process set a new NFL career rushing record with 8,390 yards, overtaking Joe Perry. It had taken Perry fourteen seasons to amass that many yards, and Brown had accomplished it in fewer than seven. He also held the league record for rushing touchdowns, with seventy-eight.

Ryan threw four touchdown passes, three to Collins and one to Brown. He also ran seven times for 20 yards total, prompting discussion of whether he was running too much. "When you're running you're at least halfway planning how the collision will occur and maybe can get set for it," he said. "Sometimes it only means a few yards, but every yard is important. I hate to waste a down throwing the ball away unless it means preventing a loss." His guts and toughness impressed his teammates.

Paul Brown's name came up in nearly every discussion of why this team was so much better than the 1962 squad. "His name lingers in the locker room like a bloody ghost, goading them to prove they can win without Paul Brown," one writer observed.[25] Parrish said the talent basically was unchanged; it was a matter of attitude. "There isn't that much difference between any two pro clubs," he said. "The one that wants to win the most usually does. The guys on this club can't wait to play the next game. I wish we were going against the Giants tomorrow. I can't wait." Part of the drive to succeed were the memories of Davis and Fleming. "This is a close ball club," Parrish said. "We've been through some rough times and that brought us together. Losing Ernie and Don was one of the bad times, and they're behind this thing, too. I don't mean there's any 'Get-This-One-for-the-Gipper' sort of speeches. But we think of those fellows."

"I think we're going all the way," he added, "but don't get the idea it's entirely to spite Paul Brown. If he had changed, he'd still be here. It's too bad. All we needed was freedom to behave like men."[26]

Jim Brown grabs the goalpost in an attempt to pull himself across the goal line in the fourth quarter of the 1964 title game. He came up short, and Lou Groza kicked a field goal on the next play to put Cleveland ahead 20–0. (Photo by Tony Tomsic)

Art Modell and Blanton Collier chat during practice at League Park in Cleveland. The two men enjoyed a warm relationship, much more so than Modell did with Collier's predecessor, Paul Brown. (Photo by Tony Tomsic)

Gene Hickerson, 66, and John Wooten, 60, lead Jim Brown, 32, on a sweep. *Cleveland Press* photographer Tony Tomsic said watching Brown and the two guards come steaming around the corner toward him was like watching a scene from a movie unfold. (Photo by Tony Tomsic)

The option blocking scheme Blanton Collier introduced in 1963 perfectly suited the instincts and athletic abilities of Jim Brown, 32, and tackle Dick Schafrath, 77. (Photo by Tony Tomsic)

Jim Brown's first autobiography, *Off My Chest,* published in 1964, addressed the black athlete's place in American society in frank terms and led to death threats against its author. (Photo by Tony Tomsic)

In a rare show of emotion, Blanton Collier exhorts his team from the sideline. (Photo by Tony Tomsic)

Police lead Cleveland quarterback Frank Ryan through an ecstatic mob of Browns fans after his three touchdown passes in the title game win over Baltimore. (Photo by Tony Tomsic)

A battered Frank Ryan talks strategy to the coaches in the press box between offensive possessions. Ryan's penchant for holding on to the ball as long as possible before throwing won him the respect of his teammates, who considered him extremely tough and brave. (Photo by Tony Tomsic)

Defensive end Paul Wiggin, who grew up in California, was amazed how deeply ingrained football was in northeastern Ohio. "It's a culture there," he said. "Football is paramount." (Photo by Tony Tomsic)

Gary Collins fends off a Pittsburgh defender. Collins caught a record three touchdown passes in the 1964 title game and as Most Valuable Player won a new Chevrolet Corvette. (Photo by Tony Tomsic)

Cleveland defensive standouts (*from left*) Galen Fiss, Vince Costello, Bernie Parrish, and Jim Kanicki take a break on the bench. All four were instrumental in the Browns' shutout of the Colts in the '64 title game. (Photo by Tony Tomsic)

Paul Warfield pulls in a pass against Pittsburgh. The Warren, Ohio, native and Ohio State Buckeye provided Cleveland with a much-needed deep threat in 1964, his rookie season. (Photo by Tony Tomsic)

Above: NFL commissioner Pete Rozelle and Art Modell confer before the 1964 championship game. The two men were instrumental in forging a lucrative bond between television and professional football in the early 1960s. (Photo by Tony Tomsic)

Left: Wooster native and former Ohio State Buckeye Dick Schafrath helps the referees determine whether Cleveland made a first down. (Photo by Tony Tomsic)

Above: Jim Brown was the all-time NFL rushing leader when he retired from professional football following the 1965 season. (Photo by Tony Tomsic)

Left: Frank Ryan wears a sling Joan Ryan sewed for him while he was recovering from elbow surgery following the 1967 season. She made it to match the coat-and-tie garb he wore while teaching at Case Western Reserve during the offseason. (Photo courtesy of Frank and Joan Ryan)

CHAPTER TWELVE

Anticipating an overflow crowd for the game against the 4–2 Giants at Municipal Stadium, the Cleveland management on Wednesday put 10,000 general-admission and standing-room-only tickets up for sale. Reserved seats had been sold out for ten days. To accommodate the working crowd, the club decided to sell the tickets between 5:00 and 9:00 P.M. Fans began lining up at the ticket window at Gate A by 10:00 that morning, and by 5:00, about 5,000 people were standing in line outside the stadium. When the windows opened, the crowd rushed forward, slamming people at the front against the stadium walls.

Twenty-one-year-old Larry Faurot of Marion managed to buy his tickets, but as he was trying to leave he was knocked to the ground and trampled. Police pulled him to safety and took him to St. Vincent Charity Hospital, where he was treated for a back injury, expected to keep him from seeing Sunday's game. James Hill, thirty, of Cleveland was about to buy his tickets when the mob knocked him out of line and against a wall. He suffered a dislocated shoulder and was taken to the hospital. Gregory Clifford, fourteen, left Patrick Henry Junior High after school to buy a ticket and was caught in the press of people. He began feeling faint and those around him lifted him up so he could breathe. Others thought he'd tried to cut to the front of the line, and they passed him back over their heads. Gregory had been to every home game that season, but he was unable to buy a ticket to this one.

Mrs. Herbert Houlehan of West 159th Street was astride the railings leading to the windows when the push began. She was immobilized, her hands and arms pressed against her sides. She was lifted off her feet and feared she was going to pass out. She wiggled down and crawled under the railing. Police helped her up and took her to the team office. Someone—she didn't know who—gave her six tickets to Sunday's game. "Right now," she said, "I feel that I never want to be in that crowd again."[1]

Modell went down to observe the melee and was chewed out, particularly by women who'd been jostled out of line. He told reporters the club would review its sales procedure, adding they could have sold 125,000 tickets if they'd had them. Sportswriters received phone calls from people who asked, "Remember me? I was in the same third-grade room with you in Hough School. Those were the good old days, huh? I was just wondering, could you help me get a couple of tickets?" Scalpers in the bars along Short Vincent Street were expecting to get as much as $25 for $5 tickets. The prices were the highest since the 1948 World Series between the Indians and Boston Braves.

Now, in late October 1963, the Browns were undefeated and looking like the Cleveland champs of old. The throng had hardly settled into the seats before all the expectations came thudding down. The Browns turned the ball over the first two times they had it: Brown fumbled on the second play of the game, leading to a New York field goal, and Frank Ryan threw an interception on the first play of the next possession, setting up a New York touchdown. The score was 10–0 less than three minutes into the game. The Giants scored on their first five possessions and were driving for another score when time ran out in the half. They led 23–0 at intermission and 33–0 after three quarters. Never before, said one observer, had so many people made so little noise. The final score was 33–6. About a third of the 84,213 who attended the game were still in the stands at the end.

The Giants came into the game three-and-a-half point favorites, so their victory wasn't completely unexpected, but their thorough domination from the outset was a surprise. Allie Sherman said the Giants played their best game in his three years as head coach, while the Browns appeared flat. "Our game plan was to go for the short yardage plays, but we didn't expect them to come so easy," Sherman said. "And we wanted to put the pressure on Ryan, and I think we did a pretty good job of that."

Ryan completed just one of nine passes for minus-6 yards in three quarters. The completion was a screen pass to Ernie Green, who was knocked out of the game on the play by a New York linebacker. Ryan limped off with a bruised thigh in the third quarter, and the Browns avoided a shutout with six minutes to go when Jim Ninowski connected with Rich Kreitling for a 10-yard touchdown. The last time they'd been shut out was by the Giants in the 1958 playoff game. For good measure, Sam Huff blocked Lou Groza's extra-point attempt.

Afterward, the Browns appeared perplexed by what had happened. One possibility was they'd become overconfident. "Everything came so easy at the start," Wiggin said. "We actually were running some teams off the field. We got a feeling of infallibility."² Blanton Collier was his usual philosophical self. "You get beat one afternoon and it's not the end of the world," he said. Ryan insisted the loss might help in the long run. "The pressure has been building up for several games," he said. "We wanted to go all the way and I think we tried too hard. We couldn't get up any momentum today. We may be a better team because of this." Groza agreed: "Sometimes it does a team good to get a beating like this. We may come back stronger than ever and beat the daylight out of some team."³

Encouraging words, but losing to the Giants so decisively made it especially trying for the fans, who'd seen way too many heartbreaking losses to New York over the years. Some of those who a week earlier were wondering whether this might be the best Cleveland team ever now were asking why it was so crummy. "They got no line, they got no backfield, they got no offense, they got no defense," a fan was overheard saying. "How they gonna win in this league?"⁴ But they still were in first place, one game ahead of the Cardinals and Giants.

The Browns defeated the Eagles 23–17 to improve to 7–1, but they didn't look good doing it. Ryan completed just four of nine passes for 70 yards and was intercepted once. Afterward, Collier addressed the team before allowing the reporters in, and when they entered they encountered a team that acted as though it had just lost. Collier was asked whether he was disappointed. "We won the game," he snapped. Ryan also was short with reporters. "I'm sorry for being so curt," he said, "but I didn't play well today at all."⁵ He couldn't have been happy, either, that he his old college teammate, King Hill, outplayed him, throwing for more than 200 yards and a touchdown.

The troubles continued the following week, as the Browns lost 9–7 to the Steelers. Pittsburgh coach Buddy Parker blamed Cleveland's woes on a lack of pass protection. But on the following Monday, Collier faulted his quarterback. "Ryan is in a passing slump," he said. "Our receivers are getting open. There's nothing wrong with our passing game from that standpoint. It's simply a matter of timing between the passer and the receivers." He compared it to a baseball team that can get runners on base but fails to drive them in. "His example certainly hits home with Cleveland Indians fans," one wag noted.⁶

Ryan couldn't figure out why he was playing so poorly, no matter how much he analyzed it, and his confidence took a hit. He understood his performance depended on his ability to put failures behind him and build on his successes, but he found himself unable to act on that understanding. "One of those deep psychological things," he said. "It was something I was buffaloed by." He was the quarterback, a team leader, and he needed to be able to rally his teammates, but he was incapable of it. "I was so concerned about my own performance," he said, "I didn't think about others."[7]

Fans had been calling for Ninowski to replace Ryan, and Collier made the switch for the next game, at home against St. Louis. Little changed. The Browns lost 20–14, dropping them into a second-place tie with the Cardinals at 7–3. Ninowski threw two interceptions and one touchdown, which came in the fourth quarter and was the last score of the game. The crowd of more than 77,000 began chanting, "We want Ryan!"

A Shaker Heights fan wrote to Collier suggesting he use the quarterbacks as messengers to bring in the plays—as Tom Landry had tried in Dallas with Eddie LeBaron and Don Meredith. "It is something new for Cleveland football," she wrote, "and let's face it, it can't be any worse an idea than what is happening now."[8]

It had been so easy for Browns fans to jump on the bandwagon, and it hurt so much to fall off. A season that had started with such promise was unraveling, leaving the Cleveland faithful disheartened and in some cases disgusted.

"They got a sick team," said one.

"Let's give Modell back to Detroit, or wherever he came from," said another.

"Lakewood's high school team, they're better," a woman remarked.

On Friday afternoon, November 22, two days before the Browns were scheduled to play the Cowboys in Cleveland, President John F. Kennedy was assassinated as he rode in a motorcade through Dallas. Commissioner Pete Rozelle immediately conferred with Dan Rooney, the Steelers' chairman and a friend. Rooney told him he believed the NFL should call off its games. Rozelle talked with Pierre Salinger, the president's press secretary and a former classmate of Rozelle's at the University of San Francisco. Salinger, rerouted to Honolulu from a scheduled trip to Japan, advised him to go ahead. "Jack would say we should play," Salinger said. Rozelle talked again with Rooney, who said he still was opposed but would support whatever decision Rozelle made.

The commissioner had little time for deliberation. Many teams traveled on Fridays and were awaiting his call. That evening, Rozelle announced the NFL would play its Sunday schedule. The American Football League already had postponed its games, as had many colleges, including Michigan and Ohio State, who were to meet in their annual rivalry on Saturday. "It has been traditional in sports for athletes to perform in times of great personal tragedy," Rozelle said. "Football was Mr. Kennedy's game. He thrived on competition."⁹

It helped that no games were scheduled to be played in Dallas or in Washington, D.C., where emotions were especially raw. Fans protested in some cities, particularly in Philadelphia, where the Eagles and Redskins were scheduled to play. People called City Hall and the *Philadelphia Bulletin* offices and said they wouldn't renew their season tickets if the game was played. Rozelle understood the sentiment against playing, noting that the nonstop television coverage of the events surrounding the assassination had intensified everyone's feelings, but he stood firm.

Rozelle attended the New York–St. Louis game, played before a sellout crowd at Yankee Stadium. "Everyone has a different way of paying respects," he told reporters. "I went to church today, and I imagine many of the people here at the game did, too. I cannot feel that playing the game was disrespectful, nor can I feel that I have made a mistake.

"If I admitted that, I would be saying that playing the games was disrespectful. I don't feel it was so."¹⁰

The Browns received about eighty phone calls of protest. One caller threatened to shoot the coaches if the game went on. Everyone suspected it was a crank call, but security was doubled just in case. Modell said he would abide by the league's decision, and the game would go on. Worried about possible retribution toward Dallas fans, he ordered the public address announcer to introduce the visitors only as the Cowboys and to refrain from saying "Dallas." It wasn't an overreaction. Due to the assassination and because it was home to an anti-Kennedy group of right-wing extremists, Dallas quickly became known as the "city of hate."¹¹ When the Cowboys arrived at Hopkins Airport, the baggage handlers refused to touch their luggage. The same thing happened with the porters when they arrived at their hotel. When the Cowboys headed out to the field before the game, Eddie LeBaron told his teammates to keep their helmets on, and they did.¹² "I was afraid of how people would react to us," said former Cowboys president Tex Schramm. "I also remember that during the game we learned Jack Ruby had shot Oswald. Everybody's mind shifted to that."¹³

About 55,000 fans showed up for the game, Cleveland's last home contest of the season. Most had bought their tickets in advance, and few were sold at the gate. The club had planned to honor retiring receiver Ray Renfro at halftime, but the ceremony was called off. "That doesn't matter," Renfro said. "I'll have lots of days. President Kennedy won't have any more." (The team did present Renfro with gifts after the game. They included a shotgun, a tractor, a hand-tooled saddle, a new car, and plane tickets and expense money for a trip to Europe for him and his wife.)

Collier told the team about the assassination before Friday's practice and informed them they'd be playing Sunday, but he didn't discuss it further. He could see they were affected by it, and there was nothing he could say to change things. The Browns went through the motions at practice and then again before the game, but they were in no mood to play. The Browns and Cowboys played sloppily, and Cleveland won 27–17. The defense picked off four Don Meredith passes, and safety Ross Fichtner returned one of them 36 yards for a touchdown. Ryan threw three interceptions, but he also connected twice for scores with Gary Collins, who set a Cleveland single-season record for touchdown catches with thirteen, breaking Dante Lavelli's mark. Asked whether he was satisfied, Ryan answered, "No sir. I didn't have a very good day. I'm still not throwing as well as I did and I don't know what's wrong."[14]

Cleveland's win, and the Cardinals' victory over the Giants, created a three-way tie in the Eastern Conference. The three teams were 8–3, with three games to play, and Pittsburgh was still in the running, with a 6–3–2 record. Hal Lebovitz sat down to figure out how many final-standing combinations were possible with those four teams. He couldn't do it, so he called Ryan. The quarterback was at home eating a sandwich and said he'd figure it out and call back. Lebovitz reminded him that tie games didn't count in figuring the percentages. "I know that," Ryan said. "Doesn't everybody?"

Ryan called back shortly. "I've established the maximum number, the most it can possibly be. It's ten to the fourth power. That means you multiply ten by itself four times. You know that don't you?"

"Sure," Lebovitz replied. "Doesn't everybody?"

Ryan explained that ten to the fourth power comes out to 10,000. "Check me out," he said. "I'm not too sharp on multiplication."

"You mean," Lebovitz asked, "there are that many combinations for the way those four teams could finish?"

"No," Ryan replied. "There are some redundancies in the total. You know what that means—duplications."

"Doesn't everybody?" Lebovitz responded.

Ryan said he would figure out the duplications and call back, which he did a few minutes later. "I calculated the redundancies, subtracted them from

10,000 and the number of possible combinations comes to 7,624. I'll bank my reputation on this. What have I to lose?"[15]

Such interviews became commonplace as Ryan garnered more attention for his play and the team's success. He was working toward his doctorate in mathematics at Rice, and writers liked to describe him as quirky, an egghead. The title of his dissertation, "A Characterization of the Set of Asymptotic Values of a Function Holomorphic in the Unit Disc," became something of a punchline in stories about him. Nate Wallack, the Browns' public-relations director, kept the title on a piece of paper in his wallet. "I don't feel I should be expected to remember it," he said.[16] Nor could he have understood it, had he read it. Ryan's abstract began, "It is known that the set of asymptotic values of a function meromorphic in [mathematical symbols] is characterized as beginning an analytic set in the extended plane." Ryan had books shipped to the team facility, and Wallack delivered them. The titles included *Cosmic Blights: An Intimate Refraction*. "He got books with titles I couldn't even pronounce," Wallack said. "Hydro-thermonuclear, that sort of thing."[17] A writer told Harold Sauerbrei he wanted to talk to Ryan about his doctoral pursuit. "I am sure Ryan will be glad to talk to you," Sauerbrei said, "but that doesn't mean you'll know what he's talking about."[18]

When Ryan arrived in Cleveland he was given the number 18, and he wore it during preseason, but then requested 13, a number few wore because of its unlucky connotation. "13 has always been a pivotal prime number. I thought it was a really wonderful number," he explained. "I never thought it was unlucky. I never believed in the association of luck."[19]

Joan acknowledged her husband's passion for mathematics made him difficult for others to relate to. Where most people would look at an orange and see its outside, the peel and the color, Ryan would envision its insides, calculating the percentage of each section to the whole. "That's the way mathematicians think," she said, noting that many seem to have a screw loose. "They're on a spectrum we don't know."[20]

What she did object to, though, was the perception that Frank was a kooky, out-of-touch genius. A newspaper reported he had an IQ of 167, but he'd never had his IQ tested. "He really has a complex about being called a genius," Joan said, "because he's working with men at Rice who really are geniuses, and it embarrasses him."[21]

Ryan clearly was highly intelligent, but more than anything else he was determined and unrelenting in his drive to succeed, both in his mathematics and football. A half dozen years earlier, he and Joan had embarked on a mission: He would earn his PhD while also succeeding as a professional football player. It required hard work and sacrifice; that's what most failed to see. "He wasn't everyman," Joan said. "Of course, that's why I married him."[22]

The writer Roger Kahn described him better than most. "He lives very hard and very deeply, committed to integrity, which is not the easiest of all the ways to do it.... He tries to insulate himself against cliché and compromise."[23]

Ryan agreed with the assessment. "I didn't see myself as going around correcting people about me," he said. "I do have some more exactness to me than most people." But, he added, "I got along with everybody. I tried to give them a good feeling for me."[24] He didn't always succeed. He could be moody, stubborn, and hard to read. "He's moody all right," Collins said. "I mean you can never be sure whether he'll say 'good morning' or 'go to hell.'"[25]

Ryan's wry sense of humor often was lost on others. Photographers showed up at training camp in 1963, and he posed for them throwing the ball left-handed. Asked about it later, he said, "Oh, that. Actually, it was Ninowski who started throwing left-handed, but I kept it up, and all the pictures were wrong. But that isn't the point. Wouldn't you think the photographers would have noticed? The point is that a professional photographer, assigned to spend a day taking pictures, should make it his business to prepare himself, to find out whether his subject throws left or right."[26] Someone suggested the photographers could have reversed the negative, and Ryan would have appeared to be throwing right-handed, though his number would be 31. A stickler for accuracy, Ryan said no, "I would have been E1."[27]

Not surprisingly, he often was misquoted. He was asked if he might become another Y. A. Tittle, a fellow Texan and the Giants quarterback and league MVP. Tittle was pushing forty and was bald. Ryan said yes, if in the next few years he lost his hair. A reporter wrote that he claimed he'd be another Tittle. Reporters heard him and Sonny Jurgensen, quarterback of the Redskins, joking about Joe Namath's $400,000 salary to play for the AFL's New York Jets. Ryan said he was going to ask for $1 million. A writer took him seriously and reported it. "I think that Frank should learn to say 'no comment,'" Joan said. "He should preserve his humor for quiet evenings with friends and family. In his attempts to be extroverted he becomes a regular Red Skelton, but he also loses some people."[28]

On top of it all, Ryan's physical appearance didn't jibe with the perception of a professional football player. He was long and lean, and his hair was turning prematurely gray, the result, he said, of too many third-and-ten situations. One writer said he looked like Jimmy Stewart playing a young lawyer. "He's everything except what a quarterback should look like, right?" guard John Wooten said.[29]

A single bar served as his face mask. It protected little more than his mouth, but it left plenty of space for him to see downfield. Unlike other quarterbacks, who turned a shoulder when dropping to pass, he backpedaled straight back, allowing him to watch as the play unfolded before him. He preferred throwing long to dumping the ball off to the backs. "I felt like if you're going to the trouble to throw the football, you should put it down the field," he said.[30] He wanted his receivers to catch the ball 20 and 25 yards from the line of scrimmage, and he hung in the pocket as long as possible waiting for a receiver to break open. "He was extremely courageous," Wooten said. "Sometimes we'd be hollering, 'Throw it! Throw it!'"[31]

Lebovitz believed Ryan's fear of again becoming a second-stringer motivated him. "He tries to ignore injuries for this reason," Lebovitz wrote. "He's afraid that once he's benched, he'll never make it back to No. 1."[32]

Ryan paid a price in injuries. He underwent knee and elbow surgery and suffered a separated sternum, a separated shoulder, and various other sprains, contusions, and gouges. He dislocated his left thumb in an exhibition game but stayed in. His teammates respected him for his toughness. "It wasn't a matter of courage," he said. "It was a thirst for success. I wanted to complete that pass. I wanted particularly to complete a touchdown pass; so I would just wait and wait until I had that opportunity. That was probably the only strong point I had as a quarterback."[33]

He undersold himself. The delivery that Sammy Baugh likened to roping a calf enabled Ryan to throw long and accurately. His gunslinging led him to scramble often from the pocket, and when he did, his athleticism made him an effective runner. "Some quarterbacks see their receivers covered and they fold up when the first man touches them," Wallack said. "If Ryan sees six inches of daylight he goes for it."[34]

But most of all, what made him successful, and resulted in the team rallying behind him, was his drive to succeed, specifically to score touchdowns. His teammates had a name for it: "Twenty and going in"—once the offense reached the 20-yard line, he was going to make sure it reached the end zone. One year, the Ryans' oldest son, Pancho, was competing in a race at Vince Costello's summer camp for boys in Millersburg. Costello and Joan were standing on a bridge above as Pancho came sprinting toward them. "I've seen that face before," Costello said, "twenty and going in."[35]

The Browns defeated St. Louis to move into a first-place tie with the Giants at 9–3 with two games to go. They were slight favorites in their next game, against Detroit, but fans worried they were jinxed against the Lions. They'd never beaten them in a regular-season game, and they'd lost nine of ten games to them overall, including three title games and the Playoff Bowl in 1960. The only time they'd beaten them was in the 1954 championship game.

The jinx continued. The Lions flattened the Browns 38–10. Ryan and Ninowski completed just eleven passes between them. New York defeated Pittsburgh, ending Cleveland's Eastern Conference title hopes. After starting 6–0, the Browns had lost four of their next seven to fall out of the title race. Collier was disappointed, but he took advantage of the situation to discuss the psychological role pressure plays in sports. He'd recently read an article by a golf pro who explained how the weight of expectations caused even the best golfers to fail at times. "[He] said there are numerous golfers with great potential, enough to be as good as Arnold Palmer and the other top ones," Collier said. "But playing on the tournament trail did something to them. They were unable to play their normal game. Something like that happened to us. I know we wanted to win, wanted to play. But we couldn't play our normal game."[36] In sum, they'd choked.

Jinx, pressure, it didn't matter. The Browns weren't going to win the Eastern Conference. Wiggin said he was disappointed for himself and his teammates, but especially so for Collier. "I've never enjoyed a season more than this one," he said. "He has been great to me. He's sincere and honest and a real gentleman."

The Browns defeated Washington 27–20 to clinch second place. Brown rushed for 125 yards and passed the mile mark, the first running back to do so in a season. Ryan threw for three scores. The next day, Brown and Ryan visited President Johnson at the White House, a meeting arranged by Representative Charles Vanik, a Cleveland Democrat. Ryan understood why Brown was invited; not only was he one of the most prominent athletes in the nation, but because he was an African American, his presence at the White House furthered Johnson's civil rights agenda. But Ryan wasn't sure about himself. He figured he was there because an uncle had been active in LBJ's 1960 presidential campaign. Johnson encouraged the players to be good role models. "He told us that maybe our nation is not perfect, but that it is up to us and him to make it a better place in which to live," Ryan said. As they were leaving the president presented them with autographed cigarette lighters. Neither man smoked, but Johnson told them to keep them on hand for guests. Someone noted the lighters were embossed with the vice-presidential seal, not the presidential. "The name's the same," Ryan said.[37]

Cleveland and Green Bay met in the Playoff Bowl, and for Vince Lombardi it was no consolation. The Packers had won the previous two NFL titles, and he wasn't excited about it and didn't figure his players would be either. "There's no second place in this league," he groused. "It is a little bit anticlimactic after three years in the championship game."[38]

For Collier, however, it was like a college spring game. It meant more practices and more chances to teach, plus further opportunities to evaluate his team. A major concern was the passing game. The Browns had attempted the fewest passes in the league: 322, more than 100 fewer than both the conference-champion Giants and the third-place Cardinals. Collier knew he could rely on Brown only so much. To win the championship, Ryan and the receivers had to produce more.

Ryan blamed his midseason slump on becoming careless and forgetting what had worked earlier in the season. The low point came in early November in the 9–7 loss to Pittsburgh, but he admitted it had been coming for several weeks. "I think I'll profit from that slump, though. I don't expect it to happen again," he said. "Next time I'll be wary of things that brought it on. I suppose Blanton was right in benching me for a game.

"I had gone so far downhill that something had to be done to stop it. Even so, I'll always wonder if we might have won the St. Louis game if I had played."[39]

CHAPTER THIRTEEN

The NFL draft in those days was held near the end of the regular season, and speculation was the Browns would choose a quarterback. They were always looking for the next Otto Graham, and despite Frank Ryan's progress, neither he nor Jim Ninowski had proven to be the long-term answer. Some good college quarterbacks were available, but Pete Beathard of Southern Cal and Bill Munson of Utah State were taken before the Browns' pick came, at eleven. As in 1957, when it chose Jim Brown, Cleveland was forced to look beyond quarterback.

The Browns were desperate for more speed on offense, especially at receiver. Other than third-year flanker Gary Collins, they had no top-flight wideouts. Ray Renfro caught just four passes in 1963 and retired after twelve seasons. Tight end Johnny Brewer was an outstanding blocker but not a great pass catcher (he later would be moved to linebacker), and split end Rich Kreitling, a former first-round draft choice, was unreliable (he once dropped a pass in front of Paul Brown, and the coach turned to *Press* photographer Fred Bottomer and said, "I told you he can't catch").[1]

The Browns also needed help at defensive back. That was evident in the Playoff Bowl when Green Bay's Bart Starr passed for 259 yards and three scores. Parrish was an All-Pro at left corner, and third-year veteran Ross Fichtner appeared set at safety, but the rest of the secondary was in flux. To meet that need, the Browns chose the best defensive back in the draft: Paul Warfield of Ohio State.

The Warren native and Harding High graduate was a track star as well as a football player. He had world-class sprinter speed and long jumped nearly twenty-six feet. He stood 6 feet, weighed 185 pounds, and played both ways for the Buckeyes. On offense he was a halfback his first two years, but he didn't carry the ball much, spending most of his time blocking for the fullback. Because of injuries, he moved to split end as a senior. He wasn't going to make a name for himself catching passes in Woody Hayes's run-oriented offense. His acclaim came on defense.

Art Modell all but assured the public that Warfield would play defensive back. He said Notre Dame head coach Ara Parseghian had told Collier that Warfield was the best defensive player he'd seen in college football. "We need some speed in that defensive backfield," Modell said, "and we're going to get it." (Such pronouncements drove Paul Brown nuts.)

The Browns held a rookie minicamp at Lakewood High School in the spring. Warfield started out at cornerback, but Collier wanted to see him at receiver as well. That was fine with Warfield, who'd always preferred offense and didn't relish tackling the bigger and faster NFL running backs. During that two-hour minicamp, Collier and his coaches decided Warfield would play on offense. He was the deep threat they needed to diversify the offense, and as a bonus he was a strong blocker. Warfield was ecstatic, more so when Collier told him he'd be working with Renfro, who'd agreed to stick around and mentor the rookie.

Collier wanted even more speed at the offensive skill positions, and the Browns took halfback Leroy Kelly from Morgan State in the eighth round. They were set at running back with Brown and Ernie Green, but they hoped Kelly would provide depth; plus, he'd played both defensive back and running back in college and was the prototypical special-teams player. At 6 feet and 200 pounds, he could roar downfield and make tackles like a defensive back, and he could return kicks like a running back. Cleveland also signed Walter Roberts, a 160-pound free agent from San Jose State, and Clifton "The Stick" McNeil, initially drafted the previous year out of Grambling. The speedy Roberts (Collier described him as "a rabbit in a wheat field") paired with Kelly to give Cleveland a potent kickoff and punt return combination.

The offense still would revolve around Jim Brown, but with the addition of Warfield, Roberts, and McNeil the passing game was transformed, providing the balance Collier sought. In the third exhibition, a 42–7 win over the Steelers at the Akron Rubber Bowl, Ninowski threw five touchdown passes, including a 99-yarder to McNeil. Pittsburgh coach Ernie Stautner said he'd never seen a Cleveland team with so much speed. In the next exhibition, Ryan threw five touchdown passes in a 35–7 victory at Detroit—two to Collins, and one each to Warfield, Roberts, and Tom Hutchinson. "I'm more convinced than ever that we have the best pair of quarterbacks in football," Collier said.

Ninowski threw eight touchdown passes in the preseason, but Collier decided to stick with Ryan as the starter. Nino was more outgoing than Ryan, and much more of a vocal leader. Years later, Joan Ryan would describe him as a "man of the people" and compare him to Bernie Kosar, the immensely popular quarterback of the Cleveland teams of the late 1980s and early '90s. "[Ninowski] never lost the love and admiration of the team," she said.² Several of Nino's teammates came up to him after Ryan was named the starter and asked what had happened. They figured it was his team and he was going to lead it. "Don't feel bad," Nino replied. "I did too." He asked to be traded, but nothing came of it. He could have complained, even split the team, but instead he accepted his responsibilities as backup quarterback: practice hard, study film, be ready to play, and help maintain the team's cohesiveness. "When you sign the contract, you sign the contract to help the whole team," he said. "If you're the second-string quarterback, you become a good second-string quarterback because you want to help the team win. But to say it wasn't difficult would be lying."³

Otto Graham didn't help matters. Speaking at the Hall of Fame luncheon in August, he said Ninowski should be running the offense. He turned to his ex-teammate Warren Lahr, the color commentator on Browns local television broadcasts. "Tell that to Blanton Collier," he said. The crowd laughed, and Graham added, "Better yet, tell it to Art Modell."⁴

Fortunately, Ninowski and Ryan got along well. It helped that Ryan had also been a backup; in fact, of the two he'd been a second-stringer more often. They were peers. Ryan also appreciated Ninowski's skill at throwing the ball and told him so. Both were leaders with strong personalities, and the team's chemistry could have become toxic, but there was no animosity between them.

The success of the passing game in the preseason didn't sit well with Jim Brown. It's not that he didn't want Ryan and the receivers to succeed, but he didn't want it to cut into his carries. When Ryan hesitated to call a play, Brown would say, "It's my turn." One time a play came in from the bench late, contradicting Ryan's call, and he switched to it. "We ran the play and it lost two yards," Ryan said. "Jim jerked me by the shoulder and called me a measly-mouthed jerk. I didn't want to engage Jim Brown in anything, so I retreated."⁵

The two men maintained a productive yet strained relationship. Because of his talent and because of the way he carried himself around the rest of the team, Brown was the undisputed leader of the offense. But as quarterback, Ryan was in charge. Brown told Ryan to call the pass plays, and he would call the running plays. But, Ryan asked, who's going to decide when to pass and when to run? That was his job as quarterback. Ryan was open to suggestions, however. The linemen told him which plays would work based on how well they were handling their men. The receivers suggested what patterns were open. The coaches added their input. "We had a lot of discourse," Ryan said.⁶ In the end, though, the quarterback made the call.

The September 5 doubleheader was a sellout—79,096 reserved seats. Standing-room-only pushed the crowd to more than 83,000. Modell was carrying forward and putting his stamp on what Paul Brown had created. The size of the crowd, the nationwide notoriety, proved Modell the Promoter was on to something. The Browns defeated Vince Lombardi's Packers 20–17 in the nightcap. Collier unleashed Jim Brown for the first time in the preseason, and he rushed for 130 yards and both touchdowns. Lou Groza kicked field goals of 42 and 43 yards.

Scripps-Howard writers picked the Giants and Cardinals as cofavorites to win the Eastern Conference. Cleveland was third. The Cardinals had been steadily improving since the franchise moved from Chicago to St. Louis following the 1959 season, and they now had one of the best offenses in the league. The Giants were getting older, but it was hard to count them out; they were the three-time defending conference champions. *Sports Illustrated* was no more enthusiastic about Cleveland's chances. With Jim Brown and "two sometimes brilliant quarterbacks," the Browns were expected to score prolifically, but the problem was the defense. It was the worst in the league in allowing yards and first downs, and it lacked depth. "It is doubtful that Collier can move the Browns any higher than third in the Eastern Division this year," the magazine said.[7]

Green Bay was the consensus choice to win the West and capture the NFL title. The Packers finished second in 1963 and did so without Paul Hornung, their star halfback, suspended for the season for gambling. With Hornung and Jim Taylor leading the way in 1962, they had lost just one game on their way to the NFL championship. They looked to be in the 1960s what the Browns had been in the '50s. The main challenge was expected to come from the Colts, led by second-year coach Don Shula, the former Cleveland defensive back and assistant to Collier at Kentucky. No matter who won the Western Conference, consensus held they would defeat the champion of the inferior Eastern Conference.

The Browns beat the Redskins 27–13 at Washington in the opener. Starting defensive tackle Frank Parker injured his knee in the first quarter, and Dick Modzelewski played the rest of the game in his place. The Browns had acquired Modzelewski in January in a trade for tight end Bobby Crespino, their first pick in 1961. "Little Mo" was thirty-three and had spent the past eight seasons with the Giants. He and his brother Ed, "Big Mo," the former Browns fullback, were sons of a western Pennsylvania coal miner and were partners in an East Side Cleveland restaurant, Mo and Junior's. New York coach Allie Sherman called Little Mo at the restaurant to inform him of the trade. Modzelewski thought Sherman was going to tell him he'd named him captain, replacing Andy Robustelli, who was considering retirement. When Sherman told him he'd traded him to Cleveland, Mo's first thought was to quit. He wanted to end his career in New York.

Mo was a fireplug, 6 feet and 250 pounds with a barrel neck and a head like a cinder block. He had played in 138 straight games, the longest streak in the NFL at the time, and he was brought in to serve as a backup to starters Parker and Bob Gain. His presence also would allow for the development of second-year tackle Jim Kanicki.

Modzelewski brought with him a champion's bearing and a positive attitude that proved infectious. On a sweltering day at practice he'd tell his teammates he was cold and needed a jacket. "Think about it, guys," he'd say. "It's not really hot. It's twenty-eight degrees and snowing." Pretty soon everyone had forgotten about the heat. He became something of a pied piper. "Guys just loved him," linebacker Dale Lindsey said. "Some people have it, and others have to buy it. He just had it."[8]

Dick Schafrath went to Mo and Junior's on the night of the trade, and he and Modzelewski talked for four hours. Little Mo said he didn't understand why the Browns weren't winning more. "He said we seemed to have too many individuals, guys who worried about whether they'd have a good year themselves, but not about the team," Schafrath recalled. "He was the biggest inspiration to me, and I think to most of the guys. We never had that feeling before."

"The way I figure it," Schafrath added, "it all started at Mo and Junior's."[9]

Modzelewski's teammates awarded him the game ball after the Washington win. It was his first in twelve years as a pro. "The Giants never gave them to the slobs on the line," he said. "I'm taking it home to my oldest son, Mark. He's been asking me for years when I'm going to bring one. It's been a long wait."[10] Mo's presence became even more important three weeks later against Dallas, when Bob Gain broke his leg and was lost for the season, ending his All-Pro career. With Parker already out, the defensive line now had just four healthy players: Paul Wiggin and Bill Glass at the ends, and Modzelewski and Kanicki as tackles.

The Browns faced the Cardinals in their home opener before nearly 77,000 fans. It was an early-season test for the Cleveland defense. St. Louis featured a fine young quarterback in Charley Johnson and a complement of talented receivers. Johnson threw three scoring passes, and the Browns trailed 30–26 late in the game. With 1:28 left, they faced a fourth and nineteen from the St. Louis 45-yard line. Collier sent McNeil in with a play, but Ryan shooed him back to the sideline. The quarterback didn't know what the coaches had in mind, and he didn't care. He knew what he wanted to run—a post pattern to Collins. They connected on a 43-yard gain to the St. Louis 2. Jim Brown scored on the next play. Cleveland was up 33–30. Johnson then completed three passes in twenty-five seconds, moving St. Louis to the Cleveland 21-yard line. Jim Bakken kicked a field goal with five seconds left, and the game ended in a 33–33 tie. The worries about the Cleveland defense appeared well founded.

CHAPTER FOURTEEN

On the morning of September 22, two days after the St. Louis game, Charles Heaton wrote a column in the *Plain Dealer* headlined "Here's to Cheer Jim Brown for Speaking Out." Heaton was much more candid than usual, but it befitted the subject. *Look* magazine had released excerpts of Brown's autobiography *Off My Chest*. Coauthored with Myron Cope, a Pittsburgh sportswriter who'd written an acclaimed magazine article about Muhammad Ali in 1963, the book offered a scathing profile of Paul Brown and provided insights into what it meant to be a black athlete in America.

Heaton described the running back as a courteous and friendly man who always had his guard up. He answered reporters' questions but never seemed comfortable around them. The reporters weren't comfortable around him, either. His teammates respected him, though not all of them liked him. He had seemed to bend some the previous season, Heaton wrote, and that had to do with Collier taking over as head coach.

The book was the first by a pro football player to lash out at the NFL's establishment. (Others would follow, including Bernie Parrish's *They Call It a Game* and Dave Meggyesy's *Out of Their League*, both published in 1971.) Brown reiterated many of the criticisms people had expressed of Paul Brown in the previous couple of years: "In the atmosphere that Paul created his players inevitably became robots. You played hard but you concerned yourself almost entirely with your performance.... You were as close to being a mechanical man as a football player can get.... The Browns lacked spirit."[1]

He had kinder words for Collier and Modell. "Paul was a coach made of wire; Blanton, on the other hand, wears like soft English woolens," he wrote. Modell called him "Big Jim." "He wasn't talking about my size. He meant that he had a regard for me, that he felt I had the character to provide a positive example for the team.

"In other words, I no longer was Paul Brown's big brute."[2]

With the publication of *Off My Chest,* Brown had become a prominent voice in the national discourse on civil rights. It was a volatile time for the movement and the country as well. Progress undoubtedly had been made. In the summer of 1963, more than 200,000 people participated in the March on Washington for Jobs and Freedom, which culminated in Martin Luther King Jr.'s famous "I Have a Dream" speech. King said 1963 "was the most decisive year in the Negro's fight for equality. Never before had there been such a coalition of conscience on this issue." *Time* magazine named him its "Man of the Year" for 1963—the first time an African American had been so honored. On July 2, 1964, President Lyndon Johnson signed the landmark Civil Rights Act into law. It banned racial discrimination in public facilities and stipulated that public institutions such as schools and hospitals that discriminated could lose federal funding. "Those who are equal before God shall now be equal in the polling booths, in the classrooms, in the factories, and in hotels, restaurants, movie theaters, and other places that provide service to the public," Johnson declared.[3]

But challenges, and unrest, remained. Just weeks after King's speech in Washington, a bomb exploded at the 16th Street Baptist Church in Birmingham, Alabama, killing four young girls. A year later, about the same time excerpts of *Off My Chest* were published, the bodies of three slain civil rights workers were found beneath an earthen dam in Philadelphia, Mississippi. The civil rights movement began shifting from the rural South to northern slums, where segregation and discrimination were an established way of life. The gross national product had risen by 25 percent from 1960 to 1964, and unemployment was falling and prices were stable. But the majority of African Americans were left out of the country's economic progress. Forty-eight percent of blacks lived in poverty in 1964, compared to 14 percent of whites. In July 1964 a riot erupted in Harlem that left one person dead and 500 injured. It was the first of many to come in American cities over the next few years, including Cleveland's Hough neighborhood.

The civil rights movement was splintering. Malcolm X dismissed King's nonviolent philosophy, arguing that passive resistance helped the white man keep his foot on the black man's neck. "That's what you mean by nonviolent, be defenseless," he said. "Be defenseless in the face of one of the most cruel beasts that has ever taken a people into captivity. That's the American white man."[4] Malcolm promoted black separatism, arguing that whites couldn't be trusted, and he called for blacks to establish "rifle clubs" to protect themselves from those who terrorized them. At the time he remained a follower of Elijah Muhammad, founder of the Nation of Islam, who preached that whites were the devil. Some in the media portrayed the Black Muslims as a religious cult that planned to take over the United States and then the world. Malcolm's message resonated in the black communities of cities such as Chicago, Detroit, and Cleveland.

Urban unrest in the North and figures such as the Black Muslims alarmed white northerners who had supported the civil rights movement in the South. Many believed blacks were going too far in their calls for equality. In 1964, 34 percent of Americans believed blacks were too demanding; by 1966 that had increased to 85 percent. Nearly one-third of whites interviewed said they felt less respect for blacks than before.

The issue spilled into the sports world in January 1964 after Cassius Clay defeated Sonny Liston for the heavyweight title in Miami. The new champion announced he was a Muslim and a follower of Elijah Muhammad. He would no longer answer to his slave name; he now was Muhammad Ali. The Browns were in Miami for the Playoff Bowl against Green Bay at the time, and Jim Brown joined Ali, Malcolm X, and a few other Black Muslim ministers at a motel to discuss the boxer's conversion. Malcolm asked Brown, "Well, don't you think it's time for this young man to stop spouting off and get serious?" Brown agreed he should. (That night, Ali told Brown privately he was going to reject Malcolm, who was breaking away from Elijah Muhammad.)[5]

Brown's discourse on what it meant to be not just a black athlete but a black man as well, proved insightful, revelatory, and controversial. He evolved from being a talented football player to a polarizing figure. "The first thing the white man must understand is the depth of our protest," he wrote. "Does he realize that the Black Muslims' basic attitude toward whites is shared by almost 99 percent of the Negro population?" Invoking the Black Muslims assured that Brown would raise hackles. He wrote that he was not associated with the Nation of Islam but instead was a member of the "more rational NAACP." And yet, "I'm all for the Black Muslims. We need every possible element going for us, whether it be a radical sect, a CORE picket line, or a team of NAACP lawyers arguing in court. The more commotion the better."[6]

Brown did not want the white man's love, nor would he turn the other cheek if attacked. And he wasn't going to kneel in the streets and pray for his rights. He preferred a "more dispassionate approach," such as that taken by the Brotherhood of Sleeping Car Porters, who used facts and figures to prove blacks were discriminated against by employers and the government.

> Shallow minds may argue that my position is a contradiction. How, on the one hand, can I acknowledge that I have known and loved white men who educated me and furthered my career but on the other hand cheer the Muslims,

who claim all white men are devils? Have I forgotten that the great majority of Cleveland football fans—fans who have treated me with immense warmth—are white?

I see no contradiction. The issue is much larger than my own relationship with white friends and fans. I give each individual the respect that he gives me, but the white race as a whole has its heel on the Negro and this is what this whole thing is about.[7]

Fans worried the book might create dissension within the team, but Heaton said he doubted it; in fact, it could prove helpful for his teammates. "Now they'll know what's been pent up in this great athlete for eight years. Many will be at least a little proud that he has spoken out.

"We are," Heaton added. "We're looking forward to telling him so this afternoon at League Park."[8]

On the same day Heaton wrote his column in the *Plain Dealer*, Brown appeared on the *Mike Douglas Show*, broadcast nationally from Cleveland's KYW-TV. Prior to the taping, a woman called the station and said she was from the "Marcy organization" in New York. "If Brown says today what he said in that article, we'll bomb his home," she threatened. Abusive calls also came to the Browns' office and to the *Plain Dealer*, and the Cleveland Police posted a round-the-clock guard on the East Side home Brown shared with his wife, Sue, and their three children.[9]

KYW executives told Brown about the threat, but he still wanted to go on. Dressed in a charcoal suit and a black tie, he was interviewed by Douglas and movie star June Allyson. He emphasized he wasn't a member of the Black Muslims. "I'm not a part of it," he said. "I probably won't ever be." He added, "The Black Muslims are not terrorists. They are a religion." Douglas asked him about the Black Muslims' aim for an African state. "That's not realistic," Brown said. "I'm an American first."

Brown said blacks in America live under "a very tough strain." He nodded toward the blond-haired Allyson. "We have to be aware of many things—for instance, the way we look at a person like June Allyson." She asked him if he hated white people. "No," he answered. "It's hard for me to envision hating an entire group."

Douglas asked him if he felt his outspokenness would hurt him. "I have to be a man first," Brown said. "Put me on Hough Avenue, and I'm just one of a group. If those Negroes aren't free, then I'm not free. I can't be an exception to the rule."[10]

Brown faced a barrage of criticism. *Look*'s letters to the editor took him to task for being ungrateful to the white race—"the race that *has* made his success possible," one writer noted.[11]

"It was indeed gratifying for me to read Jimmy Brown's views on the racial issue because for the most part nothing but silence has come from the Negro giants of the sports world," wrote Tony Hudson of West Virginia State College. "I also feel his stand took courage in view of the personal threats made against him and his family. But I hasten to add these are the dues paid for speaking out and becoming a 'controversial Negro.'"[12]

Brown also was criticized for purporting to speak for the majority of blacks. Ofield S. Dukes, deputy director of the President's Committee on Equal Employment Opportunity, was among the most prominent blacks to take exception to his stance. "As a Negro it is inconceivable to me that such a responsible magazine as *Look* would feel that the athletic prowess of Jimmy Brown would entitle him to be publicly projected as a social scientist, social commentator, and a spokesman for his race," Ofield wrote. "In his incredible statement that the Black Muslims' attitude toward whites is shared by 99 percent of the Negro population, Brown indicates his ignorance and incompetence in the area of intergroup relations, but *Look* has afforded him this public forum and Brown's contribution to social misunderstanding has embarrassed Negroes throughout the country and cast some reflections on his social intelligence and enlightenment."[13]

Murray Olderman, a national columnist for the Newspaper Enterprise Association, wrote that Jackie Robinson wanted just "what was his as a human being." But Brown wanted more—"in the syndrome of Cassius Clay or whatever his name is, who wants what is his as a racist, if he understands the term."

One of Olderman's colleagues called him and said he was considering a column in which he planned to write that whenever a black athlete became the most prominent member of his team—Wilt Chamberlain, for example—that team couldn't win a championship. Chamberlain never had won a title in college or pro basketball, and the Browns hadn't won anything since capturing the Eastern Conference crown in Jim Brown's rookie year. Olderman dissuaded his friend from writing the column, pointing out that Bill Russell was outspoken on civil rights and his Celtics were NBA champions; and Bill White, first baseman of baseball's World Series champion St. Louis Cardinals, also was a team leader and had addressed racial issues.

"But," Olderman added, "I am disturbed that Brown's views get such notoriety. I wonder what qualifies him, at 28, to stand as a spokesman for the Negro?

"I don't think a Negro who makes $50,000 for playing football, a lot more in residual benefits (in the white market) and drives a hard bargain in financial negotiations with the white man, speaks for 99 percent of the Negro population in this country, or reflects their views. Any more than John Unitas speaks for the ethnic Lithuanians in this country. . . .

"Frankly, I'm much more interested in what kind of blocking he provides on pass protection."[14]

Cleveland sportscaster John Fitzgerald confronted Brown in the locker room and told him to tone it down. "I've always admired you as a football player, Jim," Fitzgerald said. "I've never looked on you as a Negro."

"That's ridiculous," Brown responded. "You have to look at me as a Negro. Look at me, man! I'm black!"[15]

None of what his good friend had written surprised John Wooten. It was what they and other African American athletes had been talking about for years. Times were changing, the demands for equality were becoming more strident, and other young black men on the team followed Brown's lead and became more outspoken. "We as players took the position that we had to speak out," Wooten said. "We were just reacting to what was going on in the whole country. Football was no different."[16]

In deciding to write *Off My Chest*, Brown hadn't experienced an epiphany. He was responding to King's admonition, "Injustice anywhere is a threat to justice everywhere." He had seen injustice, and continued to see it, and he felt compelled to make a statement. "He never changed," Wooten said. "He said what had to be said. Once you say what you have to say, you've done it; you just go about your business."[17]

African American players had been an integral part of the Browns since their inception—Bill Willis, Marion Motley, and Len Ford are in the Hall of Fame—and those on the 1964 squad were ahead of their time in social consciousness. They partied, but they also talked economics and politics. "We never considered ourselves as athletes. We considered ourselves as men," said cornerback Walter Beach, who joined the team in 1963. Beach was well read, and his teammates called him "Doc" because he was such a deep thinker. "Football was what I did; that's not who I was," he said.[18]

The Giants drafted Beach in 1959, but he failed to make the cut and played for two seasons with the Boston Patriots of the AFL. The Patriots played an exhibition in New Orleans in 1962, distributing the itinerary for the trip beforehand. It showed the white players staying in a downtown hotel and the black players staying with black families. Beach and some of his teammates didn't believe the team should submit to such segregation, and they elected Beach to go to management and express their unhappiness. "The next morning, they gave me a ticket and released me," he said.

At one of his first practices with Cleveland, Beach confronted Jim Brown on a running play. It was a no-contact drill, but Brown threw a forearm into Beach and ran over him. No one said a word. The next time Brown came his way, Beach tackled him. The coaches shouted at Beach to get off the field. What did he think he was doing, tackling Jim Brown in a no-contact drill? Brown interceded on Beach's behalf. "Wait a minute," he said. "I ran over him last time. What was he supposed to do? Let me run over him again? He did what he was supposed to do."

Beach considered it a lesson in power dynamics. If he allowed Brown to run over him, then he was less of a man; and if he allowed Brown to defend him, then he lost his dignity. "Jim was testing me," Beach said. "He was trying to find out what kind of human being I was. He respected that I was a sovereign human being, that Jim Brown couldn't run over me."[19]

The way Brown carried himself, the things he said, and the public stances he took on civil rights allowed the other young black players to do the same. Beach, Leroy Kelly, Walter Roberts, Clifton McNeil, Charley Scales; they took their lead from Brown. "We could stand up strong and we could feel secure because of Jim," Beach said. "For my own situation, as I live my daily life, I don't really care if white people like me or not, but they [are] going to respect me. Why? Because I have integrity. Jim had integrity."[20]

Brown understood he'd be criticized for what he wrote in his autobiography. "Some people may not like what I have to say," he told Heaton. "That doesn't matter to me. The things had to be said. . . . If I can produce it won't matter. And if I can't then it doesn't matter either."[21]

He was right. The average Cleveland fan cared more about his performance on the field than his thoughts on race relations. But he already had been taking heat for his play. Otto Graham said Cleveland couldn't win a title with Jim Brown on the team. Brown was a great athlete, Graham conceded, but he didn't block or fake. Some of the current players had told him as much. "If I was the Browns' coach," Graham said, "I'd tell him that I'd trade him if he didn't block and fake." Brown couldn't compare to Marion Motley, Graham added. Brown was a great runner, but Motley was a much better all-around back. And Jim Taylor of the Packers was a better all-around player as well. "The Browns will not win as long as Brown is there," Graham said.[22]

Brown took it in stride. He said Graham was no longer a part of the Cleveland organization and so was no different than the rest of the team's followers. "Any fan has a right to his own opinion," he added. Modell was less sanguine. He considered it "tragic" that Graham saw fit to demean one of the greatest players of all time. Collier responded as well, noting that Brown had always done everything asked of him. "If there is criticism for his not blocking," he said, "it should be of me, not Brown." He added, "The only way to prove that Jim Brown isn't a good blocker is to have him do the blocking on a majority of plays and let Ernie Green carry the ball. How would you like that?"[23]

On October 23, the Friday night before Cleveland's first game of the season against the Giants, *Rio Concho*, the Western featuring Brown as an army sergeant, premiered at the Hippodrome Theater on Euclid Avenue. The film was made during the offseason, and Brown costarred with Richard Boone, Stuart Whitman, and Tony Franciosa. He was shirtless in some of the scenes, showing off his best attribute as an actor—his physique. The money was good, and he didn't have to say much. Lee Marvin assessed his performance: "Let's put it this way. Brown's a better actor than Sir Laurence Olivier would be as a member of the Cleveland Browns."[24]

Movie star was one of a number of Brown's off-field roles. He was vice president for special markets/ethnic and national groups for Pepsi, which was making a concerted effort to market to African Americans and Spanish-speakers in the United States and Mexico. Pepsi paid him $10,000 per year, and he was on call. In January, he'd begun writing a column for the *Plain Dealer*, "Jim Brown Says," in which he commented on topics ranging from Ali's conversion to Islam to whether golf is a sport. He was cochairman of the Ohio Cancer Crusade and promoted the Tell Your Neighbor campaign to support cancer research and education.

He also was in the process of establishing the Negro Industrial and Economic Union, of which he would serve as national chairman. The union would provide capital and other forms of aid to African Americans to help start or expand businesses. Its goal was for blacks to become a force within the growing American economy. "The whole purpose was to take a young black guy who was bright, had a good idea, help him to get financing for that idea, then supply him with the technical knowledge to turn that idea into a business," Brown explained. "We started businesses across America owned and operated by blacks."[25] It received grants from the Ford Foundation totaling more than $1 million.

Many of Brown's teammates attended the *Rio Conchos* premier, some dressed in tuxedos. Parrish wore a top hat and tails. The night was called "A Salute to Jim Brown," and the proceeds were earmarked for leukemia research, in memory of Ernie Davis. Brown gave a short speech beforehand and asked the audience not to be too critical of his performance. Stan Anderson, theater critic for the *Press,* described Brown as "jim-dandy when he has a chance to knock Apache heads together. His fans will know everything will be okay when he has to steer a wagonload of gunpowder into a fire.

"It is a tough assignment and only a rugged fellow could bring it off and Jim is that fellow."[26]

Few black actors had leading roles at the time. Sidney Poitier was an established star, and he became the first African American to win an Academy Award when he was chosen Best Actor in 1963 for his performance in *Lilies of the Field.* But where Poitier came across on the screen as quiet and dignified, Brown was an imposing black man, rough and ready. He broke the mold and paved the way for other black football players who became actors, such as Fred Williamson, Carl Weathers, and O. J. Simpson. (Five years later, Brown and Raquel Welch broke ground when they filmed an interracial sex scene in the film *100 Rifles.*)

American culture was changing in many ways in 1964. It was the end of the relatively calm and stable 1950s—an era when a man like Paul Brown could hold sway—and the beginning of "The Sixties." In February, Beatlemania arrived on American soil when 3,000 screaming fans greeted the Fab Four at New York's Kennedy Airport. In June, a twenty-six-year-old go-go dancer named Carol Doda performed topless at the Condor Club in San Francisco, triggering a topless wave across the country. Less than a month later, the Republicans held their national convention in San Francisco's Cow Palace and nominated Barry Goldwater. Delegates flocked from the convention hall to watch Doda perform. Musical chart-toppers in 1963 and 1964 were bouncy and uplifting tunes such as the Beach Boys' "Surfin' USA," the Supremes' "Come See about Me," and Dean Martin's "Everybody Loves Somebody." The Rolling Stones still performed in matching suits and ties, and the Grateful Dead were three years from releasing their first album. Music that challenged the status quo, such as Barry McGuire's "Eve of Destruction"—from which historian James T. Patterson derived the name of his book about 1965—were yet to come.

CHAPTER FIFTEEN

The Browns routed the Giants 42–20 at Municipal Stadium to improve to 5-1-1. The season was half over, and Cleveland was alone in first place in the Eastern Conference. But for many Browns fans, the glass was half empty. The team's defense was ranked near the bottom statistically, and its offense was inconsistent and didn't score enough. Much of the criticism was directed at Frank Ryan.

It's an old adage in football that the quarterback gets too much credit when things go well and too much blame when they go poorly. Ryan was receiving plenty of blame, even though the Browns were winning. A week earlier, in Dallas, Cleveland was trailing 16–13 in the fourth quarter, and Collier told Jim Ninowski to start warming up. Ryan had played miserably, completing nine of twenty passes and moving the offense to just one first down in the second half. But Bernie Parrish saved the day for the Browns—and Ryan—when he intercepted a pass and returned it 54 yards for the winning touchdown.

Ryan appeared headed for a slump, similar to the one he had endured in 1963, but Collier insisted he was going to stick with him. "When a pitcher gets knocked out of the box, that doesn't mean he won't be back out there in four days," he said. "That is how I feel about Frank." He offered a lukewarm endorsement after the New York game. "Frank threw better than he's been throwing," the coach said. "I'm not saying he had a great day but it certainly was a passable performance."[1] Frank and Joan were at a banquet the following week, and someone asked her to name her favorite player on the Browns. "I was a little surprised to hear her say Bernie Parrish," Frank said. "That is until I got home and saw the headline. It read, 'Parrish interception keeps Ryan from bench.'" He hadn't seen the story earlier because Joan was hiding the newspapers from him.[2]

The cynics among Cleveland fans were calling for Ryan to be replaced by Ninowski. One wrote to the *Plain Dealer*, "I was at the Giants game with six other fellows and we think Ryan was terrible. . . . I missed four games in nine years but I won't be back until Nino gets his chance." Another wrote, "Frank Ryan should be given a rest. Every week he becomes more pressed and less accurate. If James Ninowski was used more often Ryan could get this rest. With two good quarterbacks switching off and throwing to our very good receivers we could go all the way to the title."[3]

Joan heard the boos behind her in the stands when Frank threw an interception, and she'd occasionally criticize him herself. Still, the attitude of the fans ate at her. "They didn't always know as much about football as they thought," she said. Her children weren't immune to the taunting. When Pancho climbed on the school bus, the other kids chanted, "Boo, Ryan! Boo, Ryan!" His teacher sent home a note telling Joan about it. She was crushed that he had kept it from her. "They don't know what they're booing about," he told her. Then, as an afterthought, Pancho clutched her arm and said, "Don't tell Dad that they're booing me because of him. It would hurt his feelings."[4]

Part of the problem was the publicity Ryan received for his doctoral pursuit and the image of him as a walking algebra equation, but mostly it had to do with his quarterbacking. Plus, some of the Cleveland fans simply could be downright nasty. After one game, a Browns victory, the wives were milling around outside the locker room waiting for their husbands. A drunk approached them, pulled out a pocketknife, and lunged toward Joan. Police officers were nearby, and they quickly collared him. As it turned out, the fan had lost a bet and wanted to take it out on the Browns. He didn't know Joan from the other wives, but she was dressed up and clearly had some connection to the team.

The Browns beat Pittsburgh 30–17 in week eight, and they were now two full games ahead of St. Louis, which lost to the Giants. The next day, Ryan spoke to about 300 people at the Cleveland Touchdown Club. He said the win over the Steelers took pressure off him. "It's the first Monday in quite a while I've enjoyed coming into the city of Cleveland," he said. His passing statistics so far were unimpressive; he'd thrown thirteen touchdown passes against eleven interceptions. But, he pointed out, the numbers that mattered most for a quarterback were whether he could move the offense and whether his team won. His record over the past season and a half was 16–4–1. "Not another quarterback," he said, "even a Y. A. Tittle or a Johnny Unitas, can say that right now." It was true; Ryan was the winningest quarterback in the NFL. Tittle had won eleven games with the Giants the previous season but wasn't doing much in '64. Unitas and the Colts were rolling through the Western Conference—

they lost their opener to Minnesota but had won seven straight since—but Baltimore had won only eight games in 1963. By that standard, Ryan was the best quarterback in the league, despite what everyone else believed.[5]

In early November, Hal Lebovitz decided he wanted one of the Cleveland players' wives to write a column for the *Plain Dealer*. Perian Conerly, wife of former New York Giants quarterback Charlie Conerly had set a precedent. Her column, "Backseat Quarterback," became nationally syndicated. Lebovitz asked around among the wives, and Joan Ryan's name kept coming up.

Joan had been an English major at Rice, but she said the only things she'd written since she'd been married were letters and checks. She also was caring for the couple's three young boys: Pancho, six; Michael, five; and Stuart, two. Nevertheless, she accepted Lebovitz's offer. She saw it as a rare opportunity; to refuse would have been shortsighted. "My rationale was that the worst thing that could happen was that I would fail, and I could live with that," she said. "Not trying would only end in not knowing if I was up to it."[6] She planned to write from their Lyndhurst home on the special typewriter Frank was using for his dissertation. (It had math symbols on the uppercase letters). The column was to be called "Back-Seat Brown."

Joan wrote twice a week, beginning after the Washington game and running until the end of the season. A *Plain Dealer* story announced her column: "Naturally, being a pretty gal, she'll present the pro football view from the woman's angle.

"Her hubby, Frank, says, 'This is the most hilarious thing I've ever heard.' But he promises not to second-guess her. Which is fair, because Joan never second-guesses Frank."[7]

Joan later learned Lebovitz assigned Charles Heaton to serve as ghostwriter if she wasn't up to the task, but she was. She recognized quickly that to effectively write a column she needed to seize on a specific topic and expand on it. She'd see or hear something and tell herself, "That could be a column." "It becomes almost effortless," she said.[8]

Her first column, published November 11, addressed booing, a topic with which she was well acquainted. She noted how Cleveland fans used to boo former defensive back Jim Shofner, like her a Texan and an old friend of her husband. Shofner often was chasing receivers downfield as they ran for scores, and the fans believed he'd been beaten. In fact, Joan pointed out, he often was pursuing someone who'd beaten another of the defensive backs.

"Booing is a fan's prerogative; he paid for his ticket," she wrote.

"But booers have been known to be wrong. I for one, my husband for another, think they were wrong about Jim Shofner."[9] She could have said the same thing regarding her husband.

The Browns beat the Redskins 34–24 at home on November 8 to improve to 7-1-1. Cleveland now had a two-game lead, with five to go. Ryan connected with Paul Warfield on a 62-yard score, the team's longest touchdown pass of the year. It was Warfield's fifth touchdown catch of the season, and three had been for 40 yards or longer. He was emerging as the deep threat Collier had hoped for. Using an extended—and somewhat tortured—metaphor, the coach explained Warfield's effectiveness. "Good deep receivers are like long-ball hitters in baseball," he said. "The outfielders have to back up against the fence when you have long-ball hitters. So a lot of those little hits over the infield drop in. If you know the hitter can't reach the fence, you play him up close and catch balls that would be singles for a slugger. Football defenses tighten up on you, too, and make it harder to catch the short pass."[10]

Warfield was learning the intricacies of route running and how to separate himself from defenders from Ray Renfro, and he was putting his trust in Ryan, who directed him on how to vary his patterns to keep defenders off balance. If a particular play worked two or three times in succession, Ryan would call a variation of it the next time. Each time, the pattern started out looking the same, but they'd add a wrinkle. "He was doing most of the thinking for me," Warfield said. "I'm just a rookie out there excited." Warfield also studied extensively, carrying his playbook in a briefcase, and he bought into Collier's emphasis on psycho-cybernetics. "That was the largest part of my success," he said. "Most of the people on the field can match you physically, to a degree. How you're going to win is how well versed you are from the shoulders up."[11]

Warfield was the ideal complement to Gary Collins, who split out on the opposite side of the field. In his first two seasons, Collins had been most comfortable running post patterns. He'd head down the sideline and angle toward the middle of the field and the goalposts. But in 1964 he was working with Dub Jones to make himself more of a threat running corner routes and Z-outs, a play that called for him to slant inside, plant, and race back to the sideline. He lacked Warfield's straight-ahead speed, but he ran precise routes and used his size and quickness to separate himself from his defender. He was especially effective inside the 20-yard line, the "red zone." A teammate described Warfield as resembling an antelope when he ran, but Joan Ryan said Collins looked more like a giraffe. In 1963, he led the Browns with forty-three receptions, and his thirteen touchdown catches tied for most in the NFL. Warfield was wowed by his fellow receiver. "Gary Collins was the best red-zone receiver who ever played pro football," he said.[12]

With a gradually improving Ryan and two outstanding receivers, the Cleveland offense was becoming more balanced, which made Jim Brown even more of a threat. Opposing defenses no longer could concentrate on stopping him. He thrived in the option-blocking scheme, and Collier also was using him more than before on sweeps. Gene Hickerson and John Wooten would pull and lead the way, and with their outstanding speed they were ideal for getting out ahead of Brown and knocking down defenders. Tony Tomsic, a *Press* photographer, normally stationed himself on the sideline, just ahead of the line of scrimmage. As the guards came steaming around the corner toward him, with Brown trailing, it was like watching a scene from a movie unfold. "You think [Brown] is in first gear, no, no, no," Tomsic said. "He would wait patiently, and he could turn it on. It was like he had extra juice in the tank."[13] The play was even more effective because of Warfield. He split out to the weak side, opposite the tight end, and he would crack back on a linebacker. Most teams, including Green Bay, only ran the sweep to the strong side, but because of Warfield's ability to block, the Browns could run it to either side. "The thing that made us the real utopia of the sweep was Paul Warfield," Wooten said.[14]

Following the Washington game, Brown's teammates awarded him the game ball. He threw a 13-yard scoring toss to Collins and ran for another touchdown, the hundredth of his career. He was leading the league in rushing with 934 yards, more than 200 more than next-best Jim Taylor. He was accomplishing this while playing on a broken toe. He never skipped practice and refused pain medication. Modell told him he needed to see a doctor. "I know it's fractured," Brown told him. "If I have an X-ray, all it will show is that the toe is fractured. I'll still have to play with it."[15]

Next up were the Lions at home. The Browns were favored by a touchdown, but the prospect of facing a team they'd never beaten in a regular season game didn't inspire much confidence among the Cleveland faithful. The Detroit jinx had stung them in 1963, the 38–10 loss ending Cleveland's hopes for a conference title. In her column, Joan pointed out the power of superstition. Earlier in the season, the Browns had lost to Pittsburgh on a Saturday night at Municipal Stadium. She believed the Steelers beat the Browns because Galen Fiss's wife, Nancy, and longtime fan Bill Klemm didn't sit in their usual seats. Nancy always sat on the aisle, but for that game she moved over one seat to make room for Frank's brother, Bob. Klemm always arrived at the stadium forty-five minutes early and tied his binoculars, transistor radio, blanket bag, and thermos case on the rail in front of him. But he missed the Pittsburgh game because his barbershop quartet was performing in Akron. Joan and Nancy made Klemm promise to attend the rest of the home games. "The ritual of what we wear and where we sit becomes our only real security," Joan said, "since so much hinges on the unpredictable factors like the weather conditions, emotional pitch and luck."

Now, with the Browns facing a genuine bugaboo in the Lions, she quoted John Foster Dulles: "The measure of success is not whether you have a tough problem, but whether it's the same problem you had last year."

"I don't think he was talking about the Cleveland Browns," she wrote, "but [those words] are applicable, don't you think?"[16]

The fans were taking a wait-and-see approach. Imbedded deep in their psyches were the heartbreaks of the past. Bob August wrote in the *Press* that Cleveland was "a cynic's town." The Indians and Browns had disappointed too often and for too long. "All the warning signals blink caution," he wrote. "The inner voice says don't build your hopes up too high, don't expect too much, because then the letdown really hurts."[17] Witness the Browns' collapse in 1963, which left their followers more cynical than ever.

The *Plain Dealer*'s Heaton jumped on the anti-bandwagon. "Even the most loyal rooters can stand only so much of the yo-yo treatment," he wrote. "The 1958 squad was on the verge of starting a new dynasty when disaster hit in the last game. And things went downhill for several seasons. The Browns gained a reputation as losers of the 'big ones.'"[18]

More than 83,000 cynics showed up at Municipal Stadium for the Detroit game. The Lions took a 21–20 halftime lead on three Milt Plum touchdown passes. The Browns scored on two Jim Brown runs, and Groza kicked field goals of 38 and 47 yards, this despite a broken nose suffered while making a tackle on a kickoff the previous week. At forty, he was the oldest player in the NFL. At halftime, Collier and the assistants discussed plans for the second half, while the players sat stewing, itching to return to the field. Cleveland shut out Detroit in the second half. Walter Beach picked off two passes in the fourth quarter, one that set up a Groza field goal to put Cleveland up 30–21, and the other—on the final play of the game—that he returned 65 yards for a touchdown. Fans poured from the bleachers and mobbed him in the end zone. He disappeared from sight in the scrum surrounding him, and he found it unsettling. "I've got claustrophobia," he said. "I was glad to get out of there."[19]

The win took some of the pressure off the Browns, and it was evident at the Sheraton postgame party, a regular event after home games. The gatherings included the players' wives and friends, and they all moved from table to table socializing. The players split the tab, which included a dance band. "Dancing is an excellent way to relax after a tense football game," Joan explained in her column. "Some of the boys even twist a little."[20] In 1963, there was plenty of twisting as the team started 6–0. This season, however, the players hadn't been taking anything for granted. They left their wives and friends and huddled in corners of the ballroom to rehash the games. The gatherings seemed more like funerals than parties. That changed after the Detroit game. The Browns were dancing again.

Cleveland had four games remaining, including at Green Bay and at St. Louis. The Packers were struggling, but under Lombardi they were always formidable, and the Cardinals remained in the title hunt. The Browns met the Packers in Milwaukee on November 22; a Cleveland win and a St. Louis loss would clinch the Eastern Conference title. They outgained Green Bay 302 yards to 285, but lost 28–21. The turning point came early in the third quarter. The Browns led 14–7, and the Packers faced fourth down and a foot at their own 44-yard line. Cleveland lined up in a goal-line defense, but Bart Starr surprised them by throwing long to Max McGee on a play that took the Packers to the 1-yard line. Taylor scored on the next play. Jim Brown fumbled on Cleveland's next possession, and Green Bay went in for the go-ahead score. There were a few bright spots. Warfield caught seven balls for 126 yards and two more touchdowns, and Brown scored on a 1-yard run, giving him 104 touchdowns for his career, one shy of Don Hutson's NFL record. Despite a St. Louis win over Philadelphia, the Browns clinched a spot in the Playoff Bowl for the second consecutive year, though this season that would provide no consolation.

The loss didn't bode well for the postseason. The Packers weren't the best team in the West, far from it. They had lost twice to Baltimore, which embarked on an eleven-game winning streak after its season-opening loss to Minnesota. The Colts finished the season 12–2, their other loss coming in the next-to-last game, after they already had secured the conference title. It was Baltimore's first conference title since 1959, and after clinching against Los Angeles, the players threw Shula into the shower fully clothed. In the win over the Rams, the Baltimore defense sacked the L.A. quarterbacks eleven times.

Afterward, Rams coach Harlan Svare was asked who he thought was better, the Colts or Browns. The Colts, he said, because they had a better defense.

Cleveland's defense had a bad rap. It did give up more yards and more first downs than any other team in the NFL because of its "rubber band defense," but it could live with that as long as it prevented big plays. (Years later, Collins would comment that the description "rubber band defense" was hardly intimidating and didn't inspire much confidence, not like the Rams' "Fearsome Foursome" or the Vikings' "Purple People Eaters.")

The defensive line was perilously thin. The loss of Frank Parker and Bob Gain to injuries meant Dick Modzelewski and Jim Kanicki, backups at the season's start, were now the starting tackles. The Browns remained strong at defensive end with Paul Wiggin and Bill Glass. Wiggin, an All-American tackle while at Stanford, was one of six players left from the 1957 conference championship team (the others were linebackers Fiss and Vince Costello, and Gain, Brown, and Groza). Paul Brown normally eschewed West Coast players, but he made an exception with Wiggin and chose him as a "future" pick in 1956. Wiggin played his senior year at Stanford as property of the Browns, and he joined Cleveland in 1957 along with Jim Brown. He was moved to defensive end, where he became a starter in his second season. He earned his master's degree in education from Stanford in 1959 and during the off-seasons taught at the College of San Mateo in California. He and Ryan lived near each other in Lyndhurst and rode to practice together every day. It's hard to imagine another car carrying two NFL players with as much brain power.

While Modzelewski provided experience and a championship pedigree to the defensive line, Kanicki supplied youthful energy and raw power. The Browns chose the Michigan State Spartan in the second round of the 1963 draft. He was one of thirteen children, and the $14,000 he made his rookie season was three times as much as his father ever made as a foundry worker in Michigan. He weighed 270 pounds and was described by one writer as "very much like an enormous baby with soft pink cheeks," but he was strong enough to hold his ground against most anyone. His only drawback was lack of experience. He was thrust into a starting role in this, his second season, and his play was inconsistent. He was too aggressive, especially on first down. He'd fire off the line determined to reach the passer, but in those days few teams passed on first down. He was especially susceptible to a trap play, effectively taking himself out of the action. Pittsburgh's John Henry Johnson rushed for 200 yards against the Browns early in the season, and most of those came over Kanicki.

But as the season progressed, Collier taught him how to read blocks and he learned to avoid being suckered. On the field, Modzelewski told him when to rush and when to expect the run, and he was becoming more effective.

The linebackers also were a combination of experience and youthful athleticism. In the middle was Costello, who stood 6 feet and weighed 230 pounds and was one of the fastest linebackers in the NFL. A native of Dellroy, Ohio, just south of Canton, he played football, baseball, and basketball at Ohio University. He was a first baseman for two years in the Cincinnati Reds farm system and served two years in the air force before joining the Browns as a free agent in 1957. He became the starting middle linebacker as a twenty-five-year-old rookie, playing behind an intimidating front four of Don Colo, Len Ford, Gain, and Bill Quinlan. "Before my rookie year I asked the Good Lord each night in my prayers to bless my mother and father," he said. "I changed those night prayers somewhat to 'God bless Colo, Ford, Gain, and Quinlan.' I didn't want anything to happen to those big guys in front of me."[21]

One outside linebacker position was manned by Jim Houston, and the other by Fiss, a nine-year veteran and the team captain. Fiss weighed less than 210 pounds while playing linebacker and fullback at the University of Kansas, but he hit with such ferocity he earned the nickname "Earthshaker." The Browns drafted him in 1953, but like his teammates Costello and Parrish, he initially opted for professional baseball. He was part of the Indians organization and played a season as catcher for Fargo of the Northern League; one of his teammates was Roger Maris. And like Costello, he spent two years in the air force before joining the Browns in 1956. He was chosen for the Pro Bowl in 1962 and 1963, even though Collier didn't believe he tackled correctly. He didn't use his arms, as Collier taught; instead he threw his shoulder into the runner, but more often than not he was in position to make the play.

At right cornerback, opposite Parrish, Beach was proving integral to Cleveland's success on defense. Jim Shofner (he of the misguided booing) retired after the 1963 season, and Collier started Beach in the Playoff Bowl, curious to see if he was capable of replacing Shofner and making it possible to move Warfield to offense. Beach had taken a winding road to NFL starter. He spent four years in the army between high school in Pontiac, Michigan, and college at Central Michigan. After the Patriots cut him in 1962, he spent a year teaching fourth grade in Pontiac. He wrote Collier a letter before the 1963 season and received a tryout. He made the taxi squad and dressed for the final three games. "He was not a good tackler," Parrish said, "but he could cover anybody."[22]

Ross Fichtner was solid at free safety. An option quarterback at Purdue, he was drafted by the Browns in 1960 and moved to defense. Much like Parrish, he was intelligent, aggressive, and a vocal leader. He tied for the league lead in interceptions in 1962, his first full year as a starter, but he attributed his success to the fact opposing teams picked on him because of his inexperience. He remained one of the league's best ball hawks, and early in the '64 season he made two crucial interceptions: one in the tie against St. Louis and another in the fourth quarter against Philadelphia, which set up Cleveland's go-ahead touchdown. The following week against Dallas, he was knocked cold. He was unconscious for forty-five minutes and went into convulsions. "I was making a tackle," he said, "and a guy ran a 50-yard dash through my ears."[23] He shared a room at Shaker Medical Center that night with Gain, whose career ended when he broke his leg in the same game. Fichtner's left eye was knocked off its axis, and when he ran it bounced. In keeping with the times, Heaton wrote, "No complications are anticipated, however, and Ross should be ready for Pittsburgh." He wasn't. He sat out three games before returning to the lineup, though with blurred vision.

Larry Benz, a former quarterback for Ara Parseghian at Northwestern, manned the other safety spot. A native of Cleveland Heights, he went undrafted, and Parseghian called Collier and urged him to sign Benz as a free agent. He started at safety as a rookie in 1963, replacing Don Fleming. Parrish picked on him incessantly, but Benz intercepted seven passes and made the NFL All-Rookie team, and Parrish grudgingly accepted him. "If nothing else, I didn't want to train another guy," he said. "Besides, Benz was a tough little guy. When he tackled you, you knew it."[24] If the defensive backfield had a weak link, however, Benz was it. An NFL coach described him as a "hustler" but without "the speed and size to be outstanding."

The Browns defeated Philadelphia 38–24 in their final home game of the season. The crowd of 79,289 pushed total attendance for the season, including the doubleheader and other exhibitions, to 633,070, a new club record. That was more than the Indians drew in all of 1962 and nearly as much as they drew in 1964. The Indians' owners complained they couldn't attract big crowds downtown to Municipal Stadium because so many people had moved to the suburbs. Former Yankees manager Casey Stengel, noting the 80,000 people the Browns regularly drew, commented, "I guess somebody moved back."[25]

In 1964, Cleveland was a city in transition, and, in truth, many of its citizens had moved to the suburbs. The Innerbelt freeway, completed two years earlier, removed thousands of cars and trucks from downtown streets and opened the suburbs to people who previously had worked and lived in the city. More than a dozen Cuyahoga County towns surrounding Cleveland achieved city status in the early 1960s, communities such as Brecksville, Strongsville, and Solon. By 1970, Cleveland's population would shrink from a high of 915,000 residents in 1950 to about 750,000 people.

The Great Migration of African Americans from the South had helped fuel growth in the city following World War II. By 1960, blacks made up 29 percent of the population. This combination of a white exodus and black influx changed the city's racial makeup. The Hough area on the East Side went from 95 percent white in 1950 to 75 percent black within a decade. Among those who grew up in Hough and left was Tom Matte, the former Ohio State Buckeye and a Baltimore Colt running back in 1964. His father had played for the Cleveland Barons minor league hockey team, and Matte lived at 93rd Street and Hough Avenue. It was a rough neighborhood, but the conflict wasn't black against white; it was school against school. Matte and his friends made zip guns and carried knives for protection. Many of his friends were African American, among them the father of the future Ohio State basketball star Clark Kellogg. But along with the rapid change in racial makeup came tension and violence. When Matte was in ninth grade, his father moved the family to Eddy Road in East Cleveland.

The city remained de facto segregated in the mid-1960s, and the Africa American players lived in the black neighborhoods. They made a concerted effort to become involved in their community. They ate meals with their neighbors and attended the same churches. They served as Big Brothers. They campaigned for Carl Stokes, who ran unsuccessfully for mayor in 1965 and won in 1967, becoming the first black mayor of a major American city. "The Browns gave us the stage on which to carry things out," said Wooten, who lived in the Lee Harvard area. "We saw it as a road into the community in terms of being able to give back. We preached daily: Give back to your community; make your community better for everyone."[26] They were heroes for their play on the field and role models for the way they conducted themselves off of it. "They gave us ambition and hope," said Lady Gilmore, a junior at John Adams High in the fall of 1964. "We experienced a lot of pain, and we needed something to feel good about."[27]

Lady Gilmore's father had grown up in Georgia, and he ran an asphalt business in Cleveland. He loved the Browns, as did her three brothers. When the team was playing and the weather was good the neighborhood held "a cookout celebration," she said. "If you wanted to eat, 100th Street was one of the streets you wanted to come to." When the Browns were playing and the weather was cold, the houses were full of people listening on the radio or watching on television. "You could turn the heat off because of all the people in the house," she said. It reminded her of the photos she'd seen of African Americans gathered around radios listening to Joe Louis's fights—"giving them hope. . . . We were rooting for Jim Brown."[28]

The city's police force remained predominantly white, and by 1964 relations between the police and the African American community were strained. Two years later, the Hough area would explode in a weeklong riot that would leave businesses in ashes and four people dead. But as Cleveland became what historians later called "a loose and rancorous federation of walled villages," it was united in the fall of 1964 behind its football team and its hopes for an NFL championship.[29] White and black, Italian and Polish, rich and poor, everyone was rooting for the Browns.

Cleveland could have clinched the conference title with its win over the Eagles at home, but the Cardinals beat the Steelers, setting up a showdown the following week in St. Louis. The Browns were 9-2-1, and the Cardinals were 7-3-2. For St. Louis to overtake Cleveland, the Browns would need to lose their final two games, and the Cardinals would need to win their final two. The teams met at sold-out Busch Stadium on a cold, windy day with snow piled along the sidelines. Everything that could go wrong for the Browns did. Ryan was under constant pressure from the St. Louis defensive line and overthrew his receivers. When he did manage to get the ball to them, they dropped it. He was intercepted twice in the first half, once in the end zone. He didn't complete a pass until well into the second quarter, and by then the Cardinals led 14-3. The failure of the passing game exposed a weakness in the Cleveland offense. If the Browns fell behind and had to throw—and failed to do it successfully—they were deprived of their most potent weapon, the running game. Brown carried the ball fourteen times for 49 yards. Ernie Green rushed three times for 17 yards.

The Cleveland pass defense fared no better. The Cardinals' Charley Johnson completed fifteen of twenty-two passes for two touchdowns, and in the locker room afterward he puffed on a cigar and told reporters that everything he tried worked. The Cleveland defensive backs started out playing back deep, as usual, and he completed short passes in front of them. When they moved up, he threw long. "Normally, they play a zone-type defense much of the time, but today they tried man-to-man more than I've seen before," he said. "It gave us an advantage."[30]

The final score was 28–19. The Cardinals had now tied and defeated the Browns, and defensive end Joe Robb said he wasn't impressed with them. "We have a better team than Cleveland, especially if you take that big guy [Jim Brown] out of their backfield," he said. "If Y. A. Tittle can beat the Browns, we'll vote him a full share of the championship money."

Four cases of champagne had been placed on ice at the Bel Air West Motel in St. Louis, and a cab was on standby to take it to the Browns locker room as soon as it looked as though they would win. The bubbly was crated up and sent back to the dealer. Collier was flustered. "We have never worked harder preparing for a game," he said. "I've never seen a group as dedicated to win as we were this week. We lost it somewhere between the locker room and the field."[31]

The team was in a dour mood on the plane ride home. Ryan huddled with some of the offensive linemen to talk about the game plan for the Giants. Monte Clark got up and walked away angry. "You can do all the talking you want, but there's only one way to get the job done and that's to do it," he snapped. Fiss groused to a reporter, "Every time we lose, we begin searching our souls. This is no time for soul-searching. We won nine regular-season games and four exhibition games. We must have done something right."[32]

The *Plain Dealer* sent a photographer to the airport to document the team's arrival, and the photos showed grim-looking players departing the plane. Joan Ryan was among those who met the plane at the airport. The Ryans normally returned to Texas immediately after the final game of the season, which this year was December 12, and she told Modell she didn't know whether to go home and bake Christmas cookies (the NFL championship game was scheduled for December 27) or start packing for the trip back to Texas. "Bake the cookies," Modell said. "I'll even buy you the shortening."[33]

CHAPTER SIXTEEN

The Cleveland faithful felt betrayed by the St. Louis loss. "I used to be a Browns fan, but no more," one told Bob August of the *Press*. "They're dead."[1] Another team's fans wouldn't have taken the defeat so hard, but no other team was so woven into the fabric of its region. And no other fans loved their team so deeply. But, as the saying goes, the line between love and hate is a thin one. It was no surprise, then, that the love the Cleveland fans had felt for their team a week earlier had turned to bitterness. That Saturday's game against the Giants would be played at Yankee Stadium—the site of so many heartbreaking losses—layered dread on top of misery. The cynics kept hearkening back to 1958, when Cleveland seemed to have the conference title locked up and then lost to the Giants in the season finale and again in the playoff, both times in New York. Heaton called Yankee Stadium "the Browns' personal disaster area." The only encouragement came from bookies, who favored Cleveland by ten.[2]

Collier refused to allow his players to be caught up in the negativity. Instead of showing the film of the St. Louis game, he compiled a reel of highlights from earlier in the season. He also moved the final practice before the game from League Park to Municipal Stadium. When the players pulled up they were greeted by a sign that read: "NEXT GAME, BALTIMORE COLTS, DECEMBER 27." "After what we had been through in the past, it was hard not to think, 'Here we go again,'" Fiss said. "We really had to regroup, and Blanton brought us together."[3]

The game marked the return of Modzelewski to the city where he'd played on a half-dozen conference champion teams. Before the game, an old pair of sneakers arrived for him from the New York dressing room. On them was inscribed, "For the Polish Hall of Fame." Little Mo was a symbol of New York's demise. He was on the verge of another title, but with the club to which he'd been discarded. New York had declined dramatically, winning only two games all season, though it had done better against the Cardinals than the

Browns had, beating them and tying them. New York was starting five rookies, but also some great old-timers. Tittle, Frank Gifford, and Andy Robustelli were playing the final game of their Hall of Fame careers. Also calling it quits were two longtime Giant stars: running back Alex Webster, and offensive lineman Jack Stroud. What a great way for these old pros to go out: beat their old rivals the Browns and deprive them of the title at Yankee Stadium. The scenario left Cleveland fans with a collective knot in their stomachs. Tittle added to the anxiety. He said the Giants had nothing to lose and were loose, while all the pressure was on the Browns.

The New York supporters knew this would be Tittle's last game, and they cheered him wildly. The balding Texan—his head was described as resembling a bowling ball, and his face as looking like it had been hit with one—had led the Giants to three straight conference titles, the finest season of his seventeen-year career coming in 1963 when he was named the league's MVP. The 1964 season had been tough on him, though. He was best remembered for a photo taken moments after Pittsburgh's John Baker blindsided him in the second game, knocking his helmet off and gashing his scalp. Kneeling on the turf, he gasped for breath as blood ran from his head down to his cheek.

The Giants-Browns game was nationally televised, and an estimated 30 million viewers tuned in. A layer of fog lay over the stadium, and the lights were on by the one o'clock kickoff. The mud was four inches deep, according to the injured Bob Gain, who was writing a column for the *Press*. He said he could prove it by the marks on his crutches.

The Browns went ahead 3-0 on a 39-yard field goal by Groza in the first quarter, but early in the second quarter Tittle looked like his old self as he moved the Giants 80 yards in eleven plays, connecting with Dick James in the back of the end zone for a 7-yard touchdown that put New York ahead 7-3. Was it possible Tittle had some magic left? Or, from a Cleveland cynic's standpoint, was there a chance he *didn't*?

The Browns marched down the field on their next possession. Ryan dropped back to pass from the New York 13-yard line and was flushed from the pocket. He took off running, and as he was being dragged down from behind at the goal line, a Giants defensive back jammed his palm into Ryan's nose above his face mask. Ryan fumbled as he crossed the goal line, and a New York defender fell on the ball in the end zone. The officials ruled Ryan's knee was across the line when he lost the ball and signaled touchdown. The call unleashed a season's worth of frustration for the Giants. They argued vehemently—defensive back Allan Webb had to be wrestled away from the officials by his teammates—but to no avail.

On New York's next possession, Tittle tried to hit Gifford with a pass along the sideline, but Parrish intercepted at the Cleveland 40. He slogged through the mud to the New York 29, where he was knocked out of bounds. Five plays later, Ryan threw to Collins for an 11-yard score. The Browns were up 17–7.

Costello intercepted Tittle on the next possession, and with forty-five seconds remaining in the first half Ryan called timeout and trudged across the muck to the sideline. Collier leaned in close to hear Ryan. The quarterback said he wanted to run a Z-out, a pass play to Warfield. Collier liked the call and gave the go ahead.

The Z-out called for Warfield to slant inside, plant, and race back to the sideline. Ryan expected Warfield to catch the ball at the 20-yard line and step out of bounds. A field goal attempt from there by Groza would be a sure thing. Warfield was covered by Webb, a reserve safety from Arnold College in Connecticut. Webb was playing in place of an injured starter, and earlier in the week he'd found a sheepskin coat in his locker. Pinned to it was a note, written by a teammate, that read, "Please wear this. Those receivers stir up so much wind when they go past we're afraid you'll catch pneumonia."[4]

Warfield slanted inside, but instead of cutting back outside, he ran a variation of the Z-out, the Z-go, and sprinted downfield between Webb and New York's safety. Ryan lofted a pass that Warfield grabbed at the 10-yard line. He was dragged down at the 1, and on the next play Ryan flipped a pass to Ernie Green to put the Browns up 24–7.

The play was emblematic of how far the Cleveland offense—and Ryan—had come in the past two seasons. Ryan had suggested the play, and Collier had enough confidence in his quarterback to allow him to run it. Warfield had broken off his pattern, and Ryan had the poise and patience to recognize the improvisation and adapt to it.

The Browns took the opening kickoff of the second half and marched for another score, Ryan connecting with Green on a 25-yard pass play. Ryan passed to Warfield for a touchdown and to Jim Brown in the flat for another. The score at the end of three quarters was 45–7.

Collier benched his starters in the fourth quarter, and Ninowski threw 24 yards to Walter Roberts for Cleveland's last touchdown. Final score: Cleveland 52, New York 20. The Giants scored a touchdown in the waning moments, and the crowd rushed onto the field and tore down the goal posts and stole the teams' benches. The officials called the game without the extra-point try. Cleveland defensive tackle Frank Parker, 6-foot-5 and 270 pounds, had his helmet ripped off, and Monte Clark had to be restrained from going after an insult-spewing fan. It was reminiscent of the 1959 New York–Cleveland game that was held up for fifteen minutes when the Giants fans took over the field. That time the Giants won. This time, the New York fans were venting their disgust with their team's wretched season. "Giants Fail," the *Plain Dealer* headlined, "but Fans Clinch Bush League Title." Modzelewski was upset by the postgame riot because he wanted to meet up with Allie Sherman and thank him for trading him to Cleveland.

In the steamy and raucous locker room afterward, Collier awarded Ryan the game ball. The quarterback had played the game of his life, completing twelve of thirteen passes for five scores. His twenty-five touchdown passes for the season led the NFL. Ryan posed for photos, giving a thumb's up and standing between Brown and Groza. Asked whether he realized he'd thrown just one incomplete pass, he responded, "Aware of it? I sure am, and I would have completed that one if I had set myself better."[5]

Longtime Browns observers described the victory as one of the greatest in team history. It brought Cleveland its first title since 1957, and it had come with a rout of the hated Giants. Two NFL records were set: Groza scored 115 points, the most ever in a season, and Brown tied Don Hutson with 105 touchdowns for his career. Otherwise, Brown's performance was something of an afterthought in the victory. He didn't gain 100 yards—just 99—but he did end up leading the NFL in rushing for the second straight season.

Collier effusively praised his fullback and at the same time took a shot at his former pupil, Otto Graham, who'd said Cleveland couldn't win a title with Brown. "I want to pay special tribute to Jim Brown for his excellent blocking," Collier said. "The players told me they never saw Jimmy play a greater game and perform better as a team player than today."[6] Graham later responded that his earlier comments were intended to motivate Brown. "I meant they wouldn't be winning if Brown didn't block and fake," he said. "They changed. Maybe my little statement helped them."[7]

Fog held up the Browns' plane in Newark, and the team started its celebration in flight. The champagne that had gone unopened a week earlier in St. Louis now poured freely. Modell told the *Plain Dealer*'s Russell Schneider the win was the biggest thrill of his life, but he said he didn't relax until the end of the third quarter. At that point, he turned to general manager Harold

Sauerbrei and asked if he thought they'd win. "You know what he told me?" Modell said. "'It looks pretty good—but don't count on anything.' We didn't." Sauerbrei had seen every game the Browns had played, first as a sportswriter, then as a publicist, and now as general manager. This was the best of all, he told Schneider. "This one sure ends a lot of frustration," he said, "and I'm certainly happy for Art. He went way out on a limb two years ago."[8]

Collier sat with his wife, Forman, already absorbed in the game plan for Baltimore. Forman broke into sobs shortly after boarding the plane and continued crying. She told Schneider they were tears of joy, but, in fact, she was releasing the pressure under which she had lived for the past two years, since the day her husband agreed to replace his best friend as Cleveland's head coach.

The plane landed at Hopkins airport about 9:45 P.M. and was greeted by more than 5,000 fans. They'd waited two hours. The players insisted Collier be the first person off the plane, and the crowd roared when he and Forman appeared in the doorway. They threw confetti on them as they made their way to the concourse. Inside, fans packed the hallway, swallowing up the players, especially Ryan. The throng brought him to a halt—men and women in suits, blacks and whites, teens and kids on their dads' shoulders. Confetti covered Ryan's coat and a streamer hung from his head, which was bowed against the onslaught. The *Plain Dealer* published a photo of Frank and Joan embracing, Frank with the game ball in his hand. It took them forty-five minutes to reach their car.

Prior to the game, Joan hadn't known whether to pack for the trip back to Texas or to put up Christmas lights. The family never had spent a Christmas in Cleveland. But in the third quarter she went outside and began stringing up decorations on the house. Neighbors joined her, and it became a block party. "This will tickle Frank," she said. "The lights will be a perfect welcome home for him."[9]

Ryan's performance provided him with newfound confidence. The plays he called meshed with his abilities and those of his teammates. Success bred faith in himself, which in turn made him more self-assured in his play-calling and his throws. He noted that what set the Browns apart from the rest of the Eastern Conference was their wealth of players with winning attitudes: Brown, Modzelewski, Schafrath, Parrish. "I didn't know I was one," he added, "until Saturday."[10]

A few weeks earlier, Joan had received a letter, care of the *Plain Dealer* and postmarked "Sandusky." The writer said the only thing wrong with the Browns was the quarterback. The envelope didn't include a return address, but the letter was signed; so Joan went to the post office to see if she could find out where the guy lived. But the post office said no one by that name lived in Sandusky. After his performance against New York, Frank told her, "Honey, you don't have to answer him now."[11]

The next day, Ryan fell asleep in front of the television while watching Baltimore defeat Washington 45–17. (The Colts scored thirty-five points in the second half, and Shula said, "That is just what we needed to put us in tune.") "I don't remember anything past the second quarter," Ryan said. "I was so exhausted I couldn't keep my eyes open. The emotional preparation for the Giants game took a lot out of me. And I was beginning to feel the hurts from the game."[12]

When he awoke, he told Joan, "I can't understand myself why I played so well." She handed him a book she'd been reading to their boys, *The Little Prince,* by Antoine de Saint-Exupéry. She pointed to a sentence: "I was carried beyond myself by the inspiring force of urgent necessity."

"I got the message," Ryan said. "There was nothing more urgent than beating the Giants."[13]

CHAPTER SEVENTEEN

The championship game was scheduled for Sunday, December 27, in Cleveland. The Colts had the better record, but in those days the home site for the title game alternated between conferences. Nineteen sixty-four was the Eastern Conference's year to play host. The two-week interval between the end of the regular season and the championship left plenty of time for fans and scribes to speculate. The predominant sentiment was Unitas and the Colts would crush Cleveland. An opposing coach called the Browns "laugh champs," because they didn't deserve to be playing for the title. Specifically, their defense—especially the defensive backs—was a joke. Following Cleveland's win over New York, one of the Giants said of Unitas, "He'll cut the Browns to pieces."[1]

The Associated Press named Unitas the league's Most Valuable Player, and he received the Bert Bell Award as the league's top performer. He threw nineteen touchdown passes, six fewer than Ryan, but with only six interceptions (compared to nineteen for Ryan). Stoop-shouldered, with a crew cut and sporting black high-top cleats, he looked nothing like a pro football player—Ryan looked like a decathlete in comparison—but he was intelligent, daring, and a great leader. "Playing with Unitas," tight end John Mackey said, "was like being in the huddle with God."[2]

Unitas's favorite target was Raymond Berry, like Unitas a future Hall of Famer. Berry was obsessive in his preparation. He came up with eighty-eight different moves to get open, and he stayed after practice every day to work on them. In the epic 1958 overtime game against the Giants, he caught twelve passes from Unitas, including three on the fourth-quarter drive that set up the tying field goal.

Jim Parker, a Toledo native and a former Ohio State Buckeye, anchored the offensive line. Parker played left tackle early in his career, protecting Unitas's blind side. George Allen, coach of the Los Angeles Rams' dominating defensive line, the "Fearsome Foursome," said the Rams gave up trying to reach Unitas through Parker: "So all by himself he took away half your pass rush."[3] Parker later moved to guard, where, as a 280-pounder, he could pull and lead sweeps or open holes for runs up the middle. He was called "Boulevard," because his rear end was as wide as one. In the huddle Unitas would say, "Boulevard, this is critical—32 trap, right over your ass."[4]

Running back Lenny Moore scored twenty touchdowns in 1964, then an NFL record. His nickname was "Spats" because he wore tape on the outside of his cleats—one of the first players, if not the first, to sport that look. Unitas called him "Sput," for Sputnik, the Russian satellite. He was fast as a rocket. He could line up at flanker as well as in the backfield, making him a dual threat as a runner and receiver. "Lenny just glided," backup quarterback Gary Cuozzo said. "He was so smooth."[5]

The ties between the Cleveland and Baltimore franchises ran deep, dating to the early days of the All-America Football Conference. When the AAFC folded after the 1949 season, the Browns and Colts were among the three teams absorbed by the NFL (San Francisco was the other). But while the Browns flourished, the Baltimore franchise foundered. It suffered through an eighteen-game losing streak in 1949 and '50, and folded. After two seasons without a team in Baltimore, the league moved a failing Dallas Texans franchise to the city. Its new owner was Carroll Rosenbloom, a former teammate of NFL commissioner Bert Bell at the University of Pennsylvania. Rosenbloom wasn't particularly interested in owning a team, but Bell gave him little choice. He called one night and said, "Carroll, you're the new owner. I just announced it." Rosenbloom reluctantly agreed, mostly because he was between a rock and a hard place. "If I didn't take it, the folks in Baltimore would hate me," he said, "and if I did take it I'd hate myself. That's how I was forced into pro football."[6]

Rosenbloom had made millions selling khaki for military uniforms during World War II, and also in land development and electronics. He was a savvy promoter, just like Art Modell. He established fan clubs, called Colt Corrals, to strengthen ties between the team and the community. The players attended dinner parties, cookouts, even kids' birthday parties. (The city's allegiance to the team was immortalized in the movie *Diner*, in which a young woman had to pass a Colts trivia test to prove she was worthy of matrimony.) As a result, the city of Baltimore's devotion to the Colts ran nearly as deep as Cleveland's for the Browns—*nearly*, because football was more entrenched in northeastern Ohio and because of the Browns' longtime success.

The Dallas Texans, the team adopted by Baltimore, had won one game in 1952 and managed only three wins in 1953. Rosenbloom went looking for a new coach, and he approached the assistants of the NFL's best, Paul Brown. His first choice was Collier, but he turned him down to coach at Kentucky. He next offered the job to Weeb Ewbank, a former teammate of Brown's at Miami University. Like Collier, Ewbank had served as an assistant under Brown at Great Lakes and from the beginning in Cleveland. Ewbank took the Baltimore job, and among the players he inherited was a defensive back named Don Shula.

Shula came to Baltimore from Cleveland as part of a fifteen-player swap following the 1952 season. The Colts, desperate to overhaul their roster, traded five players to Cleveland, including Mike McCormack, for ten Browns, one of whom was Shula. The Painesville native grew up thirty miles from Municipal Stadium, and he was sixteen when the Browns joined the AAFC in 1946. The Browns allowed high-schoolers into games for fifty cents if they wore their letter sweaters, and Shula was a regular at Cleveland games, sitting in the bleachers with his buddies.

Cleveland chose Shula in the ninth round of the 1951 draft following his graduation from John Carroll. Joining the Browns was a dream come true, as was playing for Paul Brown. "I was just in awe of him," Shula said. He played seven seasons in the NFL for three teams before retiring, and in 1959 he joined Collier's staff at Kentucky as defensive backs coach.

Ewbank's first three Baltimore teams endured losing seasons, but in 1956 the Colts signed Unitas, who at the time was working as a pile driver on a Pittsburgh construction crew. The Steelers had drafted him in the ninth round in 1955, but he never saw the field in preseason and was cut. He and his wife, Dorothy, moved in with her parents, and he played quarterback once a week for a local semipro team, making $6 per game.

How exactly Unitas ended up in Baltimore is unclear. One story goes that Ewbank heard about him from an old friend, Unitas's former coach at Louisville. Another story has it the Colts received a letter from a fan of the semipro team, touting Unitas. Ewbank always accused Unitas of writing it. In any case, Unitas joined the Colts before the 1956 season, signing for $7,000. The team's backup quarterback had quit football to become a lawyer, and when starting quarterback George Shaw was injured, Unitas was thrust into the starting lineup. Midway through his rookie season, he led Baltimore past the Browns 21–7. At practice the following week, the team's equipment manager asked defensive end Gino Marchetti when Shaw would return. "He's never going to be the quarterback again," Marchetti said. "Unitas is the quarterback."[7]

The Colts won the NFL title in 1958 (the epic overtime victory against the Giants) and again in 1959. Unitas was named first team All-Pro both years, and in '59 threw for a career-high thirty-two touchdowns and won the first of his three Bert Bell Awards. But Baltimore began a downward slide, and following the 1962 season, in which the Colts finished fourth, Rosenbloom fired Ewbank. "It was the saddest thing I ever had to do when I let Weeb go," he said, "but I felt he had lost control of the team."[8]

Rosenbloom asked Marchetti and others for advice on who should take over as Baltimore's head coach. Marchetti recommended Shula, his former Colt teammate and roommate, who was an assistant in Detroit. Shula was just thirty-three, but he'd made a name for himself as architect of a stingy Lions defense, and his old teammates thought highly of him. While playing for the Colts, he had been part of a hard-nosed crew that included Marchetti, Artie Donovan, Don Joyce, and Bill Pellington. A sportswriter noted that "choirboys didn't survive in that company." Shula was so popular his teammates awarded him a game ball even when he wasn't playing. He'd been cut during the 1957 season and was watching a Baltimore game from the stands. The guy who replaced him was beaten for a touchdown, and afterward the players gave Shula the game ball. "He was a student all the time he played with us," Rosenbloom said. "When we cut him I was against it but I give our coaches free rein. I admired him then, and when I decided to change coaches I thought of him. I thought of some others, too, but all the recommendations I got favored Don."[9]

His popularity with his former mates, and Marchetti's endorsement, provided Shula a leg up when he took over the Colts. "That's what helped me get credibility in the eyes of these guys I used to play with, who were much better than I was," Shula said. "All of a sudden I'm going back there to coach them, and I'm just thirty-three years old."[10]

Shula was a disciple of the Browns way. He followed Paul Brown's organizational methods, from having the players write everything down in notebooks to staying in a hotel and watching a movie together the night before home games. And he relied on the teaching techniques he'd learned from Collier as a player with the Browns and as an assistant at Kentucky. "He was an intricately detailed guy," Cuozzo said. "He was very precise. And he was involved with everything."[11]

Shula knew enough to let his veterans have a say in the way things were run. The Colts were stocked with experienced and talented players on both offense and defense, men with personalities to match their considerable skills. It worked well to a degree, but the one nut Shula couldn't crack was Unitas. The quarterback told the coach to run the defense and he'd run the offense. On one occasion, Shula sent in the field-goal team, and Unitas waved it off. Instead, he called a play that went for a touchdown. Shula could be a screamer, but he quietly informed Unitas that it was his team and the quarterback would run the plays he called. Unitas refused to comply. Tom Matte, then a young halfback, occasionally brought in plays from the sideline. He'd tell Unitas the play, and Unitas would say, "That isn't going to work" and would call another play. When Matte came off the field, Shula asked why they didn't run the play he'd sent in. "John said it wouldn't work," Matte replied.[12]

"John had played with Shula," Cuozzo explained. "He was the quarterback, and Shula had never played quarterback. John was his own guy."[13]

The Colts started slowly in 1963 under Shula, losing three of their first four games, but they improved in the second half and ended 8–6. They might have finished even stronger, but for injuries to Moore and Berry. Moore suffered a knee injury and played only half the season, and without him in the lineup the Colts didn't have much of a running game. A bright spot was the emergence of John Mackey, a fullback at Syracuse who moved to tight end as a rookie in '63. He was a devastating blocker and though initially not a great pass catcher, he worked long hours with Berry and Unitas to become better. He was a new kind of tight end. Most were big, strong, and lumbering. But he was compact, powerful, and fast for his size—he stood 6-foot-2 and weighed 225 pounds—and provided Unitas with another deep threat. "He was explosive in the open field," said Ernie Accorsi, the Colts' PR director at the time. "It wasn't a matter of eluding; it was a matter of running over those defensive backs."[14] As a rookie he caught thirty-five passes for seven scores and averaged 20 yards per reception. It was the beginning of what would become a Hall of Fame career.

Heading into the 1964 season, Shula was confident in his offense but anxious about his defense. His primary concern was replacing Marchetti, whom most considered the best defensive end in pro football. He had retired after the 1963 season, and during the exhibition season it became clear the defense was sorely missing his pass rush and leadership. Fortunately, at least for the Colts, Rosenbloom convinced the thirty-seven-year-old Marchetti to unretire. "He came back just before our third exhibition against the Cardinals in St. Louis," Shula recalled, "and he played a good deal of the game with his tongue hanging out to his knee pads—and he still played better that day than any other defensive end."[15]

Marchetti stood 6-foot-4 and weighed 245 pounds and was known as "Gino the Giant," less for his size than for the impact he had on opposing offenses. He was one of the NFL's first great edge pass rushers. Statistics on sacks weren't kept in those days, but Marchetti believed he had nine in one contest. He heard someone coming up behind him after a game against San Francisco. It was Bob St. Clair, the 49ers' Hall of Fame tackle. Marchetti thought St. Clair was going to punch him. Instead, he put his hand on Marchetti's shoulder and said, "I just want to say I touched you once today."[16]

With Marchetti anchoring the defense and Unitas throwing to Berry, Mackey, and Jimmy Orr, the other end, and handing off to a healthy Moore, the Colts appeared primed for a run at the 1964 Western Conference title. They faced Minnesota in the first game of the season and, in Shula's words, "got the hell kicked out of us." Shula believed most teams disregarded Baltimore's running game in hopes of stopping Unitas, and so he planned to throw sparingly and run the ball to control the clock. In those days, teams typically ran more than they threw anyway. But the Vikings beat the Colts at their own game, rushing for more than 300 yards. The final score was 34–24.

On the flight home—"and it was a long, long trip that night from Minneapolis," he said—Shula worried about what would happen the following week against Green Bay. If the Vikings could run like they had against his defense, what would the Packers do? But the Colts prevailed, 21–20. "We had proved something to ourselves," Shula said. "I think no one was really convinced before that we were a championship team. After the Packer game, we knew we could do it."[17]

The following week, they demolished the defending NFL champions, the Chicago Bears, 52–0, Unitas throwing for three scores and Moore running for another. Shula called it "as perfectly played a game as I have ever seen." Baltimore won its next eight in a row, including another victory over Green Bay and a 17–14 revenge of its loss to Minnesota. It clinched the Western Conference title against Los Angeles on November 22. The final three games were anticlimactic: a desultory 14–3 win over San Francisco, a loss to Detroit, and a rout of Washington in the final regular-season contest. Shula figured it was good the Colts had clinched early; it allowed the backups to see some game action and gave the banged-up starters time to heal.

The Cleveland defense faced a seemingly impossible task against Baltimore: stop one of the greatest offenses in NFL history. It was going to require some imagination. That's where Bernie Parrish came in. He lived a block from Collier in Aurora, and the two rode back and forth to practice all season, talking football all the way. The two men were much different in temperament, but they shared a devotion for studying football, and they got along well. Collier made Parrish the defensive signal caller in 1964. Most teams had linebackers do it, and Galen Fiss had done it for the Browns in the past. But Collier recognized that Parrish understood the game better than anyone on the defense, and it wasn't that unusual. Shula had called signals when he played for Baltimore, as Tom Landry had with the Giants.

Fiss and Parrish were roommates, and trouble could have ensued between them when Collier made the switch, but Fiss was even-tempered and respected Parrish's knowledge of the game. Parrish watched film at home at night, which wasn't done much back then. He'd track receivers' tendencies, and then he'd go over what he'd learned with his teammates. "It reached the point where he forced most of us to watch more film to keep up with him," Fiss said. Added Paul Wiggin, "Not only did Bernie have a lot of influence on our defense in 1964, but I think Bernie left his mark on the NFL in terms of how players should prepare themselves."[18]

Collier encouraged Parrish to serve as a player-coach. Just as he had won over Jim Brown by allowing him freedom to express himself, he recognized Parrish's football brilliance and tapped into it. In contrast to Paul Brown, Parrish said, Blanton was "all ears and cooperation."[19]

Parrish was a pit bull, regularly arguing strategy with the coaches and his teammates in meetings. One day Collier said, "Bernie, it sounds to me that you'd like to be the defensive coordinator." "No, you're wrong," Parrish replied. "I want your job."[20] Collier chuckled, which angered Parrish. He was serious; he believed no one could do a better job of coaching than he could.

In the two weeks leading up to the title game, Parrish studied film of Baltimore's defense as well as its offense, and he noticed the Colts' cornerback Lenny Lyles's success with the bump-and-run defense. Lyles lined up in front of the receiver and knocked him off his route before he could get into it. The receiver either needed to make his move earlier or change his path. The bumping at the line of scrimmage disrupted the timing between quarterback and receiver.

Cleveland had employed a zone defense all season, playing off the receivers to avoid being beaten long—the rubber band defense—and Parrish figured Unitas would expect more of the same. But what if the Browns switched to a man-to-man defense and challenged the Colts' receivers before they could complete their patterns? Parrish didn't envision the classic bump-and-run; instead, he and Walter Beach would engage the Baltimore receivers before they reached the first-down marker. "We understood, based on Bernie's strategy, if it was third and eighteen we weren't going to retreat any more than fifteen yards," Beach said. "It could have been third and four; it would be the same. We narrowed the distance and gave them less room to maneuver."[21]

On its face, having Beach cover Berry appeared a mismatch. Berry was in the tenth year of his Hall of Fame career, and though hardly an imposing figure, he could run routes and catch passes better than anyone in the league. He'd caught only thirty-three passes in three years at Southern Methodist, but the Baltimore coaches saw something they liked and picked him as a "future choice" in the twentieth round of the 1954 draft. He stood 6-foot-2 and weighed little more than 175 pounds when he joined the Colts. "A skinny-assed kid," Ewbank said. "He was so frail, you shuddered every time he got hit."[22] Two years later, Unitas's first full season with Baltimore, he caught forty-seven passes for a league-leading 800 yards.

Berry and Unitas stayed after practice, working on their timing, and at night they studied film on the wall of Berry's apartment. When Moore joined the team, Berry invited him to work with them. It was all about timing, he explained, and the more they worked on it, the better they'd be. "It's like music," Berry told Moore. "The same beat has to be playing in all of our heads."[23]

Berry was said to be so blind without his glasses or contacts he couldn't read anything smaller than the *E* on the eye chart. His opponents said the only thing he could see was the ball. One of his legs was shorter than the other, and he wore a back support. He went on *What's My Line* and stumped the panel. He tried everything to gain an edge, including tinted goggles for a game in Los Angeles. When a teammate asked him why he was wearing them, he explained that the sun was going to set at 5:01, and he wanted to be ready. He enlisted his wife to throw to him during the off-season. She became proficient at the 10-yard down and out, but he also told her to throw the ball behind him, at his feet, over his head, all for him to learn to catch bad passes.

A Colts fan rented Berry a room in a vacant mansion in a Baltimore neighborhood. Fellow receiver Alex Hawkins drove by one night and saw the light on in his room. "Here we are living it up in the outside world," Hawkins said to the teammate riding with him, "and there's old Raymond in his haunted house, drawing pass routes and running his projector."[24]

Following Parrish's lead, Beach charted Berry's patterns on graph paper. The more he studied, the more confident he became. "For me it was simple," he said. "Raymond Berry didn't have the speed to hurt me deep; so I knew there was no way he could run by me. He was going to beat me on the subtle moves. Once we interrupted those subtle moves, we were in the catbird seat."[25]

Parrish would cover Orr, a smaller but faster receiver than Berry. He caught forty passes in '64, three fewer than Berry, but for more yardage and for an average of more than 21 yards per reception, best in the NFL. While Berry relied more on knowledge and precision, Orr played instinctually. He also was a good open-field runner. "When he caught the ball," Parrish said, "he was damn tricky and dangerous." The *Plain Dealer* asked an NFL coach to rate the matchup. "Orr is as clever as anyone Parrish has ever played against," he said.[26]

The Colts were confident, and with good reason. They figured they could pick apart Cleveland's zone pass defense, and if the Browns decided to play man-to-man they expected to have no trouble adapting. They doubted Beach and Parrish could cover Berry and Orr.

Arthur Daley of the *New York Times* predicted a Baltimore victory, and most people shared his view. "The statistics offer the shocking proof that Cleveland has yielded more yards to the opposition than any other ball club in the league, worse than even the New York Giants," he wrote.

"To the Colts this spells out opportunity—in capital letters."[27]

CHAPTER EIGHTEEN

Dick Schafrath and Gary Collins lived next door to each other in Aurora and rode to practice together in Schafrath's VW Bug. Collins wasn't a fan of the car. "Schaf, the truck tires are higher than our car," he complained. "This thing scares the hell out of me."[1] The defroster didn't work, and the windshield was constantly fogging or freezing over. Collins had to hang out the passenger window and clean it off as they maneuvered down the street. Sometimes they ended up driving on the sidewalk. During the two weeks leading up to the title game, Collins assured Schafrath the Browns would prevail; not only that, but he would win the Chevrolet Corvette awarded to the game's most valuable player.

"Why is that?" Schafrath asked.

"I've watched the Colts with [Paul] Warfield and Dub [Jones], and the way we've got this game planned they can't cover Paul and me one on one. He's got more speed, so they're probably going to worry more about him than me," Collins explained. "I'm going to win that Corvette."

It took a while, but Schafrath eventually came around to Collins's way of thinking. He became so sure, he booked a room and a band, Phil Palumbo and Pals from Akron, for an after-game celebration. It cost him $400. He told his wife what he'd done, and she responded, "You what?"

"I paid for this band," he said. "We're having a party."

She said, "Well you and I might be the only ones there."

Schafrath remained confident Cleveland would win, but he conceded, "My wife had me worried."[2]

The game plan Collins laid out made sense. Warfield was gaining more and more attention, both from Cleveland's opponents and in the media. *Sports Illustrated* called him the best receiver to enter the NFL in the past decade. Collier compared him to the former Browns great Mac Speedie, and as was his style, the coach spared no words in explanation.

"I always think of Mac Speedie as the finest receiver I ever had anything to do with," he said. "He would run his pattern exactly on every play. Some receivers get too impatient and cut too soon and catch the quarterback off stride, but with Speedie the quarterback could throw ahead of the cut and know Speedie would be there. Warfield is running his patterns like that now. And he has something else Speedie had, although it isn't as highly developed yet as it was in Speedie. He seems to have an instinctive knowledge of where people are as he runs. Maybe it's just extra-wide peripheral vision, but he has it. And he has what I call in the great instinctive runners a little weave, a natural move that fakes a defender out of position and adds to the knack of getting free."[3]

Collier paused, and the reporters scribbled. A look of contemplation crossed his face. He was praising Warfield, as well he should have, but he realized he was failing to provide necessary context, as any good teacher would. "This is a fine boy and a fine athlete, but he is only potentially a great receiver," he said. "He has a lot of work to do. If he wants to do it, he can be tremendous. But I don't want people to expect too much of him, especially when they start doubling him. A rookie can't always recognize double coverage; that takes time. So if he gets shut out once in a while, well, even the good veterans get shut out. What we would hope is that if a defense commits that much personnel to Warfield we can go to Collins or another receiver. Collins is especially good at catching the ball in a crowd."[4] It's unlikely the Colts paid attention to what Collier was telling the press, but they should have.

Shula figured the best way for Baltimore to defend Cleveland was to establish its running game and control the ball, thus keeping Jim Brown off the field. Brown couldn't beat them if he was on the sideline. But Cleveland's passing game also had Shula worried. At the beginning of the 1964 season, he had faced a problem just the opposite of Collier's. While Baltimore needed to strengthen its running attack to balance its passing, Cleveland needed a better passing game to balance its running. To Shula's way of thinking, his old mentor had succeeded. "Frank Ryan improved as the season wore on," he said. "He mixed up his calls, hitting Warfield a lot, but going to Gary Collins almost as much, and in a couple of games frequently throwing to Johnny Brewer, their tight end." Shula decided to employ a mix of zone and man-to-man coverage. To neutralize Warfield, the Colts planned to double-team him, just as Collins predicted. They would station Lenny Lyles close to the line of scrimmage, where he would try to disrupt the young receiver before he could run his route. "You always put pressure on a rookie," Shula said.[5]

Lyles would receive help from a safety or a linebacker. Collins would be covered primarily by one man, cornerback Bobby Boyd. Collins stood 6-foot-4; Boyd, 5-foot-10.

At fifty-eight, Blanton Collier was one of the older coaches in the league, but he had the energy of a much younger man. One writer said that if a stranger guessed his age, he'd miss by ten years. Much of it had to do with his positive outlook and his enthusiasm for studying and teaching football. At the end of a long day during training camp he was known to watch film in his room after everyone else had gone to sleep. "I guess I don't get tired because this is fun for me," he said. "I just enjoy all aspects of football."[6]

Forman often watched film with him in their den at home; it was a chance to spend time with him. One night she grew tired and headed off to bed. When she awoke, she found him still at the projector. He looked up at her, surprised: "I thought you went to bed!" He took up golf and tennis in the off-season at Forman's insistence—she believed he needed to think about something other than football—and he spent time with his growing family. One of his granddaughters mispronounced his nickname as "Dorge." It became his name with the family. On vacation in Florida one morning, he strolled the boardwalk with his girls, and later in the day talk turned to peace. A granddaughter was asked if she knew what the word meant. "Yes," she answered, "walking the boardwalk with Dorge."[7]

The Colliers had settled happily into Aurora, a small town about forty miles southeast of downtown Cleveland. They lived at 126 Willard Road in the Aurora Highlands development (their address was included in a newspaper story, which was common). Despite the strain of replacing Paul Brown and all the turmoil it entailed, plus the normal pressure of heading up a professional football team, their new life was a welcome one after the way the Kentucky stint ended. Daughters Carolyn and Kay were married and lived in Kentucky, and their third daughter, Jane, worked as a stewardess for Pan Am. Carolyn and Kay and their husbands regularly made the five-hour drive to Cleveland for home games, and Blanton insisted they bring along his granddaughters. After these games, the family members piled into a car and drove home together so they could listen to Blanton rehash the game.

Forman returned to socializing and playing hostess. A reporter described her as "a bright-eyed vivacious southern belle with a drawl sweet as liquid honey." She resumed the tradition of a pot of chili for friends and coaches after games, and Blanton would sip a glass of Kentucky bourbon. Forman served a

Kentucky ham and biscuits when she could. Her mother sent the goodies up to Cleveland—"in case we get homesick," Forman said. "You can't get old Kentucky hams outside of the Blue Grass state so we find them quite a delicacy." A family friend from Kentucky requested tickets to a Browns game, and Forman told him he could have them, but he needed to bring her something in return. "So he flew up and got the tickets," she said, "and I got a juicy Kentucky ham." Their Aurora neighbors treated them with their own versions of southern hospitality. One year, the Colliers returned home from an away game to find their garage door tied with ribbons like a giant Christmas present. Looped in the middle of the bow was a bottle of champagne.[8]

Despite his success, the impression that Collier was too nice and too soft continued to dog him, and his players continued to refute it. He didn't tear them down. He pinpointed their strengths and built on them. If a player lacked confidence, he looked for a way to build it. He didn't ignore mistakes. He pointed them out and corrected them, but he didn't dwell on them; they were in the past. "Just forget about it," he would say. "I'm not going to condemn you; your teammates aren't going to condemn you. I'm behind you all the way." He didn't want uptight players. He wanted them to feel comfortable. "Have fun," he'd say. And they did. Years later, Schafrath wrote to him, "I couldn't wait to get up every morning and get to practice. I can't recall ever using an alarm clock. I hungered for more football with each passing day. I am happy that you took the time to try and satisfy that hunger."[9]

Modzelewski, playing his first season under Collier, found his laidback manner inspiring. "Blanton makes a few calm statements and to me this does the most good," Little Mo said. "He's the teacher-type, easy to play for. We're all adult and he chews you out in his own intellectual way. He knows how to get the most out of every player."[10]

The team watched film of the previous game on Tuesdays. Collier would run a play over and over, as many as 100 times. The players kept count. "Each time you see something different, something you haven't seen before," Warfield said. "He made film-watching an art, a science, for players and coaches."[11] He talked about how much each of them relied on one another, how if one of them didn't do his job then it created a breakdown that affected them all. One game, Warfield dropped a pass he should have caught. "We have a good play drawn up here," Collier said as film of the play appeared on the screen. He ran it over and over, reviewing how each player had performed. He started on the right side of the line, opposite Warfield, with tight end John Brewer. Next came right tackle

Monte Clark, then right guard Gene Hickerson, and on down the line. "The guards, the tackles, the center—they all executed their blocks," he said. He then moved to the backfield: Collins, Ernie Green, Brown. "The backs ran their patterns," he said. Then the quarterback. Ryan dropped back seven steps before throwing, and Collier counted each of them. "The quarterback threw a perfect pass," he said. And then silence. He didn't need to say what was evident. Everyone but Warfield had done his job. "I felt like I had let down the entire team," he said.[12]

Collier's teaching, his innovations regarding positive thinking and psycho-cybernetics, even his soothing southern drawl stuck with the players off the field. They began to see things through his eyes, to think as he did. Brown visualized himself carrying the ball as he walked down the street, and he startled passersby by talking to himself. Most coaches only had a grip on players when they were on the field, but Collier was in their heads all the time, even when they were sleeping.

Cleveland's success in 1964 was the result of a number of moves Collier had made over the past two seasons. He had maintained continuity by retaining the club's longtime coaches: Fritz Heisler, the offensive line coach; Howard Brinker, the defensive coordinator; and Ed Ulinski, the linebacker coach. He also brought in two valuable assistants: Dub Jones and Nick Skorich. Jones took over the offensive meetings because of Collier's hearing trouble, and during games he sat in the press box and relayed information down to the sideline. Jones encouraged Ryan to throw deep downfield, and that became more of a strength of the Cleveland passing game. "He had a belief that if you had receivers that were fast and a quarterback who could drill it you should work it," Ryan said.[13] When the defense was on the field, Ryan talked with Jones on the phone about the next offensive series. "We all had a very clear idea of the objective of our next sequence of plays," Ryan said. "It was an extremely important facet of our success, in my opinion."[14]

Skorich joined the team as defensive line coach in 1964, following three years as head coach of the Philadelphia Eagles. He brought a high level of intensity. A native of Bellaire, Ohio, and the son of a coal miner, he smoked three packs of cigarettes during a game. He used to smoke a pipe but stopped because he bit off the stems. (He would become the team's third head coach, replacing Collier after the 1970 season.)

Collier viewed his assistants as co-coaches, and he was more interested in soliciting their input than in telling them what to do. Under Paul Brown, when the coaches sat together at meetings or meals, no one left the table until Brown did. Shortly after Collier became head coach, he and Forman had the assistants and their wives over for dinner. The conversation went on long after dessert and coffee, no one getting up. The assistants were waiting for the head coach to leave the table. "Blanton never saw himself as any different from the others," his wife said. "It never occurred to him that they were waiting for him."[15]

Personnel moves he'd made over the previous two seasons were now paying dividends. He had the foresight to move Warfield from defense to split end, thus providing Cleveland a much-needed deep threat, and he convinced Ray Renfro to stick around for a season to teach Warfield the nuances of playing the position. He added more speed in 1964 with the addition of youngsters Leroy Kelly, Clifton McNeil, and Walter Roberts, which in turn strengthened Cleveland's passing game. He strengthened the defense by giving Parrish more responsibility, moving Jim Houston to linebacker, and inserting Walter Beach into the starting lineup.

First and foremost, Collier had opened up the offense. He allowed the quarterback to call plays and make changes at the line of scrimmage. He implemented the option-blocking scheme, making the most of his talented linemen and his superstar running back, for which Jim Brown continually sang his praises. "The greatest thing about Blanton is that he knows how to utilize his forces," Brown said. "He gets more from individuals because he understands their talents and takes advantage of them."[16]

That certainly was true of Ryan. When he was with the Rams, his coaches told him he needed to do a better job of concentrating, but they never told him *how* to concentrate better. Collier, on the other hand, was sensitive to Ryan's insecurities and tried to persuade, not dictate. The two men confronted Ryan's challenges analytically, which befit both their personalities.

"I've believed for years that you can break down any action into its elements and practice each element," Collier explained. "And then when you want to perform the whole act you just pick out one element to concentrate on, to trigger your mind, to make you do those other things automatically. Now, with the passer the three things are: 1) the squaring of the shoulders and coming to balance, 2) picking out a target, and 3) throwing the ball. You practice each component until you do it almost subconsciously, almost without thinking. It's using the subconscious as a computer. You feed this information into the subconscious in practice, and then the subconscious plays back what you have stored in it."[17]

Ryan bought into Collier's approach. "He is the first coach that ever really coached me," he said. "He spent days with me, weeks. He taught me those three steps: setting, aiming, throwing. He taught me to pick out a small target on a receiver rather than just trying to hit a big blob there with arms."[18]

For all his long-winded discourses, Collier also could explain things simply, as he did with Ryan in regard to throwing to a receiver: How do you pick out a pretty girl in Grand Central Station when there are 2,000 people milling around? The first thing you do is find one, then you keep your eye on her, and you find something about her that you know you're going to recognize, and you keep looking at it. The same thing with throwing a football. Your margin of error is reduced if your focus is smaller. "So when I was throwing a ball, even in practice, I would throw at a chin instead of a face," Ryan said. "Little things like this were precious to me."[19]

The quarterback still was nervous before games, worried about fumbling or throwing an interception. Collier recognized he was overthinking his role. Ryan was so wrapped up in strategy when he got to the line of scrimmage that he forgot what he needed to do to make the play successful. The game didn't need to be so complicated. "Frank," Collier told him, "every time you try to mastermind a situation you fail more often than not."[20]

Ryan came to realize he didn't need to think through every possible scenario. Once he called the play, he needed to rely on his instincts, experience, and athletic ability. "My insight was that I shouldn't be tormented or worried or lose sleep over calling exactly the right play because there was such a tremendous variable of luck in it that I couldn't hope to be right every time," he said. "So I've become more relaxed, and when people are more relaxed they do better."[21]

Collier believed Ryan lacked maturity, which he conceded seemed odd, considering how long Ryan had been in the league. He wasn't talking about his maturity off the field; Ryan was as sophisticated and intelligent as any man on the team. "But you see he'd never really been a first-string quarterback before he came here," Collier explained. "A quarterback's got to have heart, he's got to have poise, he's got to have leadership, but he's got to have *opportunity*. Somebody has to give him the opportunity to go in there and play regardless of what mistakes he makes. Without that he can have everything else and never develop."[22]

Ryan finally had the opportunity he'd longed for and needed since joining the NFL, and under Collier's tutelage he was becoming a more focused, and at the same time a more confident and relaxed quarterback. His performance in the New York game was exhibit A. "I was coming into my abilities," he said. "I was just growing up in the sport and doing my job."[23] The result was a league-leading twenty-five touchdown passes and his first selection to the Pro Bowl.

Collins said the Browns had only a couple of extraordinary athletes—Jim Brown and Paul Warfield. "The rest of us were of average ability," he said, "and [Blanton's] teaching made the difference."[24] Collins was understating his own and his teammates' athletic abilities, but it was true that Collier made them all smarter football players. He also made them want to play and win for him, exactly the opposite of how they felt about Paul Brown in his final years. They viewed Collier as a father figure, and over the years many of them said they loved the man. "Blanton was coming from such a good place himself," Jim Brown said, "that if you were any kind of person, you never want to create any trouble for him, under any circumstances." John Wooten agreed. "Blanton believed we were a family; he treated us like we were family. . . . Most head coaches are very distant. But not Blanton. He had the ability to make you feel that you were very special."[25]

The reporters who covered the team initially were put off by Collier's calm and quiet demeanor, but they quickly warmed up to him. On Mondays he would invite them into the film room and break down the previous game, providing inside dope on what was going on with the team. It was for background so they could understand the game better and all off the record, and the reporters didn't violate his trust. Then he'd sit down with them one on one, so they would have something to use for their stories. After they were finished interviewing him, he'd ask if they had what they needed. "The man was magnificent," said radio reporter Pete Franklin. "He didn't just like reporters, he liked everyone. . . . But that was Blanton's style, and it was why we all appreciated him."[26]

Collier's hearing continued to deteriorate; he tried a variety of hearing aids and even acupuncture, an exotic treatment for the time, but nothing helped much. He managed to work around it, and those associated with the team made allowances. Ryan thought he used his hearing as a teaching tool. Collier would ask him a question. Ryan would answer, and then he'd ask the question again, saying he didn't hear. That forced Ryan to think again about the answer, and as a result he learned more by answering twice.

The players joked with Collier about his hearing on occasion, and years later they still laughed when relating a story from the 1963 Playoff Bowl. At dinner the night before the game, someone asked if they had to wear ties the next day. Collier answered, "No ties. There will be sudden death." The players roared. But for the most part, they treated him with respect. "A less intelligent group of players may have made fun of him," Monte Clark said. "But we had so much respect for Blanton that we worked with him. Besides, we were a very mature group, and we knew better than to ridicule someone such as Blanton."[27]

Press conferences could be a problem. Collier's answers sometimes didn't follow the reporters' questions. "We liked Blanton so much that no one would say, 'Hey, I didn't ask you that,'" said Tom Melody of the *Beacon Journal*. "Rather, another reporter would ask that same question a few minutes later. We sort of took care of each other and Blanton that way."[28]

The contract extension Collier signed prior to the title game was a logical reward for all he'd achieved, as well as affirmation of Modell's decision to hire him. The *Plain Dealer*'s Heaton pointed out that the coach and owner complemented each other well. "It's been a blend of success on the field plus excellent promotion which has brought record-breaking crowds to the Stadium the past two seasons," he wrote. "The combination of Modell and Collier has proved good for pro football in Cleveland."[29]

CHAPTER NINETEEN

The Ryan house was full of friends and relatives the night before the game, including Frank's mother and sister in town from Texas. George Peters, an assistant sports editor for the *Plain Dealer*, stopped by to pick up Joan's latest column. Two of the Ryan boys were in the front yard throwing a football, and neighbors were just leaving. They had dropped by with trays, mugs, and other souvenirs imprinted with the paper's front page, touting the Browns as Eastern Conference champions. They'd bought them at Higbee's and wanted Frank's autograph. Peters reminded Joan of a column she'd written earlier in the season. In it, she had noted some omens that pointed to Cleveland playing for the title. The first came in August, when Frank wrote her saying he'd rented the house in Lyndhurst though January 1 instead of their customary December 20. Next, Dottie Modzelewski, Dick's wife, told Joan she had a feeling the team was going all the way. The last time she'd felt that way was 1956, when Mo played for the champion Giants. And lastly, Frank had set up two speaking engagements for *after* the season. He'd never done that before and usually was one of the first players to head home after the last game. Confidence seemed to pervade the house, Peters said.[1]

Paul Wiggin came by to pick up Frank, and Joan stood in the hallway, the frigid air blowing in through the open front door. Frank seemed to be looking through her. "'Oh, my goodness,'" she thought to herself. "'He thinks he's going to win.' And I knew then we would."[2]

The Browns spent the night before the title game at the Pick-Carter Hotel on Prospect Avenue. As usual, they attended a movie together, as did the Colts. The name of the movie is lost to history (it might well have been the James Bond flick *Goldfinger*, released earlier that month), but the Cleveland players remembered well being hassled by the Colts. "You better go back and get some sleep," they said. And, "Why are you here? Why aren't you watching the game film?" The Colts were a rowdy bunch, especially the defensive players, with a long tradition of nastiness, dating to the championship teams of the 1950s. Ryan considered them "ugly people."[3]

Gino Marchetti was an imposing figure, as was the other defensive end, Ordell Braase, and outside linebacker Steve Stonebreaker was known to shoot his mouth off. But by far the scariest of them all was middle linebacker Bill Pellington. His teammates considered him the most intense player ever to wear a Baltimore uniform. He was a leader of the defense along with Marchetti, but while Marchetti was a gentleman and led by example, Pellington led by intimidation. If a player made a mistake, Pellington would be in his face. No one crossed him.

"I keep valiantly claiming I'm not afraid of the Big Bad Colts," Joan wrote in her column published the day of the game. "But I have to admit a small fear of the middle linebacker Bill Pellington. He was the cause of Frank's only injury in pro football."[4] In 1961, Pellington unloaded on Ryan as he was passing. The hit separated his shoulder and knocked him out of the game. Pellington was known to use his forearm as a clothesline, in practice on his teammates as well as in games. Legend has it he nearly killed a player in a College All-Star game. The kid came across the middle, and Pellington caught him in the throat. The back of his head was the first thing to hit the ground. He swallowed his tongue and doctors had to perform a tracheotomy on the field to save his life. Joan had good reason to worry.

The Colts' cockiness at the movie agitated some of the Browns. "They were acting like they'd already won it," groused second-year defensive tackle Jim Kanicki.[5] Others, especially veterans like Dick Schafrath, took it in stride. Nothing the Baltimore players could say was going to throw them off their game or motivate them further. Their confidence had been growing all week. "Monday and Tuesday, we were ready," Schafrath said. "We could have done anything. We didn't have to go to bed."[6]

The Baltimore players weren't the only ones sure of the outcome. "To be realistic about it, the championship game of 1964 already has been played," *Sports Illustrated* reported. "Baltimore won it in October by beating Green Bay for the second time." The magazine was so confident the Colts would win, it arranged for Don Shula to write a story beforehand, something along the lines of "How We Won the Championship." "Tex Maule did all the reporting," photographer Neil Leifer explained, "and the piece was written before the game, leaving only the final score and a few details to be added." Leifer set up a photo with Shula and Johnny Unitas standing behind a see-through "blackboard" on which a play was diagrammed in red paint. "The picture worked beautifully and would have made a great cover," Leifer said, "except for one small problem."[7]

The Browns had a small problem of their own. Ninowski had come down with a virus and was hospitalized. He'd lost fifteen pounds and wasn't expected to be ready by game day. Collier told Ross Fichtner he was the backup quarterback. He gave him the offensive game plan and told him to study it. Fichtner declined. He'd step in if needed, but he wasn't going to take time to learn the offense the night before the game. He told Collier he'd do better if he just threw him in and didn't give him time to think about it.

On Sunday morning, Bernie Parrish stepped off the elevator at the Pick-Carter and it seemed like all 80,000 fans were in the lobby. Colts backers swarmed all over, and a chartered bus sat outside with a sign on it: "Colt Corral No. 10." A guy in a white ten-gallon cowboy hat, red-checkered shirt, and string tie played taps on a bugle.

The Browns gathered for their pregame meal in the Pick-Carter's Aviation Room. Many of the players were too nervous to eat. Monte Clark nearly lost his lunch. "Jesus Christ," John Wooten said. "If you're going to throw up, wait till Marchetti is across the line from you."[8]

Clark had plenty to worry about. Marchetti used a vicious head slap to knock the blocker across from him off balance as he began his rush toward the quarterback. "He could be physically punishing," Clark said, "but he didn't just run you over. Sometimes he went around you. He was quicker than he looked. But most of all, he was relentless." Sitting at his locker before the game, Clark pondered whether to tape his injured knee. Would it help or hinder him in blocking Marchetti? "I'd tape it and then I'd take it off," he recalled. "I don't know how many times I did that, but there was a huge mound of tape next to my locker when I decided to go without the support."[9]

Equipment manager Morrie Kono greased Schafrath's jersey with Vaseline so Braase couldn't get a grip on him. On Saturday Schafrath's friend and attorney from Wooster, Hank Critchfield, called him. Critchfield had been talking to a friend in the Cleveland organization about the upcoming game plan. "I don't want to put any pressure on you, Dick, but I understand they're going to double Marchetti," Critchfield said. "You have Braase one on one and they think that's where it's going to break down."

"Thanks for the vote of confidence," Schafrath responded.[10]

Schafrath considered Braase the most consistent player on the Baltimore defense. "He never let up; he was constantly going," he said. "He wasn't great, but if you let up for one second, you were gone." He believed he could handle Braase on run plays because he was bigger and stronger. He was more worried about Braase's pass rush. Like Marchetti, Braase knocked his opponent off balance (mentally as well as physically) with a slap to the helmet. Schafrath was an inch taller, and he realized that when Braase lifted his arm to take a swing at him he would expose his chest. He decided to beat him to the punch, literally. He would bring his fist up into Braase's chest when he wound up to whack him. "It was an inside punch, starting at his waist and going right up into his chest," Schafrath said. All week leading up to the game, he envisioned himself doing it.[11]

Trainer Leo Murphy taped up the players and administered painkilling shots. He injected Parrish with Novocain in the ball of his foot to help him deal with a painful case of Morton's neuroma, and Parrish dosed himself with 70 milligrams of Dexedrine, his regular game-day routine.

Ninowski entered the locker room, much to Fichtner's delight, but looking a bit green. Nino had awakened that morning in the hospital feeling well enough to play. He looked sharp while warming up on the sidelines before the game, prompting Dub Jones to say, "We ought to put you in the hospital more often."

Gary Collins strode into the locker room and spied Wiggin lying on a training table. "How you feel?" he asked.

"Nervous," Wiggin said.

"Not me," Collins said, shaking his arms to show how loose he felt. "I'm going to catch five today, three for touchdowns, and I'm going to drive that Corvette home."[12]

Schafrath had arranged for his uncle, Bill Schafrath of Wooster, to be on the field as a photographer. Shortly before kickoff, Schafrath sauntered over and said, "You've been taking a lot of pictures. Make sure there's film in that."

"Something's wrong," his uncle said. "Every time I take a picture I can't see out of the lens." Schafrath studied the camera. "He'd been out there forty-five minutes taking all kinds of pictures and the lens cap was still on it," he said. Schafrath pointed it out, and his uncle removed the cap. "After the game started," Schafrath said, "he got a few photos."[13]

Tony Tomsic was on the sideline shooting for *Sport* magazine. A Cleveland Heights native, he was a staff photographer for the *Press*, but the newspaper allowed him to freelance for other publications. He worked the Baltimore sideline, because *Sport* wanted shots of Unitas. He found the turf soft but in good shape, and the weather didn't feel too cold. This wasn't Tomsic's first championship game involving the Browns. In 1950, when he was fifteen, his father had taken him to the title game. He remembered Lou Groza's last-second field goal to win it. He started tagging along with Fred Bottomer of the *Press* to Browns games when he was a teenager. Now, the twenty-nine-year-old was shooting the championship game of his hometown team. (Tomsic photographed the first Super Bowl in 1967 and the next forty-seven in a row, one of only four men to do so; his string was broken in 2015, after he suffered a stroke.)

CBS televised the game nationally, but even though it was sold out Cleveland fans had to leave town to watch the broadcast. Modell could have requested the game be aired inside the seventy-five-mile blackout radius, but he declined. The Cleveland City Council passed a resolution asking him to allow the game to be televised locally, but still he refused. He also refused closed-circuit showings in local theaters. He said it would be unfair to those who already had bought tickets. That might have made sense to a New York ad man, but it didn't sit well with Clevelanders. "Even in 1964, with actions such as these Modell demonstrated a fundamental misunderstanding of the mentality of the Browns fan," Terry Pluto wrote years later.[14]

Rozelle gave WJW Channel 8 executives permission to show the game on tape delay Monday night. It was the first time an NFL title game was rebroadcast on television, and 70 percent of Cleveland households watched.

Hotel rooms filled up quickly outside the blackout radius. "Business has been tremendous," said Dorothy Caveney, reservations manager for Holiday Inn. "We've been booking for Erie for six weeks. There must have been a lot of optimists." The chain's motels also were filling up in Toledo, Sandusky, and Ashtabula. All of the rooms had televisions, of course—and a six-person limit, Caveney emphasized. Greyhound ran buses from Cleveland to the Holiday Inn in Sandusky for $12.95, including a buffet lunch in a lounge with multiple televisions.

As the second half began, the Colts had the option of taking the ball or playing with the wind at their back. Shula chose to receive. This left Collier with the choice of which end of the field to defend. Normally he preferred to have the wind at his back at the end of the game, in case he needed a field goal to win it. But he decided to take advantage of the wind in the third quarter while it was still blowing. "If we gave it to the Colts and they got hot," he said, "we might be out of the game by the time we got it in the fourth."[15]

With a gale blowing at his back, Groza kicked the ball out of the end zone to open the half. On Baltimore's second play, Unitas dropped back, faked a throw to his right, and then threw back to his left toward fullback Jerry Hill on a perfectly designed screen pass. Hill had a convoy of blockers in front of him and plenty of open field, but he dropped the pass. He picked the ball up off the turf, and started running. As the Cleveland defenders closed in, he hurled it to the ground in frustration. As in the first half, when Galen Fiss had knifed through and thrown Lenny Moore for a loss on a screen pass, Baltimore had lost an opportunity for a long gain, if not a touchdown.

The Colts faced fourth down on their 23-yard line. Tom Gilburg, a reserve tackle, punted, and the kick went off the side of his foot for 25 yards. The Browns took over on the Baltimore 48-yard line. Ryan completed a flare pass to Jim Brown for 11 yards, but the Colt defense held, and Groza booted a 43-yard field goal for the first score of the game. Collier's decision to take the wind had paid its first dividends. "The wind was a big factor—that's what broke up the ball game," Shula said afterward. "They got us backed up in a corner at the closed end of the field and at the same time they got the momentum."[16]

On Baltimore's next possession, Unitas threw into the left flat to Hill. Fiss was about 10 yards away, but the "Earthshaker" came roaring over and knocked Hill onto his rear end after a 2-yard gain. "Legally, it could have been introduced in court as aggravated assault and battery, with intent to do bodily harm," Bob August wrote in the *Press*.[17] Kanicki then threw Unitas for a 2-yard loss. The young tackle was more than holding his own against Jim Parker, much to everyone's surprise. "Hard to tell about this boy," one NFL coach said of Kanicki before the game. "He hasn't played that much. He's big and strong and steady, but until he develops, he's below the league average as a defensive tackle." Parker, on the other hand, was in a class by himself. "There isn't another guard in football who can come close to him," the coach said. "It's like trying to move a mountain to get by him."[18]

Kanicki was lined up next to Bill Glass, and the Browns figured Glass would be double-teamed often on pass plays. Collier told Kanicki he'd have to go it alone against Parker. "You're stronger than him," Collier said. "Do what you do best, and that's hold your ground." Modzelewski also talked to

Kanicki throughout the game, as he had all season, telling him when to rush hard, when to look for the run. "I was scared to death before the game, me playing head on Jim Parker, maybe the best blocking lineman in the league," Kanicki said. "We figured that if I would hand fight instead of firing out I could do better. It worked pretty well." For his part, Parker was expecting Unitas to get rid of the ball in the usual three or four seconds, and he eased up. Kanicki didn't. "I just kept coming," he said.[19]

Unitas tried to thwart the Cleveland pass rush with screen passes, and on third down he connected with fullback Tony Lorick in the flat. But Fiss again read it and tackled Lorick after a short gain. The Cleveland captain was playing the game of his life. The Colts punted into a small gale, and this time Gilburg managed a 35-yarder that left the Browns at their own 32.

On second down, Ryan unleashed the sweep. The Browns lined up in a double-wing formation, with Ernie Green as a flanker on the left and Brown as the only back behind Ryan. Baltimore's outside linebacker, Don Shinnick, cheated toward the middle, and the defensive back opposite Green played about 7 yards off of him. Ryan pitched to Brown, and Green cracked back on Shinnick. Brown swept around end with Schafrath and Wooten leading the way and was dragged down from behind after a 46-yard gain. The Browns had a first down at the Baltimore eighteen.

It was the longest gain of the day by either side to that point, and Ryan felt the momentum swing to Cleveland. He was tempted to call another sweep, but he worried the Colts might blitz into it, resulting in a loss. He considered a run up the middle, but what if the Colts pinched inside and throttled it? He decided to go for broke and send Collins to the right corner of the end zone.

The play called for Collins to slant in a couple of yards and then break sharply toward the corner. As Ryan was about to take the snap, he noticed Bobby Boyd and safety Jerry Logan gesturing to each other, looking confused. "We couldn't hear our calls," Boyd said later. "The guy who was supposed to take the middle deep took the outside."[20] As a result, when Collins slanted back outside toward the corner, Boyd and Logan both met him. The Colts had blown their coverage, but the play wasn't going to work as designed.

Ryan set himself to throw, but seeing Collins covered he stepped forward in the pocket and waited. Collins broke off his pattern and slanted instead toward the goalposts. Ryan recognized the improvisation and fired the ball just as Baltimore defensive tackle Fred Miller grabbed a fistful of the "13" on the back of his jersey. The goalpost was positioned on the goal line in those days, and the pass sailed between the uprights. Ryan worried it would hit the crossbar, as had happened several times during the season. Later, Collins admitted that he had flinched, and though he bobbled the ball momentarily he pulled it to his chest for the touchdown. The play's success, Ryan explained, was the result of a "gross adjustment" on both of their parts. "I realized we'd gotten away with this thing," he said. "It wasn't at all the play we had called. But all good football teams do that. They realize they don't have a lock on it, so they scramble a little bit. That scramble worked really well."[21]

The Browns now unexpectedly, unpredictably, unbelievably led 10–0. The announcer for the Baltimore radio network seemed stunned as he intoned, "And all of a sudden this football game has taken on a completely different complexion." Up in the stands, Bob Migliorino and the other Cleveland fans leaped out of their seats. The guys in the row behind him splattered Migliorino and his buddy with beer. "We didn't give a damn," Migliorino said, "didn't dampen our spirits at all because we were winning." Migliorino's seat was on the 50-yard line but only twenty rows up. At 5-foot-9, he had trouble seeing the action over the heads of the players on the bench. "They were jumping around," he said. "It didn't matter. We were there. We were *there!*"[22]

Groza kicked off, and Leroy Kelly spun Lorick down at the 11-yard line. A penalty against Baltimore took it back another 5 yards. The Cleveland defense held and Gilburg punted, this time to the Cleveland 39-yard line. The Browns moved into Baltimore territory, and, facing third and long, Ryan decided to call a hook and go to Collins. It was a variation of the hook pattern in which the receiver sprinted straight ahead for 10 yards and then turned and looked back at the quarterback. On the hook and go, the quarterback pumped his arm as though to throw, and the receiver then spun and headed downfield. Boyd had been playing Collins close on hook patterns, and at halftime Collins told Ryan he thought a hook and go would work. Ryan figured this was the perfect time to try it.

Collins stopped and hooked, looking back at Ryan, and both Boyd and Logan came racing up and collided, Boyd falling to the ground. Collins sprinted toward the end zone, no one within 20 yards of him. "That was a little scary when I first threw it," Ryan said. "I realized I was lobbing it high in the air, but I was afraid I'd overthrown him. But he put his jets on, as it were, and got it. That was really a great play. It worked exactly as it was supposed to work."[23]

Collins also worried as he waited for the ball to fall into his arms. "Boy, if I'd dropped that one," he said, "I would have caught a jet right out of Cleveland."[24]

He slammed the ball twice against his left palm with glee as he leaped like a giraffe across the baseball pitcher's mound in the end zone.

The Browns now led 17–0 with six minutes left in the third quarter, and Joan Ryan couldn't believe what she was seeing. She'd been so nervous that morning she'd forgotten to put on a slip, and now, despite the freezing cold, she threw off her coat and scarf. "My body temperature had risen to the occasion," she said.[25]

The Colts were driving early in the fourth quarter, but Unitas and Moore muffed the exchange on a handoff, and Wiggin recovered at the Cleveland 47. Ryan mixed passes and runs to move the Browns deep into Baltimore territory. Brown swept 23 yards to the Baltimore 14, and on the next play Paul Warfield caught his only pass of the game, beating Lenny Lyles for a 13-yard gain to the Baltimore 1-yard line. Brown was stopped just short of the goal line on third down—he lunged forward and grabbed the goalpost and tried to pull himself across—and Groza kicked a 10-yard field goal from a sharp angle to the right. The kick gave Groza forty-nine points in championship games, the most in NFL history. Cleveland led 20–0.

Baltimore's last best scoring chance came in the fourth quarter when Unitas threw long to Jimmy Orr, who'd beaten Parrish along the right sideline. Orr bobbled the ball as he went out-of-bounds at the Cleveland 14, and the pass was called incomplete.

The Browns scored in the fourth quarter on yet another Ryan-to-Collins pass. The 6-foot-4 Collins sprinted down the right sideline in front of the Browns bench with the 5-foot-10 Boyd covering him like "a shawl over cold feet," according to one observer. The Collins-Boyd mismatch wasn't what it seemed. Boyd, a five-year veteran from Oklahoma, where he'd played quarterback for Bud Wilkinson's powerhouse Sooners, had intercepted nine passes in 1964. He was a consensus All-Pro and was chosen to play in the Pro Bowl. That he was running stride for stride with Collins was no surprise.

Ryan lofted the ball 50 yards in the air, leading Collins so that he wouldn't break stride. Boyd's right arm was draped over Collins's right shoulder, and his left hand was on his face mask as the ball dropped into the crook of Collins's right arm. ("He knocked the ball right into my arms," Collins said later.[26]) As Collins pulled it in, Boyd slid down his back and tried to yank the ball loose. He fell to the ground as Collins broke free and sprinted for the end zone. Collins's superior height and the perfect pass had made the difference.

"It was a good throw because he didn't have to pause," Ryan said. "It was the best sort of play. He was a big guy, fast and able to get those itty-bitty guys off his behind."[27] As Collins ran through the end zone, Lyles gave him a push and he disappeared into a mob of ecstatic fans flooding onto the field. A squadron of police waded in to rescue him.

The game essentially was over, but Ryan wanted more. The Browns drove to the Baltimore 12-yard line with twenty-six seconds remaining. Fans were beginning to take over the end zone, and an official told Ryan the Colts would be willing to call the game if the Browns were. "No," Ryan said, "I want one more play." Marchetti was close by and heard him. He became incensed. Why pile it on?

Ryan called a pass play intended for John Brewer. He wanted to give his friend a shot at scoring a touchdown in the championship game. "If I was really serious about scoring another touchdown I would have thrown to someone else," he said.[28] Brewer was well covered, Ryan overthrew him, and the game ended.

Joan addressed the play in her column the following week. "In defense of Frank, let me say that his motives were noble, though misdirected," she wrote. "He wanted another touchdown . . . not to dishonor the Colts, as Gino thought, but to give John Brewer a touchdown pass, which he more than deserved for his efforts all season. Frank admits he was ill-advised in his remarks."[29]

More than half a century later, Ryan still felt bad about it, and it still grated on Shula. "That was pretty hard to live with," the Baltimore coach said.[30]

The victory set off a Christmas celebration, a New Year's party, and more, all wrapped in one. A couple thousand fans stormed the field and tore down the goalposts. One man lost his false teeth while cheering, and two others reported losing their wallets. Modell's nephew Dick Rosen was assisting Kono and Murphy on the Cleveland sideline. "What should I do?" he asked as delirious and drunk fans swarmed over them, grabbing buckets, chairs, tape, anything that would serve as a souvenir. "Forget it! Just leave," Murphy shouted. "Get to the dugout as fast as you can." A cordon of blue-clad police officers escorted Brown and Ryan through the throng and off the field.

The *Plain Dealer*'s Charles Heaton described the victory as "what well may be the best performance ever in the sparkling history of this football club." That was saying a lot, considering all the titles that had come before. But none had been so surprising—*Sports Illustrated* called it "one of the biggest of all football upsets"—and no other had been witnessed by so many.³¹ The game was watched on 336 stations across the country. CBS paid $1.8 million for the rights (more than $14 million in 2017 dollars); the DuMont Television Network paid $75,000 to air the 1951 title game between the Browns and Rams (about $700,000 in 2017 dollars), the first to be televised.

The game is best remembered for the three scoring passes from Ryan to Collins, and with good reason. Collins tied Otto Graham for most touchdowns in an NFL championship game and set a record for most touchdown catches, a mark that still stands. Yet, the significance of Cleveland's defensive performance can't be overstated. Unitas completed twelve passes for 95 yards, with a long of 16 yards. John Mackey caught one pass for 2 yards. Raymond Berry caught three passes and Jimmy Orr two. The Cleveland defense, the *New York Times* stated, had reduced Unitas to "a hesitant, vulnerable passer who lost yardage making up his mind." Cleveland's defensive strategy had worked exactly as Parrish and his mates envisioned.

"It was one of those things where everything fell our way on a given day," Wiggin said. "Everything we did went right." Wiggin played eleven years for the Browns and later served as head coach of the Kansas City Chiefs and his alma mater, Stanford University. The 1964 title game was the highlight of his career. As he walked off the field, he looked up at the light standards and thought, "I could go up there right now and scream out to the city of Cleveland anything I want and it would be OK, because I am a world champion."³²

In the locker room afterward, reporters went from player to player, seeking quotes, and the players were "*yapping*," Brown said. The star running back expressed more emotion than reporters had ever seen from him. "This was beautiful," he crowed, "just beautiful." In addition to joy, Brown felt relief. He was redeemed for his outspokenness regarding Paul Brown, and he'd silenced Otto Graham and the others who said he didn't block, he only cared about himself, and Cleveland couldn't win a title with him on the team. "So it felt GOOD to get that primate off my back," he wrote later. "I said, Self, breathe this in, and don't be in any rush. You got exactly where you wanted to go. In life that is rare."³³

Collier, his glasses steamed over, was surrounded by writers shouting for an explanation, and he patiently explained the different defensive and offensive strategies. Schafrath gave him a bear hug. "I love you, Coach," he said. Collier responded, "Mule, I love you too." Then they shook with their left hands.

Modzelewski emerged from the showers and said quietly, "Let me by, I'm wet and I'll get you wet." The writers separated, but Collier stepped forward and took him by the shoulders. "Thanks," he said, "thanks."

"It was a good trade," Little Mo replied. "I never had a better season."

"I don't know how we got him," Collier told the reporters. "I don't know how they could give him up. But we were lucky we got him."[34]

Ryan had a scrape between his eyes and welts on his nose and cheek from a brutal tackle by Marchetti. The Colts pressured him throughout the game, but it rarely affected him. He was in a zone, comparable to the win two weeks earlier in New York. "I knew what I wanted to do, and I tried to do it," he said in his usual understated way. "I think it worked pretty well." He credited the offensive line and Brown's running. "Although we didn't score in the first half, we did establish the authority of our running game," he said. "Once we had hammered home that message, there was a natural reluctance by the Colts to commit themselves too soon. It removed most of the pressure from their [pass rush]."[35]

Gene Hickerson came up to Ryan and hugged him. "Let's see, we have the greatest running back in the world," he said. "We have the greatest offensive line in the world. We have the best receivers in the world. And our quarterback, well, you could say that he is adequate." The two men laughed.[36]

As he'd predicted, Collins was named the game's MVP and won the red Corvette, a three-speed convertible, and also was awarded the game ball. "We didn't give a thought about anything like a car before the game," he lied to reporters. "We just talked about winning. But I'm sure thinking about that car now."[37]

A reporter asked Parrish, "How did you fool the experts?"

"Mister," Parrish responded, "the only experts we fooled were on the field with us." Then, even awash in the celebration, he turned combative. "But like people have been saying all along, the Browns defensive backs are too small," he said. "I guess they'll just have to break up our team next season. We can't do the job."[38]

The Colts were sore losers. Marchetti said they should play two out of three and insisted Baltimore would win. Alex Hawkins said the Colts couldn't have played worse. "It makes you sick to your stomach so that you want to get out and play them again for nothing," he said. Unitas gave a short, terse interview, and when a reporter who arrived late asked a question, he responded,

"You only get one chance." A photographer asked him to pose with Shula. "See me next spring," he said.[39]

Shula placed the blame on the offense. "It never gave the defense a break," he said. "We just didn't move the ball the way this team is capable of doing. The Browns defense played well, but our lack of offense was the difference. We ruined drives by giving up the ball on fumbles and interceptions. We knew they had a fine offense, but teams had moved on their defense."[40]

Asked fifty years later whether Collier outcoached him, Shula responded, "What was the score?" Asked again, he repeated, "What was the score?" Asked a third time, he said, "When one team beats another, the coach of the winning team did a better job. That's the way it's always been, as long as the history of football."[41]

In a word, yes.

The wives, friends, and other family members were outside the locker room shrieking, kissing, and hugging. "I can't remember anything ever making me more completely happy and proud as winning with such a fine group of people," Joan said.

Frank grinned as he emerged from the locker room and kissed his mother and sister. Then, he turned to Joan and said, "Someone stole the game ball out of my locker—the one I got after we beat the Giants."

Earlier in the week, Ryan had all the players sign the ball, and he brought it to the stadium for Modell to sign. He put it on a shelf in his locker and after showering and dressing discovered it missing. He'd been awarded game balls in the past—two each from the Rams and Browns—but none meant as much. "This has to be the most rotten trick ever played on me," he muttered. "That ball meant more to me than you could ever imagine." He stormed out of the dressing room and past Fiss, who was about to hand him one of the balls used in the title game as a memento.[42]

"Frank played seven years of pro football before he quarterbacked a team to a division championship," Joan wrote in her column. "Besides that, he is a perfectionist and that game in New York is the closest he'll probably ever come to The Perfect Game. . . .

"So Frank considers this tribute by his teammates . . . something special."[43]

The loss of the ball tempered the Ryans' celebration, but they joined the rest of the team at the Sheraton. The players were introduced individually and called up to the stage. "I personally want to thank each member of this team for the darndest effort I've ever seen in pro football," Modell said. He was glowing from the antifreeze he had ingested during the game as well as the victory.

Ray Renfro had traveled from his home in Texas for the game. "I'm really proud of this team," he said. "It was a team that has been knocked plenty. People said the offense wasn't good enough and the defense was lousy. This will shut a lot of mouths."

Groza recounted that Ryan had come to him before the game and asked how he thought they'd do. "I told him we would only be as good as he was. And he was up to it today."[44]

Before leaving for Houston, Ryan issued an appeal for return of his New York game ball. "I'll gladly have another one autographed by all the Browns to give in its place next summer at Hiram," he said.[45] The theft prompted a nationwide call for its return in newspapers, television, and radio. A resident of Syracuse, New York, watching the game on television, recognized a sixteen-year-old boy roaming through the locker room during the after-game celebration and reported him to Syracuse police. The youth was known for his "collection of unorthodox sports trophies." He reportedly had once entered the Yankees' locker room with fake press credentials and stole a bat belonging to Roger Maris. He also had swiped a helmet from a Pitt-Syracuse game. How he gained access to the Cleveland locker room was unclear. Nate Wallack, the Browns' public relations director, initially said the club would send the youth an official ball. But after negative public reaction, he decided instead to send one to the police sergeant who recovered Ryan's ball. The Syracuse police department sent the game ball to Ryan in Houston.

"The recovery of the ball has now made his championship year complete," Joan wrote. The headline on her column read, "All's Well that Ends Well."

Following the game, Forman Collier and her brood gathered outside the dressing room with the players' families and friends. It seemed as though the players and coaches were in the locker room forever as they talked with reporters and posed for photos. Afterward, the Colliers headed up to Blanton's office in the stadium and rehashed the game. They were filled with joy, but relief as well. "There were many, many elements to it," Kay said. "For Daddy, I think obviously he wanted it for the team, and he wanted it for Mother, and he wanted it for Art, and I'm sure he wanted it for himself. But he was never one to put himself first."[46]

Forman was "so, so happy," Kay said. She had been watching and supporting Blanton's teams since she was twenty years old. She'd chaperoned school trips, charted shots at basketball games, played hostess to players and to boosters at Kentucky and in Cleveland. She had endured the painful and bewildering break with their best friends, Paul and Katy Brown. "She had a lot of emotion wrapped up in this. You could just feel her intensity of joy and happiness and relief," Kay said. "She always wanted Daddy to get what he deserved."[47]

Before leaving for the stadium that morning, the Collier daughters had put a bottle of champagne on ice; they'd transported it up from Kentucky with a dose of confidence. They sipped it as friends and well-wishers circulated through the house. The phone rang incessantly, and telegrams arrived from a wide variety of friends and supporters. "Congratulations," read a wire from Helen Fishback, housemother at Kentucky's Wildcat Manor. "This is real vindication." Jim Brown sent one thanking Forman for sharing her husband with the team. "Without Blanton's knowledge and integrity as a man," it read in part, "this could not have been."[48]

The next morning the Collier girls hung posters downstairs with poems and hokey sayings they made up—much as they had two years earlier when their father was named head coach of the Cleveland Browns.

Blanton came down and someone handed him a *Plain Dealer* with the headline: "Browns Capture Crown, 27–0." He sat on the stairs and held it up, posing for a Polaroid snapshot with two of his granddaughters on his lap. "The score's still the same!" he said. "The score's still the same!"[49]

EPILOGUE

One game still remained: the Pro Bowl. And it didn't end well, at least not for Frank Ryan. He was one of a half-dozen Browns chosen to play in the postseason all-star game. The others were Jim Brown, Paul Warfield, Dick Modzelewski, Bill Glass, and Jim Houston. Collier was head coach of the East, Shula of the West. The Colts still were steaming about Ryan's last-second try for a touchdown, and Gino Marchetti wanted revenge. He told reporters as much, and the papers ran with it, quoting him, "Give me one more shot at Ryan. That's all I want." In her column a week later, Joan wrote, "It was embarrassing even to Frank and me to see a pro as great as Marchetti retire in the wake of such a press buildup as he received."[1]

Early in the third quarter, Ryan dropped back to pass, and the right side of his line collapsed. Merlin Olsen roared by St. Louis guard Ken Gray and hit Ryan first, but he managed to break free. He stepped up in the pocket, and Marchetti raced by running back John Henry Johnson of Pittsburgh and grabbed him around the chest from behind. Roger Brown, all 290 pounds of him, crashed into his side, followed by Willie Davis. Ryan lay crumpled under nearly 1,000 pounds of humanity. Understandably, he wondered whether some of his East offensive teammates had plotted with Marchetti. Reporters later studied the film and concluded that Marchetti's and his mates' hits were legal. In any case, Ryan suffered a separated shoulder and concussion. He was taken to the locker room, where trainers taped up his shoulder to keep it stationary. When they tore off the tape, his skin came with it. A Houston doctor recommended surgery, but since Ryan's shoulder was raw where he'd been taped, the doctor worried about infection and decided against operating. Marchetti had indeed exacted revenge, intentionally or not.

The Ryans returned to Houston after the Pro Bowl and lived a few blocks from the Rice campus, and Frank continued working on his dissertation. He was lying in bed one night when he had an epiphany regarding a problematic aspect of his research. He rushed to his office and replicated what he'd figured out. He came home about 8:30 in the morning, and he was as ecstatic as he'd been when the Browns won the championship. He received his doctor of philosophy degree in mathematics in June 1965. "To both of us, this degree is the reward for seven years of hard work and setting other things aside," Joan said, "just as the championship was the result of five months of carefully laid groundwork, intense concentration and perfect execution."[2]

Ryan sent a copy of his dissertation to Pete Rozelle, whom he'd known since their days in Los Angeles when he was a rookie quarterback and Rozelle was general manager. He thanked Rozelle for encouraging him to work toward a PhD while also playing pro football. Rozelle responded, "I can only say that you both [Frank and Joan] are to be greatly commended for achieving such a remarkable parlay and in doing so have in every way given the NFL much more that [sic] could have given you. . . . Incidentally, if Joan could only encourage other NFL wives to become sportswriters we might in time have them in the majority and reach Utopia for quarterbacks and commissioners."[3]

The newly minted Dr. Ryan quarterbacked Cleveland to an 11–3 record and the Eastern Conference title in 1965. The Browns lost the championship game to the Packers in Green Bay, 23–12, on a field made sloppy by snow and mud. Despite having taken his team to two straight title games, Ryan remained unknown by much of the public, a reflection of the NFL's place in American society at the time, and he continued to be viewed as something of a math nerd. He was the subject of a *Sports Illustrated* profile by Jack Olsen, titled "Dr. Frank Ryan: How Smart Is Too Smart?" He appeared on the television show *I've Got a Secret*, described as a doctor of mathematics at a southwestern university. Panelists Henry Morgan, William Cullen, Betsy Palmer, and Bess Myerson failed to guess his connection to football.

Ryan was selected for the Pro Bowl again in 1965 and 1966. He led the NFL with twenty-nine touchdown passes in 1966, a Cleveland team record until Brian Sipe threw thirty in 1980. Injuries began to take their toll, and after the first three games of the 1968 season he was replaced by Bill Nelsen. The Browns waived him during training camp in 1969, and Vince Lombardi, new coach of the Redskins, signed him. He threw five passes in two years while backing up Sonny Jurgensen, then retired. He went to work as the director of information services for the U.S. House of Representatives and developed the first electronic voting system used by Congress. Lawmakers had voted by alphabetical roll call for nearly two centuries before switching to Ryan's computerized system. He later would spend ten years as athletic director at Yale, finally making it to the alma mater of his father, uncles, and brother.

Joan continued to write "Back Seat Brown" for the *Plain Dealer* until 1968, when she became pregnant with their fourth son. She kick-started her journalism career when the Ryans moved to Washington, working first for the *Washington Times,* writing two columns a week, and later for the *Washington Post.* She was a sports reporter when few women held that position. She also wrote for other newspapers and magazines and provided commentary for Washington's ABC affiliate and for NPR's *Morning Edition.* She covered everything from professional football to the Indy 500 to the Billie Jean King–Bobby Riggs "Battle of the Sexes" tennis match. Women weren't allowed in the press box when she began, and she decided against going in the men's locker rooms, instead phoning ahead to tell the teams what players she wanted to talk to and meeting them in a private room. When Frank took the Yale job and they moved to New Haven, Connecticut, she continued to produce a syndicated column for the *Washington Post* Writers Group.

The Ryans settled into semiretirement in Grafton, Vermont, in 1984 and as of this writing live there on nearly eighty acres. Frank works from an upstairs office adorned with a few photos of his playing days and of some of his "mathematics friends." He remains absorbed in mathematics, specifically the twin prime conjecture, which asserts there are an infinite number of twin primes, or pairs of primes that differ by two, for example three and five, five and seven, eleven and thirteen. As the numbers grow larger, the twin primes become less frequent. Are there an infinite number of twin primes? No one knows, and Frank is trying to find the answer. He has it narrowed to one issue he needs to resolve.

Jim Brown gained 1,544 yards in 1965, best in the league, scored twenty-one touchdowns, and was named the league's MVP. He was the NFL's all-time rushing leader, and his 127 career touchdowns were the most ever. He was thirty years old and healthy—he'd taken his share of pounding in his nine years, but he'd never missed a game.

Brown was in London filming *The Dirty Dozen* when training camp opened in July 1966. The movie was taking longer than expected, and he was absent when practices began. He had one year remaining on a two-year contract that paid him $60,000 annually. Modell stated he was suspending Brown without pay and fining him $100 each day he missed. This wasn't a smart move. Brown's movie career was taking off, and he didn't like ultimatums. He wrote the owner a letter telling him he planned to retire:

> This decision is final and is made only because of the future that I desire for myself, my family and, if not to sound corny, my race. I am very sorry that I did not have the information to give you at some earlier date, for one of my great concerns was to try in every way to work things out so that I could play an additional year.
>
> I was very sorry to see you make the statements that you did, because it was not a victory for you or I but for the newspaper men. Fortunately, I seem to have a little more faith in you than you have in me. I honestly like you and will be willing to help you in any way I can, but I feel you must realize that both of us are men and that my manhood is just as important to me as yours is to you.[4]

On July 14, 1966, Brown met with reporters on the movie set. He sat in a director's chair wearing military fatigues. "You should get out at the top," he said. "And in the last three years, with Blanton Collier and Art Modell, I have been able to do all the things I wanted to do. Now I want to devote my time to other things."[5]

Modell later admitted he shouldn't have backed Brown into a corner. "If I had told him to just forget training camp and show up when he could, I think he would have returned," he said. "But it wasn't fair to the coaches and players."[6]

Cleveland fans had trouble coming to grips with why Brown left while still so young and strong. What might the Browns have accomplished if he'd played a few more years? His departure stung less with the emergence of Leroy Kelly as his replacement. Kelly ran for more than 1,000 yards and led the NFL in rushing touchdowns in 1966. The Associated Press selected him to the Pro Bowl and named him first team. He spent ten years with Cleveland and became a Hall of Famer.

Brown continued his acting career, appearing in two dozen movies and many television programs, and he went to work building the Negro Industrial and Economic Union. He'd come up with the idea at the Pro Bowl after the 1964 championship game. In Los Angeles, he met a group of African Americans publishing a magazine called *Elegant*. "It was a good magazine and a good idea," Brown said, "but they didn't have enough money."[7] During his time working as a spokesman for Pepsi, he'd seen other black businesses struggling. He helped out how and when he could, but he could only do so much by himself; so he incorporated the union, later called the Black Industrial and Economic Union, to provide black businesses with financial and technical support. He enlisted the help of other athletes, and John Wooten and Walter Beach were among those who worked for the union. The first office was at East 105th Street and Euclid Avenue in Cleveland.

In 1967, a group of prominent black athletes met at the office for what became known as the "Ali Summit." They questioned Muhammad Ali about his opposition to the Vietnam War and his conviction to be a conscientious objector. Brown called the summit, and among those present were Ali, Bill Russell, and Lew Alcindor (later Kareem Abdul-Jabbar). They found Ali sincere in his beliefs and called a news conference to proclaim their support for him. An iconic photo by Tony Tomsic shows the summit's participants. Ali and Brown sit at a table flanked by Russell and Alcindor. Behind them stand Carl Stokes, Walter Beach, Bobby Mitchell, John Wooten, Willie Davis, and a handful of others. "It was an unforgettable moment," Beach said. "It was one of the most significant moments in my life. Ali was one of the most principled and moral human beings on the planet at the time, with the sensitivity and courage to stand."[8]

Brown continued pursuing business interests, helping others, and tackling social issues, including gang violence in Los Angeles. He is a significant figure in America's civil rights history. But, as with most things in his life, the story is more complex. He wrote a second autobiography in the late 1980s, *Out of Bounds*, which spoke to his reputation as an abuser of women. The first half of the book discussed his childhood and his time at Syracuse and with the Browns and detailed the racism he encountered. In that regard it was much like *Off My Chest*. But the second half was filled with details of his and his friends' and teammates' sexual exploits, including what they called "Creative Orgies." He explained the kind of women he preferred, using food metaphors. "I prefer girls who are young," he wrote. "When I eat a peach, I don't want it overripe. I want that peach when it's peaking." He liked his women small: "I don't mean mousy small. I mean tight. Petite. Delicate. No excess. When I get into the bedroom, I don't want to see anything that's big like me." He liked having a main girlfriend whom he could take out in public, while also enjoying women who were freaks, the ones who arrived at Cleveland Browns parties, where "we'd all bring two or three girls. . . . Those pretty girls from Cleveland were allowed to express themselves freely and creatively."[9]

He was married during most of his time with the Browns, and he and his wife, Sue, had three young children: Jim and twins Kevin and Kim. Sue had just graduated with a science degree from Tennessee State when they met, and they married not long after he joined the team. Sue was nurturing and wanted to create a home, but early on Jim informed her the standards that applied to other married couples didn't apply to him. He didn't make the rules, and so he didn't have to follow them. They divorced in 1972. In *Out of Bounds* he wrote he had no desire to marry again: "Marriage is designed to give the woman the lawful right to take most of your shit when she gets rid of you."[10]

Accusations of domestic violence and court cases dogged him for years, beginning in 1965, when he was accused of beating and sexually assaulting two teenage girls in Cleveland. One girl dropped the charge, and the other took him to court. He won the case, and she then filed a paternity suit, which she also lost. In 1968, he was accused of assault with intent to murder his twenty-two-year-old girlfriend after she was found semiconscious below the balcony of his Hollywood apartment. She declined to press charges. In 1971, he was accused of beating two women, both twenty-two, and throwing them down the stairs of his apartment. The case was dropped for lack of witnesses. In 1985, he and a twenty-two-year-old female companion were arrested on suspicion of rape and sexual battery of a thirty-three-year-old woman at his Hollywood Hills home. The charges were dismissed because of inconsistent testimony.

He ended up going to jail in 2002. Three years earlier, his new wife, Monique, had called 911 and reported he'd threatened to break her neck and was damaging her car with a shovel. A jury acquitted him of domestic threats but found him guilty of vandalism. Part of his sentence included domestic-violence counseling, which he refused, calling it dehumanizing. He also refused to pay a fine and to donate to a battered women's shelter. The judge sentenced him to six months in the Ventura County jail, and he served less than four months.

That ugly aspect of Brown's life hasn't overshadowed all he accomplished both on and off the field, and he remains a legend in Cleveland. The team unveiled a statue of him outside FirstEnergy Stadium in September 2016. Commissioned by team owners Jimmy and Dee Haslam, it shows him running with the ball tucked in his left arm, his right forearm at a right angle from his torso, primed to bang into anyone who tries to bring him down. The eighty-year-old Brown traveled from his Los Angeles home to Cleveland for the ceremony. Some of his former teammates attended, as did Cleveland's head coach, Hue Jackson, and Cleveland mayor Frank Jackson. "It's a great moment," Brown said, "because I feel it throughout my body, particularly in my heart and in my mind."

"I think it's pretty hard to argue with what Jim did as a player," Jimmy Haslam said. "I'm sure you'd get arguments from various franchises about whether he's the greatest NFL player of all time, even the greatest NFL running back, but I think it'd be pretty hard to argue that he's not the greatest Cleveland Brown of all time."[11]

Paul Brown returned to professional football in 1968 as coach and part-owner of the Cincinnati Bengals, a new franchise in the American Football League. He named it after a Cincinnati pro football team of the 1930s, and this time no one threatened to sue. "Bengals" worked as a nickname because he could animate it. Cincinnati and Cleveland didn't meet in his first two seasons, as they were in different leagues. That changed in 1970 after the NFL and AFL merged, creating two conferences within the NFL: the National Football Conference and American Football Conference. Cincinnati and Cleveland landed in the AFC's Central Division.

Blanton Collier and Brown met for the first time as opposing coaches in an exhibition at Cincinnati's Riverfront Stadium in 1970. Collier trotted toward midfield to shake Brown's hand following the game, but Brown headed directly to the locker room. Collier shrugged it off. It was his habit to shake hands after games, he said, but not Brown's. The two teams next met in Cleveland in the fourth game of the regular season. Asked whether he planned to shake hands with Brown, Collier was his usual magnanimous self. "I'll start toward the middle of the field," he said. "If he wants to shake, I'll shake. If he doesn't, I'll understand."[12] The two men spoke a few words before the game: Hello and good luck. That was it. The Browns won 30–27, and afterward Brown headed directly to the locker room. The standing-room crowd of more than 83,000 booed him.

Brown led the Bengals to the division title in 1970, Cincinnati's third year in existence. The Bengals lost to eventual champion Baltimore in the first round of the playoffs. Cincinnati returned to postseason play again in 1973 and in 1975, Brown's final season. Although his Bengal teams failed to advance beyond the first round of the playoffs, he had reaffirmed his station as one of the greatest coaches in NFL history. He already was in the Hall of Fame, inducted in 1967.

Cleveland finished 7–7 in 1970, Collier's final season with the Browns. His overall record with Cleveland was 79–38–2; his teams won four conference titles and the NFL championship. His .672 career winning percentage is nearly equal to Don Shula's and is better than those of Tom Landry and Chuck Noll; all three are in the Hall of Fame. Collier is not. He was sixty-four when he retired, still possessing the energy, health, and smarts to maintain a successful NFL career. His hearing, however, had worsened to the point where he had trouble understanding what was said on the sidelines and over the phone from the press box. He didn't want his handicap to undermine the team's success, and he decided to retire at the end of the 1970 season. He told the players after the eleventh game, a loss to the Steelers that dropped Cleveland's record to 5–6. For the first time in his eight years as head coach of the Browns, the team was in jeopardy of having a losing season. He also recognized how the losses, and the subsequent questions and criticisms of his coaching, were taking a toll on Forman, just as they had at Kentucky. On the flight back from a loss at Oakland, she held his hand and wept silently. "No one realizes what a strain my wife had been under," he told reporters. On Sundays after games, she no longer played hostess or accepted friends' invitations. "This is not a normal life at all," she said.[13]

The news of Collier's pending retirement came during a routine press conference at the Hollenden House. He hadn't intended to make the announcement that day, but in responding to a question, he let it slip. The fact he would be retiring wasn't surprising, but the way it was revealed caught everyone off guard. "The coach had to brush away some tears as he answered questions," Heaton wrote in a column published the next day under the headline "Sad Day." "And some of the newsmen had to clear their throats more than once before the queries could continue."[14]

The tributes that followed—and that continue to this day—focused as much, if not more, on Collier's impact on people's lives as on his achievements as a football coach. He was described in the press as warm, caring, loyal, a first-class gentleman. His players thought of him as a father figure, a role model, an inspiration, a confidant, and a preacher. His daughter Kay believed his equanimity and the peace he projected stemmed from his ability to forgive and forget. He never said a bad word about Paul Brown, and he contributed financially to the University of Kentucky until the end of his life. "Forget it," he'd say. "It's over, done with, put it away." In 1983, while preparing to write *Football's Gentle Giant,* Kay tried contacting Paul Brown. She called him repeatedly, to no avail. She sent a letter, registered mail, and received a notice from the postal service certifying it had been received. She heard nothing from the man she had once considered an uncle and whom her father loved like a brother.

Collier's genius as a coach was his ability to teach but also his skill at tapping into what those around him needed in order to succeed. He didn't butt heads with Jim Brown and Bernie Parrish. He let them express themselves, and both became team leaders. He didn't berate or impose his will on Frank Ryan, regardless of how things were going; he propped him up and appealed to his analytical side. He knew everything there was to know about football, but he relied on old vets such as Dick Modzelewski to help him coach and teach. He once quoted a European tennis coach who came to America and kept hearing about the importance of athletes' talent. "But what is not recognized," the tennis coach said, "is that getting the most out of that talent is a talent in itself." Blanton Collier possessed that talent more than most.

In 1975, Cleveland head coach Forrest Gregg asked Collier to return to Cleveland to tutor the team's young quarterbacks, Brian Sipe and Mike Phipps. He retired for good in December 1976. "I know I will miss football," he said, "but I will be 71 on my next birthday. It's time to do other things. One never knows how much time God is going to give us on this earth."[15]

Blanton and Forman moved to Lake Conroe, Texas, about an hour north of Houston, where daughter Carolyn and her family lived. A few years earlier, Vic Ippolito, the Cleveland team doctor, had noticed an irregularity in Collier's prostate during an annual physical and recommended he see a specialist. He kept it to himself until it later was determined to be a malignancy and he began radiation treatment. Blanton Collier died of prostate cancer on March 22, 1983, in Houston. He was seventy-six. His funeral was at Christ Episcopal Church in Lexington, Kentucky. "There was a warmth, a love in that church one seldom felt at a funeral, or anywhere," the *Plain Dealer*'s Hal Lebovitz wrote. "It always emanated from Blanton."[16] He was buried in his hometown of Paris, Kentucky.

The Kentucky Pro Football Hall of Fame inducted him in 2016. The organization already had been presenting the Blanton Collier Award for a decade. It recognizes "individuals who demonstrate outstanding integrity both on and off the football field." Jim Brown paid him a video tribute. "As a human being Blanton was unprecedented," Brown said. "He made all of us feel good; he made us feel like we were a family. Because of that, we were able to win the last championship that Cleveland has known."[17]

Kay made a scrapbook for Blanton and presented it to him on what was his last Father's Day. "It was full of shared memories," she said, "full of thanks, for little things all but forgotten along the way—and full of praise." He responded with a letter, saying he was humbled, in part because he didn't feel he measured up to all the praise and goodwill. "Just remember I love you all," he wrote, "and above all, I am Dorge—just plain Dorge."[18]

Following the 1964 season Art Modell bought out Rudy Schaefer's 20 percent of the Cleveland franchise, giving him ownership of 70 percent. Multiple shareholders in Cleveland and New York split the remaining 30 percent. "Football is my life," Modell said. "It's a labor of love. Now more than ever I'm convinced beyond any measure of doubt that Cleveland is one of the best sports centers in the world, and possibly the very best." The franchise's market value was estimated at more than $10 million.[19]

Thirty years later, Modell claimed he'd reached the $50 million debt limit the NFL placed on its franchises. He blamed Cleveland politicians and rising player salaries. He had no choice, he claimed, but to move the franchise to Baltimore. *What happened?* Modell's fiscal trouble began in 1973 when he took over operation of Cleveland Municipal Stadium from the city. He signed a twenty-five-year lease that allowed him to rent the stadium to the Browns and Indians. Under the terms of the lease, he would receive all revenue, including signage, parking, and concessions. The deal, he admitted later, "turned out to haunt me." He took out a $10 million loan to fulfill his commitment to install luxury boxes, a new scoreboard, and new restrooms. He soon discovered the stadium, completed in 1931, was in disrepair. Structural beams were wearing thin and needed to be reinforced. It was up to Modell to fix the problems. Concessions from Indians games turned out to be less than he'd figured—"They weren't drawing fleas, for crying out loud," he said.[20] He took out loans on top of loans until he found himself wallowing in debt. The state of Maryland offered him free use of a stadium in 1996 and a new stadium in Baltimore in 1997, and he jumped at the opportunity. On November 6, 1995, he announced his intention to move the team to Baltimore the following season.

The response by Cleveland fans and players was predictable. The Browns weren't just a football team; they were the soul of the city. Fans grieved as though they'd lost a family member. Grown men cried, including Lou Groza.

"It's like a fire just burned out," he said, "and all you're left with is ashes." Modell received death threats and was hung in effigy. Callers to radio shows ripped him. "I have a four-year-old whom I wanted to raise a Browns fan, like I was," said one. "And this sucker Modell has snatched that away from me. When you have grown men crying about a football team, you can't say it's only about sports. It goes way deeper than that. You ask why we still go to games, even though they're leaving? Because it's who we are. Football is in our blood. The Cleveland Browns are in our blood."[21]

The Browns defeated the Bengals 26–10 in their final home game. More than 55,000 fans showed up. They threw beer bottles and cherry bombs into the end zone, booed when the scoreboard flashed "thank you" at the two-minute warning, and used saws, crowbars, and wrenches to remove entire rows of seats for souvenirs. The official demolition of the stadium began in November 1996 and was completed the following spring. Osborn Engineering Company, which, with the architectural firm Walker & Weeks, had designed the stadium, carried out its destruction.

Modell oversaw another NFL championship when Baltimore won the Super Bowl following the 2000 season, adding insult to his betrayal of Cleveland. He sold the team to Steve Bisciotti for $600 million after the 2003 season. He died in 2012 in Baltimore, at age eighty-seven.

Cleveland never forgave Modell. When LeBron James left the Cleveland Cavaliers basketball team for Miami—a move that prompted fans to burn his jersey—polls showed Cleveland's hatred of Modell was still greater. In 2015, Modell's tombstone became a urinal. A sixty-two-year-old Browns fan posted a YouTube video of himself peeing on it. "I had no choice," he said on the video.[22]

Despite all the venom directed at him, Modell did more for Cleveland than some other owners who moved sports franchises. Dan Reeves took the Rams to Los Angeles, leaving Cleveland without an NFL team, and Walter O'Malley tore the heart out of Brooklyn when he transferred baseball's Dodgers to Los Angeles. The most notorious was Robert Irsay, who in 1984 moved the Baltimore Colts to Indianapolis in the dead of night. But Modell honored a promise that he wouldn't take the Browns' nickname, colors, or franchise records with him. The new Baltimore club, the Ravens, was designated an expansion franchise. The "reactivated" Browns returned to Cleveland in 1999. However, the organization and tradition created and maintained by Paul Brown and Blanton Collier did leave with the team. And that never has been replaced.

By the fall of 2016, it was hard to imagine the Cleveland franchise was once the most storied in pro football—the Yankees, Joe Louis, and Sam Snead rolled into one. The Browns had become a joke. A video circulating on social media satirized a pitch for 2016 season tickets. Among the selling points: The Browns play sixteen games—"A COMPLETE SEASON!" A photo of thousands of fans celebrating the Cavaliers' NBA championship was posted on Facebook under the headline "Impressive turnout as former Browns quarterbacks gather in downtown Cleveland." Cleveland finished the 2016 season with one win and fifteen losses, narrowly avoiding joining the 2008 Detroit Lions as the only non-expansion team to lose all its games in a full season since World War II. In 2017, they joined the Lions, losing all sixteen games. "People ask if there's a light at the end of tunnel," the photographer Tony Tomsic said. "You can't even see the tunnel anymore."[23]

The National Football League comprises thirty-two teams. The Cleveland Browns are one of four never to have played in the Super Bowl. But for one afternoon in December 1964, they owned bragging rights over the vaunted Baltimore Colts and the rest of the NFL.

NOTES

PROLOGUE

1. Terry Pluto, "Echoes of 1964," *Cleveland Plain Dealer,* Jan. 29, 1995.
2. Hal Lebovitz, the *Plain Dealer* sports editor, later published a thirty-six-page booklet, *Paul Brown—The Play He Didn't Call* (Cleveland: Ra-Ka, 1963), which recounted the turn of events (see especially pages 31–32). The Pro Football Hall of Fame archives, in Canton, Ohio, holds a copy. Because of the newspaper strike in Cleveland in 1962–63, the city's sportswriters were unable to write about the firing of Paul Brown and hiring of Blanton Collier when they occurred in January 1963. Bud Furillo, "End of Brown May Mean End of Pro Grid in Cleveland," *Los Angeles Herald Examiner,* Jan. 10, 1963.
3. Lebovitz, *Paul Brown,* 6.
4. Bud Shrake, "A Man in Agony," *Dallas Morning News,* Sept. 25, 1963, sec. 1.
5. Paul Brown with Jack Clary, *PB: The Paul Brown Story* (New York: Athenaeum, 1979), 262.
6. Tex Maule, *The Game: The Official Picture History of the National Football League* (New York: Random House, 1963), 81.
7. Red Smith, "Browns Prove Smarter Than Their Baseball Cousins," *Canton Repository,* Dec. 14, 1964; Don Robertson, "Frigid Welkin Rings with Fans' Whoops," *Cleveland Plain Dealer,* Dec. 28, 1964. These and many other articles are compiled in scrapbooks at the Cleveland Browns headquarters in Berea, Ohio. Where the dates, authors, and publications aren't available, clippings are cited as "Browns scrapbook."
8. Ed Seitz, "Booze at Game Can Toss Fans for Loss," *Cleveland Press,* Dec. 26, 1964.
9. Jan Mellow, "Title Game Scalpers Scratching," *Cleveland Plain Dealer,* Dec. 27, 1964.
10. John Harris, "The Last Champions: The 1964 Cleveland Browns," *Timeline: A Publication of the Ohio Historical Connection* 32 (Mar. 2015): 10.
11. "Get Ready, Folks, Here Come the Colts Fans," United Press International, Browns scrapbook.
12. Don Shula, telephone interview with the author, May 4, 2015.
13. Jimmy Brown with Myron Cope, *Off My Chest: One of the Greatest Athletes of All Time Tells the Story of His Life—On and off the Field* (Garden City, N.Y.: Doubleday, 1964), 68.
14. Kay Collier Slone, *Football's Gentle Giant: The Blanton Collier Story* (Lexington, Ky.: Life Force Press, 1985), 170.
15. Kay Collier McLaughlin, interview with the author, July 22, 2016, Louisville, Ky.
16. Don Shula, "How the Colts Met Triumph and Disaster," *Sports Illustrated,* Jan. 11, 1965, 26.
17. "Look at Me, Man!" *Time,* Nov. 26, 1965, 80.
18. Myron Cope, preface to Brown with Cope, *Off My Chest,* viii.
19. Brown with Cope, *Off My Chest,* 161.
20. Cope, preface, viii.

21. Tex Maule, "The Browns Win Big in the East," *Sports Illustrated,* Dec. 21, 1964, 24.
22. Joan Ryan, "Only Survivors," National Football League's game-day program, Nov. 4, 1979, 58, copy in the Pro Football Hall of Fame archives.
23. Terry Pluto, *When All the World Was Browns Town: Cleveland's Browns and the Championship Season of '64* (New York: Simon & Schuster, 1997), 130.
24. Bernie Parrish, *They Call It a Game* (New York: Dial, 1971), 4; Chuck Such, "Ryan Says Browns' Best Yet to Come," *Canton Repository,* Dec. 29, 1964.
25. Shula, "How the Colts Met Triumph and Disaster," 26.
26. Frank Ryan, interview with the author, Sept. 22, 2016, Grafton, Vt.
27. Tex Maule, "Upset of the Mighty," *Sports Illustrated,* Jan. 4, 1965, 11; Arthur Daley, "No Question About It," *New York Times,* Dec. 28, 1964, 41. Bob August, "Game of Lifetime for Browns' Defense," *Cleveland Press,* Dec. 28, 1964; Red Smith, "Which One Is Heffelfinger?" *New York Herald Tribune,* Dec. 28, 1964.
28. Bill Scholl, "Line Deserves Raise," *Cleveland Press,* Dec. 28, 1964; Harris, "Last Champions," 11.

CHAPTER ONE

1. Hal Lebovitz, *Paul Brown—The Play He Didn't Call* (Cleveland: Ra-Ka, 1963), 27.
2. Bob August, "Remarkable Pro Football Man—That's Collier," *Cleveland Press,* Oct. 9, 1963.
3. Kay Collier Slone, *Football's Gentle Giant: The Blanton Collier Story* (Lexington, Ky.: Life Force Press, 1985), 32.
4. Paul Brown with Jack Clary, *PB: The Paul Brown Story* (New York: Athenaeum, 1979).
5. Lebovitz, *Paul Brown,* 32.
6. Ibid., 31.
7. Melvin Durslag, "Owner of Cleveland Thinks Big," *Los Angeles Herald Examiner,* Jan. 11, 1963.
8. Paul Hornung, "Incompatibility, Lack of Titles Triggered Blowup," *Columbus Post Dispatch,* Browns scrapbook.
9. Bill Klucas, "Collier Is Browns' New Coach," Browns scrapbook.
10. Slone, *Football's Gentle Giant,* 172.
11. Jim Ninowski, telephone interview with author, Oct. 6, 2015.
12. "Collier Will Coach Browns; Sauerbrei General Manager," *Sun-Press,* Jan. 17, 1963, Browns scrapbook.
13. Frank Ryan, interview with the author, Sept. 22, 2016, Grafton, Vt.
14. Lebovitz, *Paul Brown,* 20.
15. Ibid., 21.
16. Bernie Parrish, *They Call It a Game* (New York: Dial, 1971), 95.
17. Lebovitz, *Paul Brown,* 21.
18. "The Real Blanton Collier," *Cleveland Plain Dealer Sunday Magazine,* Sept. 17, 1967.
19. Slone, *Football's Gentle Giant,* 49.
20. Kay Collier McLaughlin, interview with the author, July 22, 2016, Louisville, Ky.

CHAPTER TWO

1. Benjamin Hare, "Football at Military Training Centers during WWII," *Great Lakes Bulletin,* Feb. 11, 2006, 7.
2. Bill Scholl, "Brown and Collier Partners Again," *Cleveland Press,* Jan. 16, 1962; "Plain Dealing," *Cleveland Plain Dealer,* Jan. 17, 1962.

3. Lebovitz, *Paul Brown—The Play He Didn't Call* (Cleveland: Ra-Ka, 1963), 27.
4. Ibid.
5. Jack Clowser, "Football Limelight New to McBride," *Cleveland Press*, Feb. 10, 1945.
6. Regis McAuley, "Was Brown McBride's Top Choice?" Browns scrapbook.
7. "'Brown Raiding My Men for Pro Grid'—Widdoes," *Chicago American*, May 4, 1945.
8. Bill Levy, *Return to Glory: The Story of the Cleveland Browns* (Cleveland: World, 1965), 42–43.
9. Tex Maule, *The Game: The Official Picture History of the National Football League* (New York: Random House, 1963), 3.
10. For a detailed description of Reeves's ownership of the Cleveland Rams and the team's move to Los Angeles, see Michael MacCambridge, *America's Game: The Epic Story of How Pro Football Captured a Nation* (New York: Random House, 2004) 10, 15–17.
11. Herman Goldstein, "Call 'Em the Browns," *Cleveland News*, Aug. 14, 1945.
12. John Dietrich, "Jack in the Box," *Cleveland Plain Dealer*, May 28, 1946.
13. "Brown Raiding My Men for Pro Grid."
14. Ibid.
15. Paul Brown with Jack Clary, *PB: The Paul Brown Story* (New York: Athenaeum, 1979), 10.
16. "400 Coaches Attend Clinic," *Cleveland Press*, May 3, 1946.
17. Herman Goldstein, "Browns Have a TD Dealer—Graham," *Cleveland News*, Aug. 2, 1946.
18. Kay Collier Slone, *Gentle Giant: The Blanton Collier Story* (Lexington, Ky.: Life Force Press, 1985), 160.
19. Ibid., 262.
20. Ibid., 23.
21. Myron Cope, *The Game That Was* (New York: Thomas Y. Crowell, 1970), 217; Terry Pluto, *When All the World Was Browns Town: Cleveland's Browns and the Championship Season of '64* (New York: Simon & Schuster, 1997), 49.
22. Mickey Herskowitz, *The Golden Age of Pro Football: NFL Football in the 1950s* (Dallas: Taylor Publishing, 1974), 118; Alan H. Levy, *Tackling Jim Crow: Racial Segregation in Professional Football* (Jefferson, N.C.: McFarland, 2003), 209.
23. Cleveland Jackson, "Willis, Marion Motley to Encounter Dixie Bred Stars as Cleveland Browns, Miami Seahawks Open All-American Conference Play," *Cleveland Call and Post*, Sept. 6, 1946.
24. MacCambridge, *America's Game*, 23.
25. "Girl Band Struts as Browns Prep for Grid Opener," *Cleveland News*, Aug. 23, 1946.
26. Pluto, *When All the World Was Browns Town*, 189.
27. Jimmy Brown with Myron Cope, *Off My Chest: One of the Greatest Athletes of All Time Tells the Story of His Life—On and off the Field* (Garden City, N.Y.: Doubleday, 1964), 6.
28. "Jim Daniell Fired by Browns," *Cleveland News*, Dec. 16, 1946; "Three Browns' Grid Stars Try to Bench Wrong Men; Police Toss Them for Loss," *Cleveland News*, Dec. 14, 1946; "Saban Named Captain as Daniell Is Fired," Browns scrapbook; MacCambridge, *America's Game*, 34–35.

CHAPTER THREE

1. Bernie Parrish, *They Call It a Game* (New York: Dial, 1971), 90.
2. Paul Brown with Jack Clary, *PB: The Paul Brown Story* (New York: Athenaeum, 1979), 150.
3. Ibid., 5–6.
4. Tex Maule, "A Man for This Season," *Sports Illustrated*, Sept. 10, 1962.

5. Brown with Clary, *PB*, 161.
6. Ibid.
7. Mickey Herskowitz, *The Golden Age of Pro Football: NFL Football in the 1950s* (Dallas: Taylor, 1974), 29.
8. Ibid., 50.
9. *The NFL Century: The Complete Story of The National Football League, 1920–2000* (New York: Smithmark, 1999), 124, 125.
10. Ibid.
11. Herskowitz, *Golden Age of Pro Football*, 150.
12. Ibid., 50.
13. Ibid., 118.
14. Ibid., 25–26.
15. Kay Collier Slone, *Football's Gentle Giant: The Blanton Collier Story* (Lexington, Ky.: Life Force Press, 1985), 22.
16. Leo Murphy, interview with the author, June 24, 2015, Medina, Ohio.
17. Bill Levy, *Return to Glory: The Story of the Cleveland Browns* (Cleveland: World, 1965), 190.
18. Michael MacCambridge, *America's Game: The Epic Story of How Pro Football Captured a Nation* (New York: Random House, 2004), 36.
19. Brown with Clary, *PB*, 143.
20. Slone, *Football's Gentle Giant*, 49.

CHAPTER FOUR

1. Allen Barra, *The Last Coach: A Life of Paul "Bear" Bryant* (New York: Norton, 2005), 153.
2. Kay Collier McLaughlin, interview with the author, July 22, 2015, Louisville, Ky.
3. Don Shula, telephone interview with the author, May 4, 2015.
4. Keith Dunnavant, *Coach: The Life of Paul "Bear" Bryant* (New York: Simon & Schuster, 1996), 68.
5. Howard Schnellenberger, telephone interview with the author, Apr. 7, 2015.
6. Kay Collier Slone, *Football's Gentle Giant: The Blanton Collier Story* (Lexington, Ky.: Life Force Press, 1985), 40–42.
7. Schnellenberger interview.
8. Slone, *Football's Gentle Giant*, 84.
9. Ibid., 259.
10. Schnellenberger interview.
11. Slone, *Football's Gentle Giant*, 259.
12. Ibid., 63.
13. McLaughlin interview.
14. Schnellenberger interview.
15. Ibid.
16. Slone, *Football's Gentle Giant*, 100.
17. "People," *Sports Illustrated*, Feb. 4, 1974.
18. Schnellenberger interview.

CHAPTER FIVE

1. Tom Landry with Gregg Lewis, *Tom Landry: An Autobiography* (New York: HarperCollins, 1990), 98.

2. *The NFL Century: The Complete Story of the National Football League, 1920–2000* (New York: Smithmark, 1999).
3. Landry with Lewis, *Tom Landry*, 98–99.
4. Paul Brown with Jack Clary, *PB: The Paul Brown Story* (New York: Athenaeum, 1979), 9–10.
5. Mike Freeman, *Jim Brown: The Fierce Life of an American Hero* (New York: Harper-Collins, 2006), 49.
6. "Look at Me, Man!" *Time*, Nov. 26, 1965, 83.
7. Jim Brown with Steve Delsohn, *Out of Bounds* (New York: Zebra, 1989), 75.
8. Jimmy Brown with Myron Cope, *Off My Chest: One of the Greatest Athletes of All Time Tells the Story of His Life—On and off the Field* (Garden City, N.Y.: Doubleday, 1964), 113.
9. Ibid., 114.
10. Freeman, *Jim Brown*, 82.
11. Brown with Cope, *Off My Chest*, 113.
12. Ibid., 80.
13. "Look at Me, Man!" 83.
14. Freeman, *Jim Brown*, 100.
15. Ibid., 105.
16. Mickey Herskowitz, *The Golden Age of Pro Football: NFL Football in the 1950s* (Dallas: Taylor, 1974), 118
17. Mike Klingaman, "Catching Up with . . . Ed Modzelewski," *Baltimore Sun*, Oct. 31, 2013, available online at http://articles.baltimoresun.com/2013-10-31/sports/bs-sp-catching-up-modzelewski-20131031_1_cleveland-browns-sugar-bowl-maryland.
18. Jim Ninowski, telephone interview with the author, Oct. 6, 2015.
19. *Jim Brown: All American*, dir. Spike Lee (Home Box Office, 2002).
20. Terry Pluto, *When All the World Was Browns Town: Cleveland's Browns and the Championship Season of '64* (New York: Simon & Schuster, 1997), 166, 175.
21. "Look at Me, Man!" 80.
22. Michael MacCambridge, *America's Game: The Epic Story of How Pro Football Captured a Nation* (New York: Random House, 2004), 108.

CHAPTER SIX

1. Mickey Herskowitz, *The Golden Age of Pro Football: NFL Football in the 1950s* (Dallas: Taylor, 1974), 110.
2. Paul Brown with Jack Clary, *PB: The Paul Brown Story* (New York: Athenaeum, 1979), 180.
3. Terry Pluto, *When All the World Was Browns Town: Cleveland's Browns and the Championship Season of '64* (New York: Simon & Schuster, 1997), 39–41.
4. David Maraniss, *When Pride Still Mattered: A Life of Vince Lombardi* (New York: Simon & Schuster, 1999), 184; Frank Gifford and Harry Waters, *The Whole Ten Yards* (New York: Ivy Books, 1994), 185.
5. Pluto, *When All the World Was Browns Town*, 39–41.
6. Brown with Clary, *PB*, 255.
7. Pluto, *Browns Town*, 42.
8. Gifford and Waters, *Whole Ten Yards*, 177.
9. Brown with Clary, *PB*, 255

10. Michael MacCambridge, *America's Game: The Epic Story of How Pro Football Captured a Nation* (New York: Random House, 2004), 100–101.
11. Tex Maule, "Why the Browns Will Win," *Sports Illustrated*, Nov. 23, 1959.
12. Gifford and Waters, *Whole Ten Yards*, 194.
13. Bernie Parrish, *They Call It a Game* (New York: Dial, 1971), 94–95.
14. Jimmy Brown with Myron Cope, *Off My Chest: One of the Greatest Athletes of All Time Tells the Story of His Life—On and off the Field* (Garden City, N.Y.: Doubleday, 1964), 8–9.
15. Mike Freeman, *Jim Brown: The Fierce Life of an American Hero* (New York: HarperCollins, 2006), 107.
16. Brown with Cope, *Off My Chest*, 53, 54.
17. Ibid., 52–53.
18. Parrish, *They Call It a Game*, 95.
19. George Plimpton, *Paper Lion: Confessions of a Last-String Quarterback* (New York: Harper & Row, 1966), 284.

CHAPTER SEVEN

1. Jimmy Brown with Myron Cope, *Off My Chest: One of the Greatest Athletes of All Time Tells the Story of His Life—On and off the Field* (Garden City, N.Y.: Doubleday, 1964), 13.
2. Terry Pluto, *When All the World Was Browns Town: Cleveland's Browns and the Championship Season of '64* (New York: Simon & Schuster, 1997), 32.
3. David Harris, *The League: The Rise and Decline of the NFL* (New York: Bantam, 1986), 35.
4. Ibid.
5. Hal Lebovitz, *Paul Brown—The Play He Didn't Call* (Cleveland: Ra-Ka, 1963), 6.
6. Harris, *League*, 36.
7. Pluto, *When All the World Was Browns Town*, 36.
8. Lebovitz, *Paul Brown*, 3.
9. Shirley Povich, "This Morning," *Washington Post*, Jan. 11, 1963.
10. MacCambridge, *America's Game: The Epic Story of How Pro Football Captured a Nation* (New York: Random House, 2004), 168.
11. Sam Blair, "New Browns Work of Art," *Dallas Morning News*, Sept. 23, 1963.
12. Lebovitz, *Paul Brown*, 2.
13. "Hal Asks . . . You Comfortable in a Crowd?" *Cleveland Plain Dealer*, Nov. 22, 1964.
14. Blair, "New Browns Work of Art."
15. Ibid.
16. Ibid.
17. Charles Maher, "Modell Sets the Pace in Pro Football, *Los Angeles Times*, Aug. 2, 1966.
18. Pluto, *When All the World Was Browns Town*, 37–38.
19. Jane Artale, "Modell, Browns' Top Fan, Keeps Fingers Crossed," *Cleveland Plain Dealer*, Dec. 27, 1964, 3-C.
20. Dave Eisenberg, "The Fine Art of Running the Browns," *New York Journal-American*, Oct. 3, 1963.
21. "Hal Asks . . . You Comfortable in a Crowd?"

CHAPTER EIGHT
1. Paul Brown with Jack Clary, *PB: The Paul Brown Story* (New York: Athenaeum, 1979), 247.
2. Ibid., 252.
3. Charles Heaton, "Browns 'in Rut,' Says Plum; Hits Checkoff Rein," *Cleveland Plain Dealer*, Feb. 18, 1962.
4. "Collier to Return as Browns' Aide," Jan. 16, 1962.
5. "Graham Hasn't Changed, Still Favors Checkoffs," Bill Scholl, *Cleveland Press*, Feb. 21, 1962.
6. Jimmy Brown with Myron Cope, *Off My Chest: One of the Greatest Athletes of All Time Tells the Story of His Life—On and off the Field* (Garden City, N.Y.: Doubleday, 1964), 89.
7. Brown with Clary, *PB*, 255, 248, 247.
8. Jim Ninowski, telephone interview with the author, Oct. 6, 2015.
9. Charles Heaton, "Ninowski Gets to Call More Plays," *Cleveland Plain Dealer*, Browns scrapbook.
10. Brown with Cope, *Off My Chest*, 17.
11. Frank Gibbons, "'This Could Be the Year,' Say Brown Veterans," *Cleveland Press*, Aug. 23, 1962.
12. Hal Lebovitz, *Paul Brown—The Play He Didn't Call* (Cleveland: Ra-Ka, 1963), 7.
13. Brown with Clary, *PB*, 263.
14. Jim Brown and Steve Delsohn, *Out of Bounds* (New York: Zebra, 1989), 81–82.
15. Michael MacCambridge, *America's Game: The Epic Story of How Pro Football Captured a Nation* (New York: Random House, 2004), 168.
16. "'Overworked, May Quit,' Says Jim Brown on Coast," *Cleveland Press*, Jan. 12, 1962.
17. Ninowski interview.
18. "Collier to Return as Browns' Aide."

CHAPTER NINE
1. Tex Maule, "A Man for This Season," *Sports Illustrated*, Sept. 10, 1962.
2. Ibid.
3. Kay Collier Slone, *Football's Gentle Giant: The Blanton Collier Story* (Lexington, Ky.: Life Force Press, 1985), 123.
4. Terry Pluto, *When All the World Was Browns Town: Cleveland's Browns and the Championship Season of '64* (New York: Simon & Schuster, 1997), 29.
5. George Plimpton, *Paper Lion: Confessions of a Last-String Quarterback* (New York: Harper & Row, 1966), 291.
6. Slone, *Football's Gentle Giant*, 125–26.
7. Paul Brown with Jack Clary, *PB: The Paul Brown Story* (New York: Athenaeum, 1979), 279.
8. Slone, *Football's Gentle Giant*, 126.
9. Jim Ninowski, telephone interview with the author, Oct. 6, 2015.
10. Pluto, *When All the World Was Browns Town*, 30.
11. Ninowski interview.
12. Ibid.
13. Murray Olderman, "Unshackled Quarterbacks Make Browns Contender," Sept. 15, 1962, Browns scrapbook.

14. Frank Gibbons, "'This Could Be the Year,' Say Brown Veterans," *Cleveland Press*, Aug. 23, 1962.
15. Brown with Clary, *PB*, 277.
16. Frank Gibbons, "Browns Are Disorganized and Lacking in Poise," *Cleveland Press*, Oct. 15, 1962.
17. Gordon Cobbledick, "Plain Dealing," *Cleveland Plain Dealer*, Nov. 14, 1962.
18. "All's Not Well in Brown's Camp," *Pro Grid*, Nov. 17, 1962.
19. Shirley Povich, "This Morning," Jan. 11, 1963, Browns scrapbook; Hal Lebovitz, *Paul Brown—The Play He Didn't Call* (Cleveland: Ra-Ka, 1963), 32.
20. Charles Heaton, "Ryan Gets Passing Grade from Brown," *Cleveland Plain Dealer*, Nov. 27, 1962.
21. Frank Ryan, interview with the author, Sept. 22, 2016, Grafton, Vt.
22. Ibid.
23. Bill Van Fleet, "At Last, Ryan's the No. 1 Man," *Fort Worth Star Telegram*, 1962, Browns scrapbook.
24. Jack Olsen, "Dr. Ryan of the Browns: How Smart Is Too Smart?" *Sports Illustrated*, Sept. 27, 1965.
25. Frank Ryan interview.
26. *Fort Worth Star Telegram*, Aug. 10, 1954.
27. Frank Ryan interview.
28. *Fort Worth Star Telegram*, Sept. 12, 1955.
29. *Fort Worth Star Telegram*, Sept. 13, 1957.
30. John Dell, "All-American Friends Sunday Foes," *Philadelphia Inquirer*, Nov. 3, 1963.
31. Frank Ryan interview.
32. Megan Schneider, prod., "Joan Ryan . . . in Her Own Words," in *Still No Cheering in the Press Box*, at the Shirley Povich Center for Sports Journalism Web site, http://povichcenter.org/still-no-cheering-press-box/chapter/Joan-Ryan/index.html.
33. Frank Ryan interview.
34. Joan Ryan, "Only Survivors," Nov. 4, 1979, NFL game-day program, copy in Pro Football Hall of Fame archives, Canton, Ohio.
35. Red Smith, "Hotshot on Campus," *Connecticut*, no date available, 42, copy in Pro Football Hall of Fame archives.
36. "Ryan 'Fits Beautifully' with Plans, Coach Says," *Fort Worth Star Telegram*, Mar. 12, 1958, 14.
37. Charles Maher, "Dr. Ryan Wrestles Math, Browns," *Los Angeles Times*, July 20, 1966.
38. A three-photo sequence of the play hangs on the wall of Ryan's office at his home in Grafton, Vermont, to this day.
39. Olsen, "Dr. Ryan of the Browns."
40. Joan Ryan, interview with the author, Sept. 22, 2016, Grafton, Vt.
41. Roger Kahn, "C-(Frank Ryan)/2," *Saturday Evening Post*, Nov. 20, 1965, 92–95.
42. Jack Gallagher, "The Brainy One Told Students They Were on Candid Camera," *Houston Post*, Mar. 1, 1965.
43. Frank Ryan interview.
44. Jimmy Brown with Myron Cope, *Off My Chest: One of the Greatest Athletes of All Time Tells the Story of His Life—On and off the Field* (Garden City, N.Y.: Doubleday, 1964), 73–74.
45. Pluto, *When All the World Was Browns Town*, 56.
46. Brown with Clary, *PB*, 262, 282.

47. Jim Brown and Steve Delsohn, *Out of Bounds* (New York: Zebra, 1989), 104.
48. Dave Eisenberg, "The Fine Art of Running the Browns," *New York Journal-American*, Oct. 3, 1963.
49. Denny Lustig, "Man on the Street," in Lebovitz, *Paul Brown*, 15.
50. Ibid.
51. Ibid.
52. Robert Dolgan, "What Players Think about Firing," in Lebovitz, *Paul Brown*, 13.
53. Ibid.
54. Ibid., 12.
55. Ibid., 13.
56. Brown with Cope, *Off My Chest*, 56.
57. William V. Levy, *Return to Glory: The Story of the Cleveland Browns* (Cleveland: World, 1965), 182–83.

CHAPTER TEN

1. "Is Pro Football New Folk Religion?" *Cleveland Press*, Sept. 27, 1963.
2. Paul Wiggin, telephone interview with the author, May 25, 2016.
3. John Thorn, "Introduction: Why Canton?" *The Pro Football Hall of Fame 50th Anniversary Book*, ed. Joe Horrigan and John Thorn (New York: Grand Central, 2012), xvii, xviii.
4. Stephen Mahoney, "Pro Football's Profit Explosion," *Fortune*, Nov. 1964, 155.
5. Ibid.
6. Ibid., 153.
7. Ibid., 155.
8. Tex Maule, "The Cowboys Can Ride High on Better Defense," *Sports Illustrated*, Sept. 9, 1963.
9. *Cleveland Press*, undated clipping, Browns scrapbook.
10. Loren Tibbals, "Scribbles," *Akron Beacon Journal*, Jan. 29, 1963.
11. "Davis Knew End Was Near," Associated Press, May 20, 1963, Browns scrapbook.
12. Ibid.
13. Terry Pluto, *When All the World Was Browns Town: Cleveland's Browns and the Championship Season of '64* (New York: Simon & Schuster, 1997), 238–39.
14. "Tragic Death of Fleming Casts Pall over Browns," *Canton Repository*, June 5, 1963.
15. Charles Heaton, "Eyes of Football World Are on Browns, Collier Says," *Cleveland Plain Dealer*, July 23, 1963.
16. Jim Ninowski, telephone interview with the author, Oct. 6, 2015.
17. Jimmy Brown with Myron Cope, *Off My Chest: One of the Greatest Athletes of All Time Tells the Story of His Life—On and off the Field* (Garden City, N.Y.: Doubleday, 1964), 206–8.
18. Ibid.
19. Chuck Such, "Aggressiveness Emphasized in Browns Camp," *Canton Repository*, July 12, 1963.
20. Bob Sudyk, "'Team Must Believe Play Will Work'—Collier," *Cleveland Press*, July 19, 1963.
21. Ibid.
22. Brown with Cope, *Off My Chest*, 206–8.
23. Maxwell Maltz, *Psycho-Cybernetics: A New Way to Get More Living Out of Life* (New York: Pocket Books, 1960), vii.

24. Kay Collier Slone, *Football's Gentle Giant: The Blanton Collier Story* (Lexington, Ky.: Life Force Press, 1985), 266.
25. Dick Schafrath, interview with the author, June 23, 2015, Berea, Ohio.
26. Ibid.; "Alex Haley Interviews Jim Brown," *Playboy,* February 1968, available online at http://www.alex-haley.com/alex_haley_jim_brown_interview.htm.
27. Slone, *Football's Gentle Giant,* 271–72.
28. William V. Levy, *Return to Glory: The Story of the Cleveland Browns* (Cleveland: World, 1965), 198.
29. Charles Heaton, "Browns' Offense Falters," *Cleveland Plain Dealer,* Sept. 9, 1963; Chuck Such, "Browns Insist Exhibition Egg Will Hatch Division Title," *Canton Repository,* Sept. 9, 1963.

CHAPTER ELEVEN

1. Charles Heaton, "Collier Enrolls First Browns in Contenders Class," *Cleveland Plain Dealer,* Sept. 14, 1963.
2. Ibid.
3. Ibid.
4. Paul Wiggin, telephone interview with the author, May 25, 2016.
5. Heaton, "Collier Enrolls First Browns in Contenders Class."
6. Gordon Cobbledick, "Plain Dealing," *Cleveland Plain Dealer,* Sept. 15, 1963, 2-C.
7. "'I Told You So,' Browns Chorus," Sept. 17, 1963, Browns scrapbook.
8. Jim Ninowski, telephone interview with author, Oct. 6, 2015.
9. Bob August, "Remarkable Pro Football Man—That's Collier," *Cleveland Press,* Oct. 9, 1963.
10. Dick Schafrath, interview with the author, June 23, 2015, Berea, Ohio.
11. John Wooten, telephone interview with the author, Apr. 20, 2015.
12. Terry Pluto, *When All the World Was Browns Town: Cleveland's Browns and the Championship Season of '64* (New York: Simon & Schuster, 1997), 216.
13. Dale Lindsey, telephone interview with the author, July 7, 2016.
14. Schafrath interview.
15. Ibid.
16. Ibid.
17. Gordon Cobbledick, "Plain Dealing," *Cleveland Plain Dealer,* Oct. 15, 1963.
18. "Parker Calls Frank Ryan Best Running QB in League," *Columbus Dispatch,* Oct. 7, 1963.
19. Frank Gibbons, "Browns Have Fans' Tongues Awaggin'," *Cleveland Press,* Oct. 8, 1963.
20. Chuck Such, "Battling Browns Reach for Elusive Pot of Gold," *Canton Repository,* Oct. 14, 1963, 19.
21. Kay Collier Slone, *Football's Gentle Giant: The Blanton Collier Story* (Lexington, Ky.: Life Force Press, 1985), 272, 154.
22. Wiggin interview.
23. Slone, *Football's Gentle Giant,* 148.
24. Ibid., 153.
25. Sandy Grady, "Paul's 'Ghost' Goads Browns to Victory after Victory," Browns scrapbook.
26. Ibid.

CHAPTER TWELVE

1. "Fans Hit the Line and Get Crushed," *Cleveland Press*, Oct. 24, 1963.
2. Bill Scholl, "'Browns Jelled in Second Steeler Game'—Wiggin," *Cleveland Press*, Nov. 11, 1964.
3. Fritz Howell, "Browns' Football Bubble Bursts with 33-6 Loss to New Yorkers," Associated Press, Oct. 28, 1963, Browns scrapbook.
4. Gordon Cobbledick, "Plain Dealing," *Cleveland Plain Dealer*, Oct. 29, 1963.
5. Bill Scholl, "Pass Thefts Save Browns from Philly Willies," *Cleveland Press*, Nov. 4, 1963.
6. Chuck Such, "Collier Says Browns Have Selves to Blame," *Canton Repository*, Nov. 12, 1963.
7. Frank Ryan, interview with the author, Sept. 22, 2016, Grafton, Vt.
8. Cobbledick, "Plain Dealing."
9. Judy Battista, "Jack Would Say We Should Play," in "The Untold NFL History of That Day in Dallas," *NFL.com*, accessed Jan. 26, 2018, http://www.nfl.com/jfk.
10. Ibid.; "334,892 See NFL Despite Protests," Associated Press, Browns scrapbook.
11. Manny Fernandez, Richard Fausset, and Alan Blinder, "A Silence Fell on Dallas in 1963. Not This Year," *New York Times*, July 17, 2016, 16.
12. Michael MacCambridge, *America's Game: The Epic Story of How Pro Football Captured a Nation* (New York: Random House, 2004), 187.
13. Battista, "Jack Would Say We Should Play."
14. Chuck Such, "Cleveland's on Its Way, Say Players," *Canton Repository*, Nov. 24, 1963.
15. Hal Lebovitz, "NFL Eastern Finish Has Possibilities; How Many? Ask Browns' Mathematician," *Cleveland Plain Dealer*, Nov. 30, 1963.
16. Roger Kahn, "C-(Frank Ryan)/2," *Saturday Evening Post*, Nov. 20, 1965, 92–95.
17. Jim Trinkle, "Ryan Considered Serious Student," *Fort Worth Star Telegram*, Oct. 17, 1964, 14.
18. Kahn, "C-(Frank Ryan)/2."
19. Frank Ryan interview.
20. Joan Ryan, interview with the author, Sept. 22, 2016, Grafton, Vt.
21. "Our Frank's Now Dr. Ryan of Rice, *Cleveland Plain Dealer*, June 6, 1965.
22. Ibid.
23. Kahn, "C-(Frank Ryan)/2."
24. Frank Ryan interview.
25. Kahn, "C-(Frank Ryan)/2."
26. Ibid.
27. Jack Olsen, "Dr. Ryan of the Browns: How Smart Is Too Smart?" *Sports Illustrated*, Sept. 27, 1965.
28. Gary Cartwright, "Frank Ryan: How the Unwanted Quarterback Made Good," *Sport*, June 1964.
29. "Cleveland Browns Frank Ryan Last NFL Championship QB (1964)," YouTube video, 6:23, posted by Steven Watson, Sept. 9, 2014, https://www.youtube.com/watch?v=L8PlflBYtaE&t=13s.
30. Frank Ryan interview.
31. "Cleveland Browns Frank Ryan."
32. Terry Pluto, *When All the World Was Browns Town: Cleveland's Browns and the Championship Season of '64* (New York: Simon & Schuster, 1997), 283.

33. "Cleveland Browns Frank Ryan."
34. Trinkle, "Ryan Considered Serious Student."
35. Joan Ryan interview.
36. Bill Scholl, "Browns Cracked under Pressure, Collier Believes," *Cleveland Press*, Dec. 10, 1963.
37. Edwin Kernan, "LBJ Tells Brown, Ryan, They Can Help Nation," *Cleveland Plain Dealer*, Browns scrapbook.
38. "Playoff Bowl Proves Boring to Packers," *Cleveland Press*, Dec. 20, Browns scrapbook.
39. Bill Scholl, "Frank Ryan Promises Cleveland Better Years Ahead," *Pro Football Illustrated*, Jan. 18, 1964, 6.

CHAPTER THIRTEEN

1. Tony Tomsic, telephone interview with the author, Nov. 18, 2016.
2. Joan Ryan, interview with the author, Sept. 22, 2016, Grafton, Vt.
3. Jim Ninowski, telephone interview with the author, Oct. 6, 2015.
4. Charlie Powell, "Graham: 'Browns Can't Win with Brown,'" *Canton Repository*, Aug. 11, 1964.
5. Tim Warsinskey, "Former Cleveland Browns QB Ryan Marvels at CWRU, Cautions about 'Vicious' NFL," *Cleveland Plain Dealer*, Sept. 28, 2013.
6. Terry Pluto, *When All the World Was Browns Town: Cleveland's Browns and the Championship Season of '64* (New York: Simon & Schuster, 1997), 113.
7. "So, in the East: Browns? Cardinals? Cowboys?" *Sports Illustrated*, Sept. 7, 1964.
8. Dale Lindsey, telephone interview with the author, July 7, 2016.
9. Jack Mann, "Mo Put Go in Browns," *New York Herald Tribune*, Dec. 28, 1964.
10. Bill Scholl, "His 1st Game Ball Has Mo Beaming," *Cleveland Press*, Sept. 14, 1964.

CHAPTER FOURTEEN

1. Bernie Parrish, *They Call It a Game* (New York: Dial, 1971); Dave Meggyesy, *Out of Their League* (Berkeley, Calif: Ramparts Press, 1971); Jimmy Brown with Myron Cope, *Off My Chest: One of the Greatest Athletes of all Time Tells the Story of His Life—On and off the Field* (Garden City, N.Y.: Doubleday, 1964), 36.
2. Brown with Cope, *Off My Chest*, 67, 93–94.
3. Stephen B. Oates, *Let the Trumpet Sound: The Life of Martin Luther King Jr.* (New York: Harper & Row, 1982), 279, 301.
4. Ibid., 251.
5. Randy Roberts and Johnny Smith, *Blood Brothers: The Fatal Friendship between Muhammad Ali and Malcolm X* (Philadelphia: Basic Books, 2016), 200.
6. Brown with Cope, *Off My Chest*, 166–67.
7. Ibid., 168.
8. Charles Heaton, "Here's Cheer to Jim Brown for Speaking," *Cleveland Plain Dealer*, Sept. 22, 1964.
9. Don Robertson, "Police Guard Jim Brown's Home," *Cleveland Plain Dealer*, Sept. 23, 1964.
10. Ibid.
11. Letters to the editor, *Look*, Nov. 17, 1964, 6.
12. Ibid.
13. Ibid.

14. Murray Olderman, "What Makes Brown Negro Spokesman?" *Akron Beacon Journal*, Sept. 29, 1964.
15. "Look at Me, Man!" *Time*, Nov. 26, 1965, 86.
16. John Wooten, telephone interview with the author, Apr. 20, 2015.
17. Ibid.
18. Walter Beach, telephone interview the author, Oct. 11, 2016.
19. Ibid.
20. Ibid.
21. Heaton, "Here's Cheer."
22. Charlie Powell, "Graham: 'Browns Can't Win with Brown,'" *Canton Repository*, Aug. 11, 1964.
23. "I'd Trade Him, Graham Says of Jim Brown," *Cleveland Plain Dealer*, Aug. 12, 1964.
24. "Alex Haley Interviews Jim Brown," *Playboy*, February 1968, available online at http://www.alex-haley.com/alex_haley_jim_brown_interview.htm.
25. Jim Brown with Steve Delsohn, *Out of Bounds* (New York: Zebra, 1989), 58.
26. Stan Anderson, "Brown Plunges Hard Against Apaches, *Cleveland Press*, Oct. 24, 1964; "Razzmatazz Launches Jim Brown Film," *Cleveland Press*, Oct. 24, 1964.

CHAPTER FIFTEEN

1. Charles Heaton, "Collier Exonerates Ryan; Blames Fumbles, Penalties," *Cleveland Plain Dealer*, Oct. 27, 1964.
2. "Ryan Flees NFL 'Animals,'" Associated Press, Nov. 3, 1964.
3. "PD Readers Sound Off," *Cleveland Plain Dealer*, Oct. 29, 1964.
4. Joan Ryan, interview with the author, Sept. 22, 2016, Grafton, Vt.
5. "Ryan Drops Hermit Role; Glib after Victory Tonic," *Cleveland Plain Dealer*, Nov. 3, 1964.
6. Ibid.
7. "Mrs. Frank Ryan to Call Signals as PD Columnist," *Cleveland Plain Dealer*, Nov. 10, 1964.
8. Joan Ryan interview.
9. Joan Ryan, "Booing Shofner Was a Mistake," *Cleveland Plain Dealer*, Nov. 11, 1964.
10. Tex Maule, "Not Much Defense, but Two Long-Ball Hitters," *Sports Illustrated*, Oct. 19, 1964.
11. Paul Warfield, telephone interview with the author, July 6, 2015.
12. Ibid.
13. Tony Tomsic, telephone interview with the author, Nov. 18, 2016.
14. John Wooten, telephone interview with the author, Apr. 20, 2015.
15. Terry Pluto, *When All the World Was Browns Town: Cleveland's Browns and the Championship Season of '64* (New York: Simon & Schuster, 1997), 167.
16. Joan Ryan, "Who's Superstitious? Don't Wear THAT Dress," *Cleveland Plain Dealer*, Dec. 11, 1964.
17. Bob August, "Forget Those Doubts, Browns Almost There," *Cleveland Press*, Nov. 26, 1964.
18. Charles Heaton, "Browns Must Erase 'Laugh Champs' Tag," *Cleveland Plain Dealer*, Nov. 24, 1964.
19. Bill Scholl, "Game Football to Beach," *Cleveland Press*, Nov. 16, 1964.
20. Joan Ryan, "'Prophet Mo' Better Than Tranquilizer," *Cleveland Plain Dealer*, Dec. 11, 1964.

21. Chuck Such, "Browns 'Measure Up' to Last Title Squad," *Canton Repository,* Nov. 5, 1964.
22. Pluto, *When All the World Was Browns Town,* 103.
23. "1964 Browns Safety Ross Fichtner," YouTube video, 1:34, posted by cleveland.com, Sept. 15, 2014, https://www.youtube.com/watch?v=yK4F3rxoNEo.
24. Pluto, *When All the World Was Browns Town,* 102.
25. Red Smith, "Browns Prove Smarter Than Their Baseball Cousins," *Cleveland Press,* Dec. 16, 1964.
26. Wooten interview.
27. Lady Gilmore, telephone interview with the author, Oct. 14, 2016.
28. Ibid.
29. David Stradling and Richard Stradling, *Where the River Burned: Carl Stokes and the Struggle to Save Cleveland* (Ithaca, N.Y.: Cornell University Press, 2015), 11.
30. Bill Scholl, "Browns Played into Our Hands," *Cleveland Press,* Dec. 7, 1964.
31. Bill Scholl, "'Toe' in Doorway Fails to Frighten Cards Out of Title," *Cleveland Press,* Dec. 7, 1964 .
32. Chuck Such, "Browns Suffer from St. Louis Blues, Lose 28–19," *Canton Repository,* Dec. 7, 1964.
33. Joan Ryan, "It's Time for Turning Point," *Cleveland Plain Dealer,* Dec. 9, 1964.

CHAPTER SIXTEEN

1. Bob August, "Bookie Doesn't Share Brown Fan Pessimism," *Cleveland Press,* Dec. 8, 1964.
2. Charles Heaton, "Browns Must Avert 'Chokeup' Label," *Cleveland Plain Dealer,* Dec. 8, 1964.
3. Terry Pluto, *When All the World Was Browns Town: Browns and the Championship Season of '64* (New York: Simon & Schuster, 1997), 118.
4. *New York Times,* Dec. 13, 1964.
5. Russell Schneider, "Ryan Was at His Best Is Unanimous Viewpoint," *Cleveland Plain Dealer,* Dec. 13, 1964.
6. Chuck Such, "Passing Antics of Ryan Leave Little Doubt," *Canton Repository,* Dec. 13, 1964.
7. "Otto Withdraws Brown 'Needle,'" *Akron Beacon Journal,* Dec. 15, 1964.
8. Bill Levy, *Return to Glory: The Story of the Cleveland Browns* (Cleveland: World, 1965), 16–22.
9. "Christmas Lights Go Up," *Cleveland Plain Dealer,* Dec. 13, 1964.
10. "Ryan's Key Passes against Giants Inspired by Urgency," *Cleveland Plain Dealer,* Dec. 15, 1964.
11. "The Letter Said: 'Only Thing Wrong with Browns Was QB,'" *Los Angeles Times,* Dec. 28, 1964.
12. *Cleveland Press,* Dec. 14, 1964, Browns scrapbook.
13. "Ryan's Key Passes against Giants Inspired by Urgency."

CHAPTER SEVENTEEN

1. Tex Maule, "The Browns Win Big in the East," *Sports Illustrated,* Dec. 21, 1964, 24.
2. Tom Callahan, *Johnny U: The Life and Times of John Unitas* (New York: Crown, 2006), 220.

3. *NFL Century: The Complete Story of The National Football League, 1920–2000* (New York: Smithmark, 1999), 153.
4. Frank Gifford with Peter Richmond, *The Glory Game* (New York: HarperCollins, 2008), 37.
5. Gary Cuozzo, telephone interview with the author, Sept. 29, 2016.
6. Mickey Herskowitz, *The Golden Age of Pro Football: NFL Football in the 1950s* (Dallas: Taylor, 1974), 142.
7. Callahan, *Johnny U,* 95.
8. Herskowitz, *Golden Age of Pro Football,* 143.
9. Don Shula, "How the Colts Met Triumph and Disaster," *Sports Illustrated,* Jan. 11, 1965, 27.
10. Callahan, *Johnny U,* 198.
11. Cuozzo interview.
12. Tom Matte, telephone interview with the author, Apr. 23, 2015.
13. Cuozzo interview.
14. "#42, John Mackey: The Top 100: NFL's Greatest Players | NFL Films, 2010," YouTube video, 3:57, posted by NFL Films, Aug. 16, 2016, https://www.youtube.com/watch?v=r-s3uSaZUfs&t=2s.
15. Shula, "How the Colts Met Triumph and Disaster," 27–28.
16. "#42, John Mackey."
17. Shula, "How the Colts Met Triumph and Disaster," 29.
18. Terry Pluto, *When All the World Was Browns Town: Cleveland's Browns and the Championship Season of '64* (New York: Simon & Schuster, 1997), 241.
19. Bernie Parrish, *They Call It a Game* (New York: Dial, 1971), 101.
20. Pluto, *When All the World Was Browns Town,* 244.
21. Walter Beach, telephone interview with the author, Oct. 11, 2016.
22. Herskowitz, *Golden Age of Pro Football,* 139.
23. Mark Bowden, *The Best Game Ever: Giants vs. Colts, 1958, and the Birth of the Modern NFL* (New York: Atlantic Monthly Press, 2008), 68.
24. Herskowitz, *Golden Age of Pro Football,* 95.
25. Beach interview.
26. Bob Smith, "Unitas and Great Receivers Keep Baltimore on March," *Akron Beacon Journal,* Dec. 22, 1964.
27. Arthur Daley, "Daley Says Colts Have Too Many Guns for Browns," *New York Times,* Dec. 27, 1964.

CHAPTER EIGHTEEN

1. Terry Pluto, *When All the World Was Browns Town: Cleveland's Browns and the Championship Season of '64* (New York: Simon & Schuster, 1997), 261.
2. Dick Schafrath, interview with the author, June 23, 2015, Berea, Ohio.
3. Tex Maule, "Not Much Defense, but Two Long-ball Hitters," *Sports Illustrated,* Oct. 19, 1964.
4. Ibid.
5. Don Shula, "How the Colts Met Triumph and Disaster," *Sports Illustrated,* Jan. 11, 1965, 27.
6. "The Real Blanton Collier," *Cleveland Plain Dealer Sunday Magazine,* Sept. 17, 1967.
7. Chuck Such, "Collier: Wife, 3 Girls Top Rooters," *Canton Repository,* Dec. 17, 1964.

8. Jane Artale, "Mrs. Collier Calls Plays That Make Happy Transplanted Kentucky Home," *Cleveland Plain Dealer,* Oct. 29, 1963.
9. Kay Collier Slone, *Football's Gentle Giant: The Blanton Collier Story* (Lexington, Ky.: Life Force Press, 1985), 202.
10. Hal Lebovitz, "Hal Asks: Is There a Greater Coach Than Collier?" *Cleveland Plain Dealer,* Jan. 2, 1966.
11. Slone, *Football's Gentle Giant,* 260.
12. Paul Warfield, telephone interview with the author, July 6, 2015.
13. Frank Ryan, interview with the author, Sept. 22, 2016, Grafton, Vt.
14. Slone, *Football's Gentle Giant,* 149.
15. Ibid., 139.
16. Ibid.
17. Jack Olsen, "Dr. Ryan of the Browns: How Smart Is Too Smart?" *Sports Illustrated,* Sept. 27, 1965.
18. Ibid.
19. "Cleveland Browns Frank Ryan Last NFL Championship QB (1964)," YouTube video, 6:23, posted by Steven Watson, Sept. 9, 2014, https://www.youtube.com/watch?v=L8PlflBYtaE.
20. Olsen, "Dr. Ryan of the Browns."
21. Ibid.
22. Ibid.
23. Frank Ryan interview.
24. Slone, *Football's Gentle Giant,* 37.
25. Ibid., 202.
26. Pluto, *When All the World Was Browns Town,* 79.
27. Ibid., 70.
28. Ibid.
29. Charles Heaton, "Success of Browns Wins New Contract for Collier, *Cleveland Plain Dealer,* Dec. 24, 1964.

CHAPTER NINETEEN

1. George Peters, "Pinch Hitting: Who's Afraid of the Big, Bad Colts?" *Cleveland Plain Dealer,* Browns scrapbook.
2. Joan Ryan, interview with the author, Sept. 22, 2016, Grafton, Vt.
3. Frank Ryan, interview with the author, Sept. 22, 2016, Grafton, Vt.
4. Joan Ryan, "Middle Back Defense Key," *Cleveland Plain Dealer,* Dec. 27, 1964.
5. John Harris, "The Last Champions: The 1964 Cleveland Browns," *Timeline: A Publication of the Ohio Historical Connection* 32 (Mar. 2015): 10.
6. Dick Schafrath, interview with the author, June 23, 2015, Berea, Ohio.
7. Neil Leifer, with Dian K. Shah, "Tricks of the Trade," *Sports Illustrated,* May 9, 2016.
8. Bernie Parrish, *They Call It a Game* (New York: Dial, 1971), 11.
9. Chuck Heaton, "1964 Browns Holding Reunion to Celebrate Team's Last Crown," *Cleveland Plain Dealer,* July 15, 1984.
10. Schafrath interview.
11. Ibid.; Terry Pluto, *When All the World Was Browns Town: Cleveland's Browns and the Championship Season of '64* (New York: Simon & Schuster, 1997), 129.

12. "Collins' Jest Becomes Record on Field," *Canton Repository*, Dec. 28, 1964.
13. Schafrath interview.
14. Pluto, *When All the World Was Browns Town*, 160.
15. Tex Maule, "Upset of the Mighty," *Sports Illustrated*, Jan. 4, 1965, 11; "Colt Coach Offers 'Windy' Excuses," *Akron Beacon Journal*, Dec. 28, 1964.
16. "Colt Coach Offers 'Windy' Excuses."
17. Bob August, "Game of Lifetime for Browns' Defense," *Cleveland Press*, Dec. 28, 1964.
18. Bob Smith, "Enemy Mistakes Key to Browns' Success," *Akron Beacon Journal*, Dec. 23, 1964.
19. Harris, "Last Champions."
20. Maule, "Upset of the Mighty."
21. Frank Ryan interview.
22. Harris, "Last Champions."
23. Frank Ryan interview.
24. Bill Scholl, "Here's How Collins Set Pass Snagging Mark," *Cleveland Press*, Dec. 28, 1964.
25. Joan Ryan interview.
26. Scholl, "Here's How Collins Set Pass Snagging Mark."
27. Frank Ryan interview.
28. Ibid.
29. Joan Ryan, "Joan Writes Off Ryan Injury as 'Show Biz,'" *Cleveland Plain Dealer*, Jan. 13, 1965.
30. Don Shula, telephone interview with the author, May 4, 2015. .
31. Charles Heaton, "Browns Capture Crown, 27–0," *Cleveland Plain Dealer*, Dec. 28, 1964; Maule, "Upset of the Mighty."
32. John Harris, "Last Champions."
33. Jim Brown with Steve Delsohn, *Out of Bounds* (New York: Zebra, 1989), 106–7.
34. Maule, "Upset of the Mighty," 13.
35. Ibid.
36. Pluto, *When All the World Was Browns Town*, 156.
37. Scholl, "Here's How Collins Set Pass Snagging Mark."
38. Parrish, *They Call It a Game*, 26.
39. "Colt Coach Offers 'Windy' Excuses"; Harry McClelland, "Colts Shaken Up by Shellacking," *Cleveland Press*, Dec. 28, 1964.
40. "Colts Shaken Up by Shellacking."
41. Shula interview.
42. "Collins' Jest Becomes Record on Field."
43. Joan Ryan, "All's Well That Ends Well," *Cleveland Plain Dealer*, Dec. 30, 1964.
44. "Collins' Jest Becomes Record on Field."
45. "Who Took Ryan's Ball?" *Cleveland Press*, Dec. 28, 1964.
46. Kay Collier McLaughlin, interview with the author, July 22, 2016, Louisville, Ky.
47. Ibid.
48. Kay Collier Slone, *Football's Gentle Giant: The Blanton Collier Story* (Lexington, Ky.: Life Force Press, 1985), 166–67.
49. McLaughlin interview.

EPILOGUE

1. Joan Ryan, "Joan Writes Off Ryan Injury as 'Show Biz,'" *Cleveland Plain Dealer,* Jan. 13, 1965.
2. Joan Ryan, "Hubby Gets PhD Despite Jokes," *Cleveland Plain Dealer,* June 4, 1965.
3. Pete Rozelle to Frank Ryan, May 24, 1965, copy in the Pro Football Hall of Fame archives, Canton, Ohio.
4. Ryan Cortes, "Jim Brown Retires While on the Set of 'The Dirty Dozen,'" *The Undefeated,* July 13, 2016, http://theundefeated.com/features/jim-brown-retires-while-on-the-set-of-the-dirty-dozen/.
5. Tex Maule, "The Curtain Falls on a Long Run," *Sports Illustrated,* July 25, 1966.
6. Terry Pluto, *When All the World Was Browns Town: Cleveland's Browns and the Championship Season of '64* (New York: Simon & Schuster, 1997), 180.
7. Maule, "Curtain Falls on a Long Run."
8. William C. Rhoden, "Ex-Brown Walter Beach Recalls Black Athletes' Support for Ali," *New York Times,* Sept. 28, 2014.
9. Jim Brown with Steve Delsohn, *Out of Bounds* (New York: Zebra, 1989), 125, 117, 118, 122.
10. Ibid., 120.
11. Pat McManamon, "Browns Unveil Statue of Hall of Fame Running Back Jim Brown," *ESPN,* Sept. 18, 2016, http://www.espn.com/nfl/story/_/id/17577952/cleveland-browns-unveil-statue-hall-fame-running-back-jim-brown
12. Kay Collier Slone, *Football's Gentle Giant: The Blanton Collier Story* (Lexington, Ky.: Life Force Press, 1985), 192.
13. Dan Coughlin, "Wife OK's Decision," *Cleveland Plain Dealer,* Dec. 2, 1970, 1-F.
14. Slone, *Football's Gentle Giant,* 192.
15. Chuck Heaton, "A Champion Dies: Blanton Collier Guided Browns to Last Title," *Cleveland Plain Dealer,* Mar. 24, 1983, Section F.
16. Kay Collier Slone, *Football's Gentle Giant: The Blanton Collier Story* (Lexington, Ky.: Life Force Press, 1985), 293.
17. "Blanton Collier, Pro Football HOF Induction," YouTube video, 13:23, posted by Franky Minnefield, July 27, 2016, https://www.youtube.com/watch?time_continue=2&v=e4bPdW_MO6s; "Blanton Collier," YouTube video, 4:52, uploaded by homersodidshe, May 17, 2016, https://www.youtube.com/watch?v=0ns0vmZWXE8. That changed in June 2016, when the Cleveland Cavaliers won the National Basketball Association championship.
18. Slone, *Football's Gentle Giant,* 297.
19. "Modell Purchases Control of Browns," *Cleveland Plain Dealer,* July 2, 1965.
20. "A Busted Play," *Sports Illustrated,* Dec. 4, 1995.
21. Steve Rushin, "The Heart of a City," *Sports Illustrated,* Dec. 4, 1995.
22. Alison Knezevich, "Balto. Co. Dismisses Charges against Browns Fan Accused of Urinating on Modell's Grave," *Baltimore Sun,* Feb. 11, 2015 http://www.baltimoresun.com/news/maryland/crime/bs-md-co-serbu-charges-dismissed-20150211-story.html.
23. Tony Tomsic, telephone interview with the author, Nov. 18, 2016.

INDEX

A&M, 46
ABC, 69
Accorsi, Ernie, 170
Akron Beacon Journal: on Brown's firing, 101; on Collier's coaching style, 183
Albert, Frankie, 40
Alcindor, Lew (Kareem Abdul-Jabbar), 203
Ali, Muhammad, 138, 140, 142, 203
"Ali Summit," 203
All-America Football Conference (AAFC), 22–23, 25, 29, 32–34, 36, 37, 159–60, 167
Allegheny Athletic Association, 99
Allen, Bill, 89
Allen, Ermal, 43, 47, 49
Allen, George, 166
All-NFL (*Sporting News*), 104
Allyson, June, 141
American Football League (AFL): formation of, 71; NFL merger with, 205; 1963 season and Kennedy assassination, 124; 1963 season and size of, 98; players' salaries, 128
American Professional Football Association, 99
Anderson, Edwin, 76
Anderson, Stan, 146
Andrews, Vinnie, 67
Andrie, George, 106
Arnett, "Jaguar" Jon, 51
Arnett, Jon, 93
Arnsparger, Bill, 21, 47
Artale, Jane, 72
Associated Press, on Unitas, 166
Atlanta Constitution, on Collier's coaching, 84
August, Bob, 11, 152, 160, 189

"Back-Seat Brown" column (Ryan), 149–50, 201. *See also* Ryan, Joan Busby (wife)
"Backseat Quarterback" column (Conerly), 149
Baker, John, 161
Bakken, Jim, 137
Baltimore Colts: and Arnsparger, 21; band and majorettes of, 4; Colt Corrals (fan club), 4, 167; early history of, 167–69; image and reputation of, 184–85; move to Indianapolis by (1984), 209; NFL joined by, 37–38, 167; 1958–59 seasons, 62, 168; 1962 season, 86; Shula hired as coach for, 169–71; Unitas hired by, 51, 168. *See also* Shula, Don; *individual names of players*
Baltimore Colts 1963–64 season: Browns' and Colts' offense/defense matchup (1964), 135, 166–67, 170–74, 175–77, 180; games played in second half of season, 148–49; Los Angeles Rams game, 153–54; NFL Championship game and reaction, 1, 3–11, 184–98; Western Conference champions (1964), 165, 171
Baltimore Ravens, 209
Barra, Allen, 42
baseball, popularity of (1963), 98
Baugh, "Slingin'" Sammy, 89
Beach, Walter "Doc," 9–11, 143–44, 152, 155, 172–73, 180, 203
Beacon Journal (Akron): on Brown's firing, 101; on Collier's coaching style, 183
Beall, Frank, 88
Bell, Bert, 38, 40, 71, 167
Benz, Larry, 9–10, 156
Berry, Charles, 61
Berry, Raymond, 9, 166, 170, 171, 173–74, 194
Bird, George "Red," 31
Bisciotti, Steve, 209
Bixler, Paul, 18, 104
Black Muslims, 139–42
Blanton Collier Award, 207
Bossard, Harold, 3
Boston Patriots, 143–44
Bottomer, Fred, 188
Boyd, Bobby, 10, 177, 190–92
Braase, Ordell, 185, 186
Bradshaw, Charlie, 48
Bratkowski, Zeke, 80, 93
Breslin, Patricia, 68

230 INDEX

Brewer, Johnny, 132, 176–78, 193
Brinker, Howard, 18, 104
Brodie, John, 51
Brooklyn Dodgers (AAFC), 33–34
Brooklyn Dodgers (baseball team), 209
Brotherhood of Sleeping Car Porters, 140
Brown, Jim: biographical information, 52–55; Browns' and Colts' offense/defense matchup (1964), 172, 176; and Collier's coaching style, 179, 180, 182; and Davis's death, 102; on early African American players, 30; and Eastern Conference championship (1964), 162–64; and fans, 101, 158; film career and sponsorships of, 80, 145–46, 201–3; football legacy of, 204–5; hired by Cleveland Browns, 50–58; "Jim Brown Says" (*Plain Dealer* column), 145; and Modell, 16, 145, 201–2; NFL Championship (1964) game, 5–7, 10, 189–90, 192–94, 198; 1958–60 season, 59, 61, 62, 64; 1962 season, 85–86, 94–97; 1963 season, 106, 110, 111, 114, 117–20, 122; 1964 season, 133–35, 137, 151, 152, 154; *Off My Chest*, 7, 64, 138–46; *Out of Bounds*, 203–4; and Paul Brown, 13–14, 50–58, 74–81, 138; in Pro Bowl (1964), 199; violence toward women and criminal record of, 203–4; visualization techniques used by, 107, 108; at White House, 130–31
Brown, Katy, 12–13
Brown, Mike, 19
Brown, Monique, 204
Brown, Paul: biographical information, 13, 18, 30–31; Cleveland Browns' name, 13–14, 25; Cleveland Browns' 1946–55 titles, 50; Cleveland Browns' 1958–60 seasons, 59–66; coaching style of, 35–41, 56, 179–80; and Collier, 12–19, 28–34, 39–41, 83–85, 95, 198, 205–7; and Jim Brown, 13–14, 50–58, 74–81, 138; late career of, 205–6; legacy of, 49; "A Man for This Season" (*Sports Illustrated*) on, 82–83; McBride's hiring of, 23–25; Modell and firing of, 1–3, 13–14, 69–70, 78–80, 85–87, 94–97, 133; on offensive strategy, 74–81, 132; *PB*, 13, 27, 35, 52, 77, 86; play-calling by, 3, 36, 78, 82, 87, 97, 109; and Plum, 74–77, 82; reaction to firing, 101, 108, 109, 113; retirement of, 97; and Rosenbloom, 167; and Shula, 168, 169; talent discovered by, 116
Brown, Roger, 199
Brown, Sue, 141, 204
Brown, Swinton "Sweet Sue," 52–53
Brown, Theresa, 52–53
Bryant, Paul "Bear," 5–6, 41, 42–49, 83, 91
Bugle Boys, 4

Call and Post (Cleveland), on Willis and Motley, 30
Cannon, Jimmy, 64
Canton Bulldogs, 99
Canton Repository, on football popularity, 99
Cassady, Howard "Hopalong," 76
Caveney, Dorothy, 188
CBS, 60, 67, 188, 194
"Characterization of the Set of Asymptotic Values of a Function Holomorphic in the Unit Disc, A" (Ryan), 127
Charlotte Observer, on Brown's firing, 1
Chicago Bears, 73, 171
Chicago Rockets, 37
Chicago Tribune, Ward and, 22–23
Christian Century, on football popularity, 98
Cincinnati Bengals, 205–6, 209
Civil Rights Act (1964), 7, 139
civil rights movement, 139–42. *See also* race relations
"clamping," 9
Clark, Monte, 103, 107, 159, 163, 179, 183, 186
Clay, Cassius. *See* Ali, Muhammad
Cleveland Browns: Cleveland Rams' origin of, 23–25; early halftime shows of, 31; early team players hired by Brown, 25–34; Jim Brown hired by, 50–58; midwestern players preferred by, 27, 52; move to Baltimore and modern-day team, 208–10; naming of, 13–14, 25; NFL joined by, 37–38, 167; 1946–55 titles of, 50; 1958–60 season, 59–66, 160, 163; 1962–63 season, 110–20, 121–31; pregame tradition of, 36, 184–85; Skorich as head coach of, 179. *See also* Brown, Paul; Cleveland Browns and offense/defense strategies; Cleveland Browns 1964 season; Collier, Blanton; Modell, Art; Municipal Stadium (Cleveland); race relations; *individual names of players*
Cleveland Browns and offense/defense strategies: "clamping," 9; Collier's quarterback pick (1963), 101–9; four-three defense of Landry, 59–60; in 1963–64 season, 132–37, 154–56, 166–67, 170–74, 175–77, 180; option blocking, 113–14; by Paul Brown, 27, 36–37, 74–81, 132; Split-T offense, 89–90; "stereotyped" offense, 16, 62, 76, 82, 85; T-formation offense, 27–29; Z-out, 162
Cleveland Browns 1964 season, 146, 147–59; and city of Cleveland, 156–58; early season, 135–37; as Eastern Conference champions, 160–65; exhibition game (1963), 100; fans' criticism of Ryan, 147–50; games played in second half of seasons, 147, 148, 150–56, 158–59; NFL

Championship game and reaction, 1–11, 184–98; and "Sixties" culture, 146
Cleveland (city): League Park, 32; Mo and Junior's (restaurant), 136; in 1964, 156–58. *See also* Municipal Stadium (Cleveland); *individual names of newspapers; individual names of teams*
Cleveland Indians, 14, 32, 86, 122, 155, 156. *See also* Municipal Stadium (Cleveland)
Cleveland News, on Musical Majorettes, 31
Cleveland Panthers, 25
Cleveland Press: and McBride, 23; NFL Championship (1964) game, 11
Clifford, Gregory, 121
Coast Guard Academy, 76
Cobbledick, Gordon, 87, 101, 112, 119
Cohen, Vincent, 55
College All-Star Games, 21, 23, 66, 72, 107, 177
Collier, Blanton: assistant coaches of, 179–80; biographical information, 16, 18; coaching style of, 105–8, 175–83; death of, 207; hearing of, 6, 22, 40, 43, 77, 174–75, 182–83, 198; hired as Browns' head coach, 12–19, 110–20; innovations of, 27–29; and Jim Brown, 138, 145; late career of, 205–7; legacy of, 49, 207; marriage and family of, 177–78 (*see also individual names of family members*); on 1963 season losses, 123–24, 130; and Paul Brown, 12–19, 28–34, 39–41, 83–85, 95, 198, 205–7; as Pro Bowl coach (1964), 199; rehired by Cleveland Browns (1962), 81; and reporters, 182–83 (*see also individual names of media outlets; individual names of reporters*); and Rosenbloom, 168; at University of Kentucky, 5, 12, 15, 21, 22, 41, 42–49, 104–5, 198; in U.S. Navy, 20–22, 27. *See also* Cleveland Browns and offense/defense strategies; Cleveland Browns 1964 season
Collier, Carolyn "Sis" (daughter), 6, 12–13, 22, 43, 177, 207
Collier, Jane (daughter), 6, 12–13, 22, 177
Collier, Kay (daughter). *See* McLaughlin, Kay Collier
Collier, Mary Forman "Forman" (wife): biographical information, 21–22, 42–43; and husband's career, 12, 15, 18, 28, 42, 48, 164, 177–78, 180; and husband's retirement, 206, 207; at NFL Championship (1964) game, 6, 197–98
Collins, Gary: on Browns' and Colts' offense/defense matchup (1964), 175, 176; and Collier's coaching, 179, 182; as MVP, 195; NFL Championship (1964) game, 187, 190–95; 1962 season, 88; 1963 season, 126, 128; 1964 season, 132, 150–51

Colo, Don, 155
Colt Corrals (fan club), 4, 167
Columbus Dispatch, on Collier as head coach, 14
Conerly, Charlie, 59–60, 141, 149
Conerly, Perian, 149
Cope, Myron, 138–46
Corley, Ed, 55
Costello, Vince, 11, 108, 111, 129–30, 154, 155, 162
Cotton Bowl, 54–55
Craft, Russ, 38
Crespino, Bobby, 135
Critchfield, Hank, 186
Cronkite, Walter, 60
Crow, John David, 91
Crowley, James A. "Sleepy Jim," 27
Curci, Frank, 49

Daley, Arthur, 1, 11, 174
Dallas Cowboys, 94, 98, 106, 119, 124–26, 136
Dallas Texans, 167
Daniell, Jim, 26, 33–34, 38
Davis, Ernie, 78, 79, 80, 102–3, 146
Davis, Willie, 57, 65, 199, 203
Dawson, Len, 51, 75
Deeb, Norm, 46
Detroit Lions: Cleveland Browns' trades with (1961), 76; fans of, 70; 1963 season, 108, 130; 1964 season, 151–53; ownership of, 101; Playoff Bowl (1960), 65–66; 2008 season, 210
Dial, Buddy, 90
Dietrich, John, 25
Diner (film), 167
Dirty Dozen (film), 201
Donovan, Artie, 169
Dukes, Ofield S., 142
Dulles, John Foster, 152
DuMont Television Network, 194

Elegant (magazine), 202
Ewbank, Weeb, 41, 59, 168, 173

fans: of Baltimore Colts, 3–4, 167; of Browns, in late 1940s, 37–38; and Browns' Eastern Conference championship (1964), 3–4, 164, 191; on Browns' move to Baltimore, 209; criticism of Ryan by, 147–50; of Detroit Lions, 70; and football popularity in 1963, 98–101, 121–22; of Jim Brown, 117; and Municipal Stadium doubleheaders, 73; reaction to Paul Brown's firing, 101
Faurot, Larry, 121
Fawcett Stadium (Canton), 100
Fichtner, Ross, 9, 126, 132, 156, 186
Fishback, Helen, 198

232 INDEX

Fiss, Galen, 10, 62, 118, 151–52, 154, 160, 172
Fiss, Nancy, 151–52
Fitzgerald, John, 143
Fleming, Don, 103–4
Flynn, Tommy, 31
Fondren, Walter, 90
Football's Gentle Giant (Collier), 207
Ford, Len, 56, 143, 155
Ford, William, 101
Ford Motor Company, 100
Fortune, on football popularity, 100
four-three defense, 59–60
Franklin, Pete, 182
Freeman, Bobby, 61, 62
Freeman, Mike, 52–53
Furillo, Bud, 2

Gabriel, Roman, 80
Gain, Bob, 9, 136, 154, 155, 161
Game, The (Maule), 3
Gehrig, Eleanor, 23
Gibbons, Frank, 86, 117
Gifford, Frank, 59–64, 161, 162
Gilburg, Tom, 189, 190
Gilliland, R. J., 4
Gillman, Sid, 57, 91–94
Gilmore, Lady, 157–58
Glass, Bill: on Collier, 6; on Jim Brown, 57; NFL Championship (1964) game, 5, 189; 1963 season, 111; 1964 season, 154; and Plum trade, 76; in Pro Bowl (1964), 199; psychology techniques used by, 107
Graham, Otto: at Coast Guard Academy, 14, 76; and Collier, 29, 105–6; criticism of Browns by, 134, 144–45, 163; hired by Cleveland Browns, 27–28; legacy and retirement from Cleveland Browns, 8, 50–51, 74; and Paul Brown, 33–39
Grand Union, 69
Gray, Ken, 199
Green, Ernie, 11, 102, 122, 133, 158, 162, 179, 190
Green Bay Packers: and Lombardi, 65; 1961 season, 75, 79; 1963 season, 131, 135; 1964 season, 153, 171; and Starr, 132
Gregg, Forrest, 207
Grier, Rosie, 60
Groza, "Big Spot," 32
Groza, Frank, 32
Groza, Lou: biographical information, 32; on Browns' move to Baltimore, 208–9; Eastern Conference championship (1964), 161, 163; hired by Cleveland Browns, 26; legacy of, 103; NFL Championship (1964), 11, 189, 191, 192; 1958–60 season, 61; 1962 season, 86;

1963 season, 111, 113, 116, 122, 123; 1964 season, 135, 154

Halas, George, 73, 99
Hall of Fame (Canton, Ohio), 98
Hall of Fame (Kentucky), 207
Harburuck, Charles, 69
Harnett, John J., 25
Haslam, Dee, 204
Haslam, Jimmy, 204
Hawkins, Alex, 173, 195
Hay, Ralph, 99
Hayes, Woody, 115, 132
Heath, Stan, 35
Heaton, Charles: and "Back-Seat Brown" column (Ryan), 149; on Browns' loss to St. Louis (1964), 160; on Collier's coaching style, 183; on Collier's death, 207; on Collier's retirement, 206; on NFL Championship (1964) game, 193; on 1963 season, 101, 109, 112; on 1964 season, 152, 156; on *Off My Chest* (Brown), 138, 141, 144. See also *Plain Dealer* (Cleveland)
Heffelfinger, William "Pudge," 99
Heisler, Fritz, 18, 104, 112, 179–80
Herskowitz, Mickey, 30
Hickerson, Gene, 62, 103, 108, 114–15, 151, 179, 195
Hill, James, 121
Hill, Jerry, 10, 189
Hill, King, 80–81, 90–93, 123
Holiday Inn, 188
Hornung, Paul, 14, 51, 79, 114, 135
Hough neighborhood (Cleveland), 157, 158
Houlehan, Herbert (Mrs.), 121
Houston, Jim, 95, 111, 155, 199
Houston, Lin, 26, 111
Houston Post, on Brown's firing, 14
Howell, Jim Lee, 59
Hudson, Tony, 142
Huff, Sam, 57, 60, 62, 64, 77, 122
Hunt, Lamar, 71
Hutchinson, Tom, 109, 112, 133
Hutson, Don, 7, 153

injuries, Collier on avoidance of, 116–17
Ippolito, Vic, 35, 207
Irsay, Robert, 209

Jackson, Leroy, 78
James, Dick, 161
"Jim Brown Says" (*Plain Dealer* column), 145
Johnson, Charley, 136–37, 158
Johnson, John Henry, 154, 199
Johnson, Lyndon, 7, 130–31, 139, 142

Jones, Dave, 67, 179–80
Jones, Dub, 38, 104, 105, 112, 150–51, 175, 187
Jones, Edgar "Special Delivery," 27
Jones, George, 25
Jordan, Henry, 65
Joyce, Don, 169
Jurgensen, Sonny, 128, 200

Kahn, Roger, 94, 128
Kanicki, Jim, 9–11, 106, 136, 154, 185, 189–90
Kareem Abdul-Jabbar (Alcindor), 203
Katcavage, Jim, 60
Kellet, Don, 4
Kelley, Whitey, 1
Kelly, Leroy, 133, 144, 191, 202
Kennedy, John F., 79, 124–26
Kentucky Pro Football Hall of Fame, 207
Kentucky Wildcats, 16, 18
King, Martin Luther, Jr., 139, 143
Kirkpatrick, Lee, 21
Klemm, Bill, 151–52
Knox, Chuck, 49
Knox, Frank, 20
Kono, Morrie, 13, 95, 110, 186, 193
Kosar, Bernie, 133–34
Kramer, Jerry, 114
Kramer, Ron, 51
Kreitling, Rich, 85, 122, 132
KYW TV, 141

Lahr, Warren, 134
Landry, Tom, 14, 50, 59–65, 206
Lavelli, Dante "Gluefingers," 26, 38, 65, 126
League Park (Cleveland), 32
Leahy, Frank, 23
LeBaron, Eddie, 125
Lebovitz, Hal, 16–19, 72, 126–27, 129, 149–50
Lee, Jim, 59
Leifer, Neil, 185–86
Lindsey, Dale, 115, 136
Lipscomb, Gene "Big Daddy," 87
Lloyd, Dave, 76
Logan, Jerry, 190, 191
Lombardi, Vince, 59, 65, 75, 114, 131, 200
Look (magazine), 138, 142
Lorick, Tony, 190, 191
Los Angeles Dons, 23, 37
Los Angeles Herald-Examiner, on Brown's firing, 2
Los Angeles Rams, 51, 57, 80, 91–94, 153–54, 180, 209
Los Angeles Times: on Jim Brown, 56; on Modell, 73
Lyles, Lenny, 172, 176–77, 192
Lynch, Dick, 117

MacCambridge, Michael, 40
Mackey, John, 9, 11, 166, 170, 194
Malcolm X, 139–40
Maltz, Maxwell, 107–8, 150
"Man for This Season, A" (*Sports Illustrated*), 82–83
Manning, Peyton, 75
Marchetti, Gino: defensive end talent of, 111; and early Colts' history, 168, 169; NFL Championship (1964) game, 6, 170–71, 185–87, 193, 195; in Pro Bowl (1964), 199
"Marcy organization," threats by, 141
Market Melodies (ABC), 69
Marshall, George, 37–38, 79, 87
Marshall, Jim, 115
Marvin, Lee, 145
Massillon Tigers (pro team), 24, 99
Massillon Washington High School Tigers, 13, 18, 30–31
Matson, Ollie, 93
Matte, Tom, 157, 170
Maule, Tex: "A Man for This Season," 82–83; on NFL Championship (1964) game, 185; on NFL formation, 24; on 1958–59 seasons, 62, 63; on 1962 season, 3; on Paul Brown, 76–77, 82, 101. See also *Sports Illustrated*
May Company, 3–4
McBride, Arthur "Mickey," 23–25, 29, 36, 40, 67
McCormack, Mike, 17, 78, 84, 86, 95, 97, 103
McGee, Max, 153
McLaughlin, Kay Collier: birth of, 22; on father's career, 12–13, 44–45, 47–48, 85, 206–8; *Football's Gentle Giant*, 207; Jim Brown interviewed by, 118; Kentucky home of, 177; at NFL Championship (1964) game, 6, 197–98; on parents' marriage, 42–43
McNeil, Clifton "The Stick," 133, 144
Melody, Tom, 183
Meredith, Don, 126
Miami Seahawks, 32
Michaels, Lou, 10
Michaels, Walt, 28, 61
Michigan State University, 74
Migliorino, Bob, 4, 191
Mike Douglas Show (KYW TV), 141
Miller, Fred, 190
Miller, Jim, 47
Minnesota Vikings, 98, 171
Mitchell, Bobby, 56–57, 61, 65, 76–79, 82, 86, 203
Mo and Junior's (Cleveland restaurant), 136
Modell, Art: anti-Semitism toward, 72; biographical information, 2, 68–69; and Browns' Eastern Conference championship (1964), 1, 159, 163–64; Browns' move to

Modell, Art (cont.)
  Baltimore by, 208–9; and Browns' strategy of (1963–64) season, 135; characterization of, 2, 72; and Collier's coaching success, 183; on crowd control problems, 122; on Davis's death, 102; death of, 209; on early football broadcasting, 101; early ownership of Browns by, 67–73; and Jim Brown, 16, 145, 201–2; 1964 season, 151; Paul Brown's firing by, 1–3, 13–14, 69–70, 78–80, 85–87, 94–97, 133; television blackout by, 70–71, 188; on Warfield, 133
Modzelewski, Dick "Little Mo": Browns' Eastern Conference championship (1964), 160; Browns' strategy of (1963–64) season, 135–36; on Collier's coaching, 178; NFL Championship (1964) game, 9, 189–90, 195; 1958 season, 60; 1964 season, 154; in Pro Bowl (1964), 199
Modzelewski, Dottie, 184
Modzelewski, Ed "Big Mo," 56, 135
Modzelewski, Mark, 136
Molloy, Kenneth, 53–54
Montana, Joe, 75
Moore, Lenny, 9–10, 167, 170, 173, 192
Morrison, Fred "Curly," 67
Morrow, John, 96–97, 103
Motley, Marion, 29, 30, 39, 105–6, 143, 144
Muhammad, Elijah, 139–40
Municipal Stadium (Cleveland): Cleveland Rams championship game (1945) at, 25; construction of, 31–32; crowd size (1963), 117, 121–22; doubleheaders at, 73; financial problems and demise of, 208–9; NFL Championship (1964) game at, 1, 2; ticket sales, 4, 73, 100, 121–22, 156
Murphy, Leo, 40, 84, 186, 193
Musical Majorettes, 31

NAACP, 140
Namath, Joe, 128
Nation of Islam, 139–40
Nationwide Insurance, 67
Neale, Greasy, 38
Nealon, Clark, 14
Neely, Jess, 90
Negro Industrial and Economic Union, 145, 202–3
Nelsen, Bill, 200
Newspaper Enterprise Association, 142–43
New York Giants: and Beach, 143; and Browns' Eastern Conference championship (1964), 160–65; Eastern Conference championships (1958, 1959) of, 59–65, 160, 163; and Huff, 77; and Landry, 50; 1962 season, 3, 94; 1963 season, 117–18, 122, 125, 130, 131, 135–36; 1964 season, 4, 147
New York Herald Tribune, on NFL Championship (1964), 3
New York Jets, 128
New York Times: on Browns' and Colts' offense/defense matchup (1964), 174; on Brown's firing, 1; on NFL Championship (1964), 194
New York Yankees (AAFC), 23, 33
New York Yankees (baseball), 50
NFL: and All-Pro teams, 34; Browns and Colts entrance to, 37–38, 167; draft (1956), 51; draft (1963–64) season, 132–33; early African American players in, 29; football popularity in 1963, 98–101; formation of, 24–26; and Jim Brown's early career, 57; Maule on, 82; and Modell's early ownership of Browns, 70; National Football Conference and American Football Conference created by, 205; 1963 season and Kennedy assassination, 124–25; players' graduation policy of, 26; television rights and blackout, 70–71, 188
NFL Century, The, 50
NFL Championship (1964), 1–11, 184–98; coaching and management of teams, 1–3; fans' expectations for, 3–4; game and reaction, 1–11, 188–98; game day preparation, 184–88; players in, 6–11. *See also* Cleveland Browns 1964 season
Ninowski, Jim: Browns' strategy of (1963–64) season, 133–34; injury (1962), 87; NFL Championship (1964) game, 162, 186, 187; 1963 season, 102–9, 112, 122, 124, 130; 1964 season, 147–48; and Paul Brown, 16, 74–75, 77, 80–81, 83, 85–87, 94
Noll, Chuck, 114, 206
North, John, 49
Northwestern University, 14, 21, 27–28, 148

O'Connell, Tommy, 74
Off My Chest (Brown, Cope), 7, 64, 138–46
Ohio Cancer Crusade, 145
Ohio State University: early Cleveland Brown players hired from, 25–26, 29, 31; 1963 season and Kennedy assassination, 124; Paul Brown at, 13, 20, 23–25, 27; Schafrath at, 115; and Warfield, 132
Olderman, Murray, 142–43
Olsen, Jack, 200
Olsen, Merlin, 199
O'Malley, Walter, 209
100 Rifles (film), 146
option blocking, 113–14

Orr, Jimmy, 9, 171, 174, 192, 194
Out of Bounds (Brown), 203–4
Owen, Steve, 59

Paley, William, 67
Paper Lion (Plimpton), 108
Parilli, Babe, 74
Parker, Buddy, 123
Parker, Frank, 117, 135, 136, 154, 163
Parker, Jim, 9, 166, 189, 190
Parrish, Bernie: Browns' and Colts' offense/defense matchup (1964), 171–72, 174; and Collier's coaching style, 180; and Fleming, 103–4; NFL Championship (1964) game, 8–11, 162, 164, 186, 187, 192, 194, 195; 1962 season, 94–96; 1963 season, 111, 120; 1964 season, 147–48, 155; and Paul Brown, 17, 65; *They Call It a Game*, 138
Parseghian, Ara, 14, 133, 156
Paschall High School (Ft. Worth, Texas), 89
Paul, Gabe, 72
PB (Brown), 13, 27, 52, 62, 77, 86
Peaks, Clarence, 51–52
Pellington, Bill, 169, 185
Pepsi Cola, 80, 145, 202
Perry, Joe, 120
Peters, George, 184, 185
Philadelphia Eagles: and Cleveland's first NFL game, 38; 1962 season, 86; 1963 season, 119–20, 123, 125; 1964 season, 156, 158; and Skorich, 179
Phillips, Red, 93
Phipps, Mike, 207
Pittsburgh Steelers: early broadcasts of, 100; exhibition game (1963), 100; 1956 season, 51; 1959 season, 39; 1962 season, 87; 1963 season, 117, 123, 124, 130, 133–34; 1964 season, 148, 151–52, 158; and Rooney family, 71, 73
Plain Dealer (Cleveland): "Back-Seat Brown" column, 149–50, 201 (*see also* Ryan, Joan Busby [wife]); on Browns' and Colts' offense/defense matchup (1964), 174; on Browns' Eastern Conference championship (1964), 163–64; on Collier's coaching style, 183; on Collier's death, 207; on Collier's hiring as Browns' head coach, 16–19; on early NFL and AAFC, 25; on football popularity (1963), 101; "Jim Brown Says" column, 145; on Modell, 72; on NFL Championship (1964) game, 193, 198; on 1964 games played in second half of season, 147–48, 152, 159; on 1962 season, 87; on 1963 season, 109, 112, 119; on *Off My Chest* (Brown), 138, 141, 144

Playoff Bowl (1960), 65–66
Playoff Bowl (1963), 131
Playoff Bowl (1964), 140
Plimpton, George, 108
Plum, Milt, 39, 52, 61, 64–65, 74–77, 82, 111, 152
Pluto, Terry, 95, 188
Poitier, Sidney, 146
Povich, Shirley, 69
President's Committee on Equal Employment Opportunity, 142
Press (Cleveland): on Browns' Eastern Conference championship (1964), 161; on Browns' loss to St. Louis (1964), 160; on Browns' offensive strategy, 132; on Collier's coaching, 117; on Jim Brown, 146; on NFL Championship (1964) game, 189; on 1962 season, 86; on 1964 season, 151; and Tomsic, 187–88
Pro Bowl (1962), 97
Pro Bowl (1964), 199
Pro Football Hall of Fame (Canton, Ohio), 98
Psycho-Cybernetics (Maltz), 107–8, 150

Quinlan, Bill, 35, 65, 155

race relations, 138–46; in city of Cleveland, 157–58; and civil rights movement, 139–42; early African American players, 7, 29–30, 53–54, 143; *Off My Chest* (Brown) on, 138–46; at University of Kentucky, 46
Ratterman, George, 74
Reeves, Dan, 24–25, 101, 209
Renfro, Ray: at NFL Championship (1964) game, 197; playing by, 39, 84, 88, 125–26, 132, 133, 180; Warfield mentored by, 133, 150, 180
Rice University, 8, 90–91, 93
Rio Concho (film), 145–46
Robb, Joe, 159
Roberts, Walter, 133, 144, 162, 180
Robustelli, Andy, 60, 64, 136, 161
Rooney, Art, 71, 100
Rooney, Dan, 71, 124
Rosen, Dick, 193
Rosenbloom, Carroll, 1, 40, 167, 168–71
Rote, Kyle, 59
Rozelle, Pete, 71, 82, 99–100, 124–25, 188, 200
Rupp, Adolph, 42
Russell, Bill, 142, 203
Russell, Jack, 96
Rutledge, Ed, 46–47, 49
Ryan, Frank: biographical information and mathematics career of, 8, 88–94, 126–30, 200–201; Browns' and Colts' offense/defense matchup (1964), 176; Browns' strategy of

Ryan, Frank (cont.)
(1963–64) season, 133–34, 137; "A Characterization of the Set of Asymptotic Values of a Function Holomorphic in the Unit Disc," 127; Cleveland Browns' hiring of, 80, 81, 93–94; and Collier's coaching, 16–17, 179, 180–82; fans' criticism of, 147–50; late football career of, 199–201; NFL Championship (1964) game, 8, 11, 161–65, 184–85, 189–98; 1963 season, 102–9, 112, 117–19, 122–24, 126–27, 130; 1964 season, 158–59; physical appearance of, 128–29; in Pro Bowl (1964), 199; stolen game ball of, 196–97; "twenty and going in" quarterback style of, 129–30; visualization techniques rejected by, 108; at White House, 130–31. *See also* Ryan, Joan Busby (wife)
Ryan, Frank "Pancho," Jr. (son), 94, 129–30, 148, 149
Ryan, Joan Busby (wife): "Back-Seat Brown" column of, 149–50, 201; biographical information, 91–92, 127, 129–30; and Browns' Eastern Conference championship (1964), 164–65; on Collier, 150; on fan's criticism of husband, 147–50; journalism career of, 201; in Los Angeles, 93–94; on Marchetti, 199; and NFL Championship (1964) game, 8, 159, 184–85, 192, 193, 196, 197; on Ninowski, 133–34; on postgame parties, 153; on superstition in games, 151–52
Ryan, John (grandfather), 88
Ryan, Michael (son), 94, 149
Ryan, Robert W. (father), 88
Ryan, Stuart (son), 149
Rymkus, Lou, 27, 33

Saban, Lou, 27
St. Clair, Bob, 171
St. John, Lynn, 24
St. Louis Cardinals: 1962 season, 87, 88; 1963 season, 124, 125, 131, 136–37; 1964 season, 148, 153, 158–59, 160
Salinger, Pierre, 124
Sanna, Nay, 14
Sauerbrei, Harold, 15, 127, 164
Scales, Charley, 119, 144
Scarry, Mo, 30
Schaefer, Rudy, 67, 208
Schafrath, Bill, 187
Schafrath, Dick: and Browns' and Colts' offense/defense matchup (1964), 136, 175; on Collier's coaching, 178; NFL Championship (1964) game, 185–87, 190, 194; 1963 season with Collier as head coach, 113–16; tackle position of, 103; visualization techniques used by, 107
Schenkel, Chris, 100
Schmeling, Max, 32
Schneider, Russell, 163–64
Schnellenberger, Howard, 44, 46–49
Schramm, Tex, 71, 125
Schwartzwalder, Ben, 54, 103
Scripps-Howard, on Browns' strategy of (1963–64) season, 135
Shaker Heights Country Club, 85
Shaw, George, 168
Sherman, Allie, 97, 122, 136
Shinnick, Don, 11, 190
Shofner, Jim, 149–50, 155
Shula, Don: on Browns' and Colts' offense/defense matchup (1964), 135, 176–77; hired as Colts' coach, 169–71; legacy of, 49, 206; NFL Championship (1964) game, 5, 6, 8–10, 188–93; 1964, games played in second half of season, 153–54; as Pro Bowl coach (1964), 199; Western Conference Championship (1964), 165
Sipe, Brian, 207
Skorich, Nick, 179–80
Slone, Bob, 12
Smith, J. Glen, 4
Smith, Jim Ray, 95, 103, 115
Smith, Red, 3, 61–62
Speaker, Tris, 25
Speedie, Mac, 33, 38, 175–76
Split-T offense, 89–90
Sport (magazine), 187–88
Sporting News, All-NFL of, 104
Sports Illustrated: on Browns' strategy of (1963–64) season, 135; on Collier at Kentucky, 49; on Collins, 175; "A Man for This Season," 82–83; and Maule, 63; on NFL Championship (1964) game, 8, 11, 185–86, 193–94; on Ryan, 200
Starr, Bart, 132, 153
Stautner, Ernie, 133
Stengel, Casey, 156
Stephens, Larry, 80
Stewart, Dave, 30–31
Stokes, Carl, 157, 203
Stone, Avatus, 53–54
Stonebreaker, Steve, 185
Strauss, Joseph, 33
Stribling, Young, 32
Stroud, Jack, 161
Summerall, Pat, 61–62
Syracuse Nationals, 55
Syracuse University, 53–55

Taylor, Jim, 79, 114, 144, 151
television: and football popularity in 1963, 98–101; NFL blackout policy, 70–71, 188; NFL Championship (1964) game on, 188, 194
Texas Christian, 54
T-formation offense, 27–29
They Call It a Game (Parrish), 138
Thompson, William S., 25
Thomson, Bobby, 61–62
Thorpe, Jim, 99
Tibbals, Loren, 101
ticket sales: and Cleveland Indians, 156; Municipal Stadium doubleheaders, 73; in 1963 and 1964, 4, 100, 121–22
Timken, Henry H., Jr., 99
Timken, W. R. "Tim," Jr., 99
Tittle, Y. A., 128, 148, 161
Tomsic, Tony, 151, 187–88, 203. See also *Press* (Cleveland)
Topping, Dan, 23
Touchdown Club, 119, 148
Triplett, Mel, 64
Tyer, Jim, 115

Ulinski, Ed, 18, 179–80
Underwood, Buckshot, 47
Unitas, Dorothy, 168
Unitas, Johnny: Browns' and Colts' offense/defense matchup (1964), 166–67, 171–74; hired by Baltimore, 51, 168; NFL Championship (1964) game, 1, 8–11, 188–90, 192, 194, 195; 1963 season, 108–9; 1964 season, 148–49; and Shula, 169–70
University of Alabama, 46
University of Kentucky: Collier at, 5, 12, 15, 21–22, 41, 42–49, 198; Shula at, 135, 168
University of Michigan, 124
University of Oklahoma, 89–90, 192
U.S. Navy, Collier and Paul Brown in, 20–22, 27

Van Brocklin, Norm, 65, 92
Vanik, Charles, 130
Varden, Mary Forman. See Collier, Mary Forman "Forman" (wife)
Violent World of Sam Huff, The (CBS), 60
visualization techniques, used by Cleveland Browns, 107–8, 150

Wade, Billy, 92–93
Wallack, Nate, 29, 127, 129, 197
Walsh, Ed, 53–54
Ward, Arch, 22–23, 26, 37
Warfield, Paul: Browns' and Colts' offense/defense matchup (1964), 132–33, 175; and Collier's coaching, 176, 178, 180, 182; injury of, 151; NFL Championship (1964) game, 11, 162, 192; 1964 season, 150–51, 153, 155; in Pro Bowl (1964), 199
Washington Post: Joan Ryan at, 201; on Modell's ownership of Browns, 69
Washington Redskins, 79; and Jurgensen, 128; 1962 season, 86, 87; 1963 season, 111–12, 113, 125, 135–36; 1964 season, 150–51; Ryan with, 200; Western Conference Championship (1964) loss, 165
Washington Times, Joan Ryan at, 201
Waterfield, Bob, 93–94
Watkins, Tommy, 76
Webb, Allan, 162
Webster, Alex, 55, 59, 161
Weitz, Myron, 96
White, Bill, 142
Widdoes, Carroll, 25–26
Wiggin, Paul, 98; Browns' strategy of (1963–64) season, 136; late career of, 194; NFL Championship (1964) game, 9, 10, 11, 184, 187, 192, 194; 1963 season, 98, 106, 111, 119, 123, 130; 1964 season, 154
Willis, Bill, 29–30, 65, 143
Wilson, George, 108
Wilson, "Touchdown Tommy," 80, 102
WJW (television station), 188
Woods, Joe, 96
Wooten, John: at "Ali Summit," 203; on city of Cleveland, 157; on Collier's coaching style, 182; and Jim Brown, 143; NFL Championship (1964) game, 186, 190; 1962 season, 84; 1963 season, 103, 106, 113–16; 1964 season, 151; on Ryan, 129
World's Fair (1939), 71

X, Malcolm, 139–40

Yale University, 201
Yaworsky, Walt, 43

Z-out, 162

www.ingramcontent.com/pod-product-compliance
Lightning Source LLC
Chambersburg PA
CBHW022056160426
43198CB00008B/249